the
best
creative
NONFICTION

Volume Volume Volume Volume Volume Volume
1

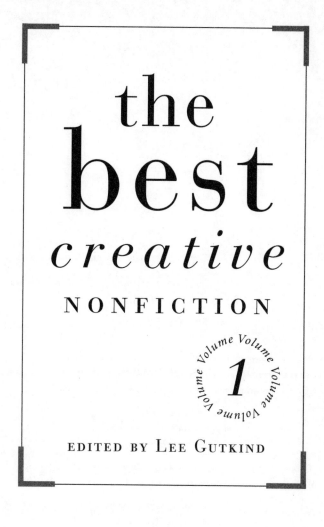

the
best
creative
NONFICTION

Volume *Volume Volume Volume* 1 *Volume Volume*

EDITED BY LEE GUTKIND

W. W. NORTON & COMPANY

New York London

coordinating editors

HATTIE FLETCHER

DINTY W. MOORE

IRINA REYN

contents

Fame and Obscurity (with Appreciation to Gay Talese) and Our Search for the Best Creative Nonfiction

LEE GUTKIND

In a volume entitled *The Best Creative Nonfiction,* you are probably expecting work by the literary giants—Annie Dillard, John McPhee, Tom Wolfe, Joan Didion—but instead you get Sunshine O'Donnell. J. D. Schraffenberger. Eula Biss. Olivia Chia-lin Lee. Household names, they're not. Perhaps even more obscure are the publications from which the work has been reprinted. *Ninth Letter. Isotope. Gastronomica. Hanging Loose.* Not to mention (are you ready for this?) *PMS.*

These are literary journals. Actually, more than 600 literary journals are published annually in the United States. (*PMS,* by the way, stands for poem, memoir, story.) Circulation for the most well-known, such as the *Paris Review,* is barely 6,000—a pinprick compared to the scope of popular magazines such as *Vanity Fair,* which circulates 1.2 million issues and reaches more than 6 million readers monthly.

Literary journals may not attract the same audience as the "slick" mags, but they have long provided a place for writers—famous and not so famous—to showcase interesting and often controversial work.

Transition, launched in 1923 (and now out of print), featured early segments of *Finnegans Wake*, by James Joyce, and essays, poems, and stories by Gertrude Stein, Ernest Hemingway, Hart Crane, Samuel Beckett, Dylan Thomas, and Rainer Maria Rilke. Some of these writers were just finding their voice back then—as writers Bonnie Rough and Heather Sellers, in *Ninth Letter* and the *Alaska Quarterly Review*, respectively, are today. Literary journals publish not just new and emerging writers; many well-known literary figures choose to be published in journals, because, in contrast to the slicks, literary journals are read religiously by serious readers, writers, editors, and agents—publishing insiders.

A primary reason to write—a challenge and joy—is to be daring with form and content. Writers want to try out new ideas and break structural barriers. You can't do that very often in popular publications. But in literary journals generally, and in creative nonfiction specifically, writers can experiment.

Now, here is where things may get a little messy and even more confusing, because many people don't know exactly what creative nonfiction is all about. Creative nonfiction, you may have heard it said, is a non sequitur, an oxymoron—a contradiction in terms. Monica Hsiung Wojcik, a young writer whose work, from a writing course in the genre at Princeton University, appears in this collection, says, "My mother, a non-native English speaker, refers to the course as 'Non-creative Fiction.' 'What's the difference?' she says."

Fiction means, basically, that the writer has made up some stuff. Some parts of a short story or a novel may be true, or based on truth or fact, but the writer has also taken liberties to make the work more dramatic. So, it is fiction. Nonfiction, obviously, means the opposite—that nothing has been fabricated. The story is true and accurate and can be confirmed by anyone who wants to investigate.

Until recently, most nonfiction has been written in a rather formulaic manner. In newspapers and many magazines, the dry facts have been paramount. Reporters took their job description seriously and reported "the facts, ma'am, just the facts," as Detective Joe Friday (portrayed by actor Jack Webb) said on the old *Dragnet* TV series. Friday dissuaded witnesses, victims, and suspects from going off on tangents, from imagining, speculating, editorializing, and fantasizing. Friday's world was cut and dried, two dimensional, just like that of traditional journalism, in which the reporter—the person conducting the investigation and gathering the information—is generally prohibited from enlightening a reader with personal observation.

Creative nonfiction gives the writer more artistic freedom—not in regard to the truth but in constructing the story. Ultimately, the primary goal of the creative nonfiction writer is to communicate information, just like a reporter, but to shape it in such a way that it reads like fiction.

Creative nonfiction writers tell stories, utilizing dialogue, description, characterization, point of view, while at the same time remaining true to the facts. This is a daunting challenge—and for a long while only the best writers experimented with the form. In the 1930s and 1940s, George Orwell, Ernest Hemingway, and Ernie Pyle proved that it's possible to be a good reporter *and* storyteller, simultaneously informing and enlightening readers. In the 1950s and 1960s, Gay Talese and Tom Wolfe sparked the "New Journalism" movement, still a viable term in some quarters today. Truman Capote coined the idea of the "nonfiction novel" with his masterful *In Cold Blood*.

Which is not to say that traditional journalists do not write creative nonfiction. To the contrary, they are hungry to do so, although newspapers and magazines sometimes make it difficult for them to satisfy their creative energies and urges. This is why they publish freelance work in other venues, as do Karl Taro Greenfeld, a reporter and editor at *Sports Illustrated*, whose essay is taken from the *Paris Review*, and Michael Rosenwald, a reporter for the *Washington Post*, who invites the reader along as he undergoes a complete physical exam for *Popu-*

lar Science magazine. Both pieces are successful because, as Greenfeld describes the mission of creative nonfiction, they "allow the writer to entertain, while still informing and educating." Rosenwald and Greenfeld both write in scenes, in a cinematic and carefully plotted progression.

Editors at the *Seattle Post-Intelligencer* permitted reporter Carol Smith to use creative nonfiction techniques to piece together a story of a mysterious woman calling herself Mary Anderson who in 1996 checked into a luxury boutique hotel and never checked out. "In many ways, the story of Mary Anderson is the antithetical newspaper story," Smith says. "There was no news peg. There was no resolution. We had already written the 'news account' when it happened. There was, in fact, no reason to write another story. And yet, it received a huge reader response. Readers connected with the questions it raised about who we are, and how we live in the world. To me, there is no higher calling for creative nonfiction."

The intersection between journalism and creative nonfiction has led some people to call this kind of writing "literary journalism" or, as previously mentioned, "New Journalism." "New" or "literary" journalism focuses on other people, mostly. Writers (the first person) may be included, observing and commenting, but they are generally not the protagonists, the primary subjects of their stories. But in recent years a shift to personal narrative has changed the shape of—and infused energy and electricity into—the entire publishing and writing world.

Highly praised memoirs have been written over the years, such as Thoreau's *Walden*, James Baldwin's *Notes of a Native Son*, and Hemingway's *A Moveable Feast*, but the "memoir craze," as people refer to it today, began with perhaps a half-dozen books published in the early and mid-1990s in which writers recounted their lives in as dramatic a way as possible, writing as close to fiction as they dared. Books such as *This Boy's Life*, by Tobias Wolff, *The Liars' Club*, by Mary Karr, and

Angela's Ashes, by Frank McCourt, were immensely popular and whetted the public's appetite (to an alarming degree, some might say) for personal narratives.

Many of these writers first started working in other genres: Wolff was (and continues to be) a well-respected fiction writer; Karr first established her credentials as a poet. One of the main reasons why creative nonfiction has become so popular so quickly is because writers who have achieved and practiced the dramatic literary techniques that creative nonfiction allows have crossed genres.

The "memoir craze" arguably has also led to an explosion of first-person narrative; everyone, it seems, wants to tell his or her story. And in our increasingly connected world, it has become easier for would-be writers to find audiences. Online publications—especially blogs—have reshaped and enlarged the publishing world in a heretofore unimaginable revolution of style and freedom.

Blog is short for weblog—an online journal, frequently updated and intended for public consumption. Some blogs have a particular focus or mission—politics, say, or celebrity gossip—but even more blogs, numbering perhaps in the millions, are published online by anyone with access to a computer and a rudimentary knowledge of software who thinks he or she has something to say. The downside of this phenomenon is that, as it turns out, most people don't have much to say and don't want to work too hard to say it well. Because there are no controls or guidelines, including that of good taste, blogs can be vulgar, inflammatory, vindictive, accusative, and hurtful. On the other hand, blogs can be remarkably intercultural and interdisciplinary, connecting ordinary people from throughout the world in a very direct and intimate way. Blogs can also be a launching pad and proving ground for new and undiscovered writers, which is why we have included excerpts and entries from blogs in *Best Creative Nonfiction*.

Our editors have devoted considerable time and effort to surfing the web, looking for sparks of nonfiction prose that bristle with wisdom, humor, pathos, and promise. We can't know what we've missed in our disorganized and sporadic search, but we think we have found some representative voices—such as Mimi, a transplanted Londoner establishing herself in New York City by any means possible, and Oliver, a Londoner whose blog is devoted to applying for myriad ludicrous employment opportunities for which he is not qualified.

The blogs are presented just as readers might discover them online—with no order or introduction. As you look through *Best Creative Nonfiction*, you will come upon them intermixed with the magazine and journal essays. Suddenly you will meet hotcoffeegirl recounting her experiences as a narcoleptic, or a ranting waiter confronting the swift passage of time.

The blogs excerpted here are rough and raw, but also piercing and provocative—which is how we hope you feel about the creative nonfiction genre after you discover this collection at the library or bookstore. Leaf through it and read the work we have selected by writers whose names may not immediately impress you, but whose ideas and voices will make an impact and make you feel angry, irritated, charmed, motivated, or enraptured. For that is what the best literature of any genre—poetry, fiction, or nonfiction—is all about: triggering emotions, inspiring ideas, breaking stylistic boundaries, and questioning societal norms. That is what creative nonfiction can do best. In this anthology, we have attempted to provide you with some of the best examples of what we think is the best genre.

THE WORK ANTHOLOGIZED here has been culled by our editors from hundreds of print and online publications. We reached out through advertisements and e-mails to editors from around the world, inviting them to nominate pieces for inclusion in *Best Creative Nonfiction*. We also convened a prestigious nominating board of editors, teachers, and writers to select for consideration their favorite pieces of nonfiction prose published within the last year or so. This volume is the result of efforts and insight from many of the most knowledgeable professionals in the literary community.

This is the first *Best Creative Nonfiction*. The journal *Creative Non-fiction*, of which this will serve as issue no. 32, and our publishing partner, W. W. Norton, intend to publish *The Best Creative Nonfiction* annually, each summer. Look for the striking pastel-striped cover. Behind it is an unusual and unforgettable literary experience for readers, writers, and bookstore browsers seeking a porthole into literature that makes a personal connection with the writer and captures real life with the power of cinema and the integrity of fact.

acknowledgments

Undertaking a new annual anthology is a huge project—especially an anthology of the best writing in a genre. After all, a nearly boundless amount of potential material must be whittled down to a book-size collection. This inaugural issue of *The Best Creative Nonfiction* could not have been assembled without the help of many people:

- A Nominating Board of editors and writers read with an eye to this anthology and made recommendations: Robert S. Boynton, Kristen Cosby, Taha Ebrahimi, Brenda Miller, Mimi Schwartz, Bryant Simon, and Kathleen Tarr.
- Editors from more than three hundred publications and presses nominated work from the pages of their journals, newspapers, magazines, and book lists.
- Amy Cherry, at W. W. Norton, generously offered insight and encouragement.
- Andrew Blauner, our agent, has been consistently supportive of *Creative Nonfiction*'s endeavors.
- The staff at the journal *Creative Nonfiction*—assistant editor Donna Hogarty, editorial assistant Jess Adamiak, and adminis-

trative assistant Julia Ressler—secured permissions and assembled a complete manuscript in near-record time.

Finally, *Creative Nonfiction* would like to thank the Juliet Lea Hillman Simonds Foundation and the Pennsylvania Council on the Arts for their generous and ongoing support, which makes all our work possible.

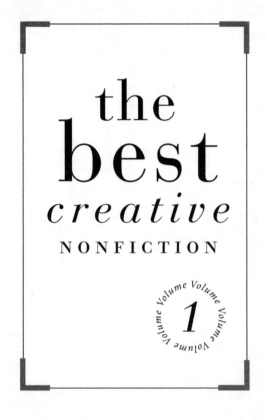

the
best
creative
NONFICTION

Volume Volume Volume Volume Volume

1

The Cipher in Room 214

Who Was Mary Anderson and Why Did She Die?

CAROL SMITH

"People respond to stories," says Carol Smith, a reporter for the Seattle Post-Intelligencer. "It's the way we're wired to receive information. Newspaper accounts are filled with the drama of people's lives, and yet most newspaper stories are reports rather than narratives. In our rush to put out information, we too often ignore the very human need to read a story with characters, suspense, drama and theme." Smith responds to the "human need" of which she speaks in this story about an unsolved mystery.

Mary Anderson is fading, as surely as a forgotten Polaroid. Her case file has been archived, a thick stack of dead ends and unanswered questions, shut in manila folders and buried in the county's morgue. Records of the police investigation have been destroyed. The man who retained the institutional memory of the case resigned from the King County Medical Examiner's Office four years ago.

This is just the way Anderson apparently wanted it.

AN ARTIST'S SKETCH OF THE MYSTERIOUS WOMAN. (*Seattle Post-Intelligencer*)

If there was anything out of the ordinary about the woman's arrival at the Hotel Vintage Park in downtown Seattle that autumn day, it was only the weather—a near-record 80 degrees. That much is recorded.

The woman herself slipped by unnoticed. She had called an hour or so earlier to reserve the room. She took a cab, got out around the corner with two bags and walked into the lobby alone on Oct. 9, 1996. She signed the register "Mary Anderson." No one spotted the hesitation marks in her handwriting. There were no tags on her luggage.

The desk clerk recalled nothing exceptional about her—no accent, nor anything to make her seem out of place in the luxury boutique hotel. Neatly groomed with artfully shaped brows and a pearly manicure, she carried an expensive olive-green, woven-leather purse and paid about $350 in cash for two nights in an elegant room at the end of a long, richly carpeted hallway.

This is where the trail of Anderson's life ends. No one knows precisely what happened next. Was she absorbed in the final details of erasing her identity—perhaps flushing away a driver's license and address book, ripping the label off a prescription bottle? Did she anticipate the confusion her act would cause? Did she have second thoughts?

What we do know is this: She made no phone calls. Ordered nothing from room service. Instead, in some unknown sequence, she put out the "Do Not Disturb" sign, applied pink Estée Lauder lipstick and combed her short auburn hair. She wrote a note on hotel stationery, opened her Bible to the 23rd Psalm and mixed some cyanide into a glass of Metamucil.

Then she drank it.

People who choose cyanide are trying for a clean getaway from this life. With cyanide, there is no question about outcome, or intent.

Her note, its corner tucked under the bottle of Metamucil to keep it from slipping off the hotel desk, read:

> *"To whom it may concern: I have decided to end my life and no one is responsible for my death."*
>
> *Mary Anderson.*
>
> *"P.S. I have no relatives. You can use my body as you choose."*

When the guest in Room 214 did not check out at noon on the 11th, front-desk manager Josh Quarles signaled the bellman to look in on her. The bellman knocked. But there was no answer. A deadbolt blocked his entry.

"At that point, we knew somebody was inside the room," Quarles said. Thinking she might be a sound sleeper, or hearing-impaired, Quarles went with the bellman and engineers to bypass the lock.

Inside the room, Mary Anderson had propped herself against the pillows on the bed. She appeared to have fallen asleep, a King James Bible clasped to her chest. Quarles checked her pulse. Nothing.

When police arrived, they found the room "neat and orderly," half a dozen stretch velour separates in hues of emerald green, fuchsia, navy and black hanging in the closet. She had a cobalt blue Himalaya Outfitters jacket and black leather gloves from Nordstrom. Her purse contained $36.78 in cash, but no ID. No key. No credit cards. She had packed slippers for comfort. Size 10.

Police noted her final coordinates—"head to the west, and feet to the east"—like a ship gone down at sea. There were, according to official reports, "no signs of a struggle." At that point, everyone assumed that this was a routine suicide case. Investigators had a name, contact phone number and address from the hotel registry.

What they didn't realize was this: Everything they thought they knew about Mary Anderson was a lie. Her name—an alias, likely made up on the spot based on a later signature analysis. The New York address she'd given the hotel—non-existent. The phone contact she left—a wrong number.

Mary Anderson was a non-entity, a puzzle. A cipher.

Nine years later, Anderson's file is the coldest of cold cases—one with low odds of being solved. It doesn't have enough sex appeal for tabloid television. It doesn't arouse public anger, or horror, in the same way as a murder. Some would argue, why bother with it? She asked for her death. She got it. On her terms. Case closed.

And yet . . . her death raises other questions: How can a person live to middle age without leaving any ties to the world? What about her dry cleaner? The cosmetics counter sales lady? Did they wonder about a troubled woman in their midst?

Somewhere, someone must realize that she doesn't come around anymore. To push through life and touch no one, to develop no gravity that pulls anyone else into your orbit, seems impossible.

Even in her death, Mary Anderson has traction, a pull on certain strangers.

Jerry Webster is one of them.

Webster, the former chief investigator for the King County Medical Examiner's Office, is the closest Anderson has to a proxy "next of kin."

He is the man in charge of her affairs, at least on paper. His initials are next to the order not to release her personal effects from the Medical Examiner's Office until she is identified. It was he who finally ordered her body embalmed and buried at the county's expense.

Webster, a wiry, indefatigable man of 61, now runs a small Kent-based mortuary with an office in a shopping plaza on Capitol Hill. He does what he can to dignify any death. One of his proudest moments was when he accompanied the bodies of three Chinese men, found dead in a container on a ship in Elliott Bay, home to Fujian province in 2000.

It matters to him who the dead are.

There are only a few cases in his 18-year career as a cop, and later in his 10 years as an investigator for the ME's office, that still haunt him. Mary Anderson's is one. It's a paradoxical mystery: If Mary Anderson wasn't who she said she was, then who killed her?

"It didn't appear it was going to be a complex case, or a difficult one," Webster said. "Then things started to go wrong."

Investigators ran her fingerprints through the FBI's Integrated Automated Fingerprint Identification System. They checked with Canadian and American missing-person records, with Interpol and the Royal Canadian Mounted Police. They checked with cyanide manufacturers, and tried to trace her possessions. They sought the help of the media, casting for leads. Within a few months, she was officially categorized what she remains today: a Jane Doe.

THE TERRITORY OF the unidentified is its own purgatory. The unknown are not easily laid to rest. The Internet is full of galleries of the disappeared and the reconstructed—some missing parts of their bodies, faces, minds or memories—arrayed in an eerie, endless lineup. The lives of the missing seem interrupted in the most mundane ways—they left to go jogging, or to the corner store. They were last seen getting into cars, or leaving bars. They didn't arrive at baby show-ers or jobs. They departed their lives abruptly, without explanation: "She said she'd call back, but she never did."

And under each photo, a refrain: Do you know? Do you recognize? Please call with information.

The advent of the Internet has offered both real hope and false promise to searchers.

"Let's say you entered (a set of criteria) into the National Crime Information Center database—190 pounds, brown eyes, age 50 to 60—you'd get thousands of hits—60 pages of them," Webster said. "Then you have to go through one by one."

According to Todd Matthews of Tennessee, who helped build the Doe Network, a Web archive of missing and unidentified people, there are nearly 6,000 unidentified bodies known to law enforcement agencies, and more than 100,000 missing—enough to fill Safeco Field more than twice over.

"And that represents just 10 to 50 percent of cases," said Matthews, who in 1998 staked a reputation by using the Internet to solve one of the most famous missing-person cases of the 20th century—the decades-old mystery of a 1968 murder victim then known only as "Tent Girl."

But the sheer power of the Web still can't overcome one fundamen-tal limitation—unless someone is reported missing somewhere, there is little hope of making a match with an unidentified body. That is why, of the thousands of cases that have sifted through Matthews' hands, Anderson's stands out.

Cold-called by a reporter a continent away, Matthews immediately knew her case from its bare-bones description before a name was mentioned. "You're talking about Mary Anderson," he said. She pulls on him, too, for this simple reason: At least those listed as missing have something Anderson claimed she did not: someone who is looking for them. Who missed them. Who, presumably, loved them.

Perhaps the most puzzling thing about Mary Anderson's death is the deliberateness with which she chose it. The mind wants to make sense of it, to find a reason. Was it depression? Mental illness? A constellation of disappointments?

Webster is bothered by a different set of questions. "I'm convinced she left us clues to who she was, and we missed them," Webster said, leaning back in his closet of an office at his mortuary. A few months into the investigation, Webster remembered that there was a copy of *Seattle Weekly* on the desk, a pressed maple leaf set on a page.

"The maple leaf might have been a clue," he said. Or perhaps it was pointing to one. Based on the symbolism of the leaf, he and his team redoubled their efforts to search in Canada.

Steen Halling, a professor of abnormal psychology at Seattle University, shares the view that there were no accidents about the way she died. "She was very methodical," said Halling, who also recalled the case. "As in death, so she likely was in life." Halling read something else into her choice as well: "I wonder if there was a bit of a challenge in it," he said. "If you're going to find out who I am, you're going to have to work at it."

INVESTIGATORS DID WORK at it, putting in countless hours and chasing dozens of leads.

"It's the only case I never solved in my 10 years," said Arleigh Marquis, the medical examiner's primary investigator on the case. Marquis has identified people from leads as slim as a copied key. Like Webster and Matthews, he still thinks about Mary Anderson.

Anderson refused to yield to their probing.

"We examined her hands to see whether they suggested an occupation," Webster said. Sometimes forensic investigators can judge, by the softness of the skin, or a pattern of calluses, what work a subject might have done. Nothing.

Her use of cyanide, however, likely meant that she had some education. For a time, investigators thought she might have worked for a mining company or a chemistry lab—either medical, or university—where she would have had access to the poison. But a search produced nothing.

Her skill at hiding her identity may have been its own clue. Could she have worked for an intelligence operation? Was she a spy?

"That's entirely possible," said Marquis, now the medical examiner for Snohomish County. Her appearance was vaguely Eastern European, although her command of the written English language indicated that she was a native speaker, he said.

He also wouldn't rule out that she had family, despite her note. "When people tell me that, I automatically don't believe it," he said. "It's more a request not to look."

Marquis believes that she was likely familiar with Seattle and had been to the hotel before, perhaps had a significant memory associated with it. The ZIP code she wrote in the hotel registry was for Astoria, N.Y., but checks there didn't reveal any information.

There were other false leads. She had a copper IUD implanted in her uterus, the implied intimacy of it suggestive of a relationship. But the part number was worn away, so investigators couldn't trace its origin. And no lover came to claim her. Scars beneath both breasts indicated some form of cosmetic breast surgery—indicating that she had the means, and desire, to care for her appearance. That, too, led nowhere. Dental records didn't help either.

They tried to trace her clothing and makeup to their point of purchase, but all were from department stores located in multiple states. The lot her Metamucil came from was shipped initially to Phoenix, but could have gone anywhere after that. Her family Bible had no family listed.

When all the leads had been exhausted, this is all they knew of Anderson: She was about 5 foot 7 and approximately 240 pounds. She had short, brownish hair and brown eyes. She was likely between age 33 and 45. She had never borne children. She owned two pairs of eyeglasses and shopped at midrange department stores. The brand names she wore, The Villager (by Liz Claiborne) and Alfred Dunner, were available at what was then The Bon Marché, or at J.C. Penney. In Canada, she could have bought those brands at Sears or Hudson's. She preferred bright lipstick: Starlit Pink or Rich and Rosy. She wore Estée Lauder Private Collection perfume.

But even "facts" can be subjective. Light eyes turn darker after death, Matthews of the Doe Network said. And it's sometimes hard even in life to differentiate eye color. Hair can be color-treated. Age estimates are subjective at best.

Identifying details get reported differently by different people, and such creeping inconsistencies are the bane of searchers.

Some things are provable: An autopsy confirmed she was in good health. But the psyche doesn't yield to the scalpel; there are no forensic tests for a broken spirit.

IF ANDERSON CHOSE an invisible death, it may well have been the result of an invisible killer. Depression—undiagnosed depression in particular—is an insidious threat. According to the U.S. Centers for Disease Control and Prevention, suicide is among the top 10 causes of death in the United States, outstripping homicide.

"It's a lethal condition that is underdiagnosed and undertreated," said Dr. David Dunner, professor of psychiatry at the University of Washington and director of the Center for Anxiety and Depression. Only about half of those who have it seek help, and only about half of those who seek help are diagnosed properly and treated. Of those who are diagnosed, only half are treated adequately, he said. "Unfortunately, suicide is an outcome with a fairly high percentage, although the exact figure is unknown," he said.

Experts estimate the mortality rate for severe depression to be about 15 percent. The risk of suicide is about 20 times greater for people with depression than for the general population. And although men have triple the rate of suicide, women attempt it three times more often than men, psychologists say. Women are more vulnerable to depression, in part because of hormonal interplay with mood disorders, Dunner said. Rates of depression are twice as common in women than in men.

People who are depressed may go in and out of feeling suicidal. It is very difficult to predict. A feeling of hopelessness, however, is one commonality among those who contemplate suicide, Dunner said. Survivors of suicide attempts talk about it as though they were taken over by a "black cloud."

No one knows what Mary Anderson's state of mind was, but her deliberate invisibility could itself be a clue.

At a certain age, women can begin to feel unnoticed, said Halling, the psychology professor at Seattle University. Women who are seeing their looks begin to change, and who have not yet achieved the revered status of elder or grandmother, may begin to feel lost in a society that focuses on shallow views of women's worth.

Perhaps it's revealing, then, that she picked Mary Anderson as her alias. Mary Anderson was the name of the woman who invented the windshield wiper in 1905. Was it deliberate irony to choose as a namesake the inventor of a ubiquitous device we look past daily with little notice? Or merely happenstance?

For both sexes, middle age is a time of dealing with accrued life issues, the "baggage" of messy lives, said Pepper Schwartz, a professor of sociology at the University of Washington. The changes such unresolved life issues cause in people may be subtle enough that those around them don't see them spiraling into depression. "People forget just exactly what the person used to be like, so nobody is figuring out how to respond," Schwartz said. "Pretty soon it's a real big problem."

Looking at the Anderson case from the outside, Schwartz said, her method suggests that she really wanted to die. "That's an important part of that description. . . . I think it's important to know she was beyond caring." Isolation can lead to that level of despair, she added. "We're very much a herd animal, and a coupling animal," she said. "We need to have people in close intimate relationship. We get strange when we don't. If we stay isolated, we feel unimportant, irrelevant and start to get self-destructive."

WIND RAKES THE branches of the trees that shelter the headstones spread across Crown Hill Cemetery. Tucked into a modest residential area on the edge of Ballard, the graveyard is one of the few remaining family-owned cemeteries in Seattle.

In the green-shingled cemetery office, caretaker Phillip Howell pulls a yellowing card from an old steel file cabinet. "Here she is," he says. The card reads: Doe, Jane, Grave No. 197-A.

Howell heads across the brown grass to the far corner of the cemetery.

"Quite often this is a happy place," he says, sounding wishful. "It's a place where people come to be together and remember. But this back here is kind of a sad area. There's one person who was murdered a couple of spaces away."

A few feet from the back fence, just over from a high bank of dirt from already-dug graves, he stops and feels for the slight indentation that tells him he has arrived.

"This is it," he says. Anderson shares the space with another, a man buried as indigent. The county spent $479 on her burial. There was no service. There is no marker on her grave.

But there are people who remember. Quarles, who found her at the hotel, does. "I've thought about her a lot over the years," he said. "It shouldn't be that easy to just disappear."

Webster still wishes he knew her real name, if only to lay the matter to rest for whatever family she had.

Matthews, too, wants to give her a name. "Everyone deserves that," he said.

And Halling, of Seattle University, offered this. "If you wanted to, you could disappear. She made herself anonymous, but still a presence."

In that sense, she got what she perhaps didn't get in life: notice.

The sun is setting, and the caretaker winds his way through the cemetery back to his office. Dotted around the graveyard are monuments to memories of others—a perpetual garden with a bench and wintering pansies at the grave of a teenager, a mausoleum housing a man buried seated in his wheelchair—each as idiosyncratic as the person it memorializes.

Behind him, a blanket of fallen maple leaves carpets Mary's grave.

Badlands

Portrait of a Competitive Eater

JOHN O'CONNOR

"Badlands," which originally appeared in the literary journal Gastronomica, *introduces readers to the expanding sport of competitive eating. The narrator has a strong presence, whether he's trying to finish a Colossal burger with Badlands or keeping an eye out for "urges contrary to swallowing" as a judge during a championship event. The writer's involvement—his immersion in the topic—helps readers delve even deeper into the event.*

Badlands was hungry. And by hungry I don't mean peckish, or pleasantly empty, or that he had that faint grumble you get an hour or so before dinner. No, this was a different breed of hunger altogether. It was a murderous, desert island hunger, the kind you feel deep in your eyeballs, when all of your rational faculties have atrophied and your brain feels like it's dribbling out of your nostrils and the only thing you desire in this world is FOOD, any kind of food, RIGHT NOW.

Let it be said that Badlands is not accustomed to this kind of hunger. Normal hunger, sure. He's usually hungry. In fact, a satiated Badlands is a rare creature indeed. But tonight was different. Tonight it was as if a small mammal, say, a badger (those most capable burrowers of the weasel family), had crawled down his gullet, hollowed out his stomach, and lay there growling and scratching away at his insides.

You see, Badlands does not usually fast before contests, as he believes this can lead to "shrinkage" of his stomach, thereby reducing his intake of food. He'll eat a normal breakfast the day of an event, sometimes lunch, too, and maybe even a snack shortly before the start whistle. All of which sets Badlands at ideological odds with the vast majority of competitive eaters, called "gurgitators," who generally hold that an empty stomach equals increased stuffing capacity. Physiologically speaking, both theories are half-baked. But for some reason a few acolytes of the fasting school have had recent success on the circuit, so tonight Badlands was experimenting, and it was clear from the look on his face that the experiment was killing him.

To make matters worse, George Shea, the brains and impeccable hair of the International Federation of Competitive Eating (IFOCE) that organized the contest, had asked gurgitators to arrive well ahead of time as insurance against start whistle snafus, which are routine at these gatherings. Tonight's event was the second annual World Pelmeni Eating Championship (pelmenis are a Russian pasta—think tortellini crossed with pierogi), one of the year's biggest contests, with a modest media presence and a semi-respectable cash prize, and George wanted everyone present mega-early and ready to cram.

So Badlands had driven the hour from his house in Copiague, Long Island, in wrist-slitting rush-hour traffic and by successive miracles had found a parking spot two blocks from the Atlantic Oceana Ballroom in Brighton Beach, Brooklyn, parallel-parked his mammoth SUV in two beautiful, for-the-record-book turns, and lumbered through the Oceana's clouded glass doors, slightly out of breath and major-league agitated, right on time.

That was at six P.M. Now it was eight, and it had been early morning since he'd last eaten. Nothing all day, not even a Slim Jim.

After a circumnavigation of the Oceana's sprawling insides, I found Badlands slumped in a chair near the kitchen, its swinging doors divulging an anthill-like scrum of waiters while offering a glimpse of the boiling madness inside, a war zone of grease-strewn men and crashing metal. Badlands looked sedated. His eyelids sagged; a meaty sliver of tongue was clamped between his teeth; and his hands were clasped across his broad belly. A 420-pound, six-foot-five-inch semi-vegetative Black Goliath.

I revived him with a knuckle punch to the bicep.

SMACK! His eyes shot open; his size fourteens flew off the floor; and his massive body lurched forward.

Blinking, frowning, he struggled to his feet. "You alright?" I asked.

"Yeah, yeah. I'm feeling good," he said. "My stomach is stretched and I'm ready to go."

"You looked half-dead."

"Aw man, I was visualizing."

One of Badlands's precontest rituals entails visualizing the eating of whatever food is at hand, like a skier might imagine slipping through a slalom course prior to a race. It's akin to meditation: a cleansing of the chakra bowels to achieve unobstructed intestinal harmony.

Badlands's jeans rode low off his waist, hitched up his thick shanks, and his 5-XL black Sean John jersey had an ironing board look to it, the sleeves coming to points at the shoulders like a kite. He also wore a matching baseball cap, the brim flattened and flipped to the back. Despite his fervent attempts to keep the jersey clean, in about thirty minutes it will be streaked white down the front from the soupy extract of pelmenis.

"I guzzled a half gallon of water before I left home," he said. "Just a little something to keep myself stretched. I haven't had anything to eat since breakfast, and I'm worried how that'll affect me. Plus, my bladder is about to go, man."

A few days earlier, Badlands had explained to me one of the pillars of his gurgitational philosophy, namely that with every food comes an ideal strategy for attack, a strategy to be measured against an eater's individual speed and capacity. Over the past couple of weeks, Badlands had been searching for his pelmeni strategy, guzzling gallons of water and plowing through bowls of ravioli and pierogi at his kitchen table while his eleven-year-old son, Brandon, timed him on the microwave.

"Pelmenis are a relatively easy food to speed-eat because they're soft," Badlands had told me, "but the pasta gets tough after a while and is hard on the jaws." To address this problem, he'd been chewing a wad of Big Red—twenty-one sticks at a time—for an hour a day. "You gotta have strong jaws in this game," he'd said. "You cannot come to the table with weak jaws and expect to go the distance. A lot of people don't realize that, and they try to take shortcuts."

The grand prize at the Pelmeni Championship was fifteen hundred dollars, and Badlands hoped tonight would be the payoff for all his Chef Boyardee workouts. The standing record, held by Oleg "the Russian" Zhornitskiy (who's actually Ukrainian), was 244 pelmenis in six minutes. Badlands thought he could do at least 250.

"I'm through with this fasting stuff though, man," he said, rubbing his stomach and arching back on his heels. "It's wrecked my energy level."

A few other gurgitators milled around nearby—Ed "Cookie" Jarvis, "Hungry" Charles Hardy, "Gentleman" Joe Manchetti, Sabatino "the Great" Manzi, "Krazy" Kevin Lipsitz—all of them big, big dudes. Sabatino had a cartoonishly oblong gut, like a yoga ball held in suspenders, and a swinging, bovine double chin. Cookie packed most of his extra weight in several intimidating saddlebags fore and aft of his waistline. And Hungry seemed to hold his spare pounds primarily in his neck and shoulders, which appeared as solid as armor. Despite this awesome display of flesh, Badlands could easily claim Fat Bastard supremacy over them all.

In fact, Badlands's sheer bulk is a little intimidating at first. On instinct I tend to be wary of people who are taller than me, let alone 250 pounds heavier. And Badlands not only looms over me, he looms around me. When I hug him (we always greet each other with a soul brother handshake) it's a little like being in the arms of a grizzly, except, I imagine, gentler. But his liquid brown eyes, pudgy shaved head, and cylindrical jowls give him the sublime and placid mien of the Buddha. It also helps that he's possibly the nicest person I've ever met.

From the looks of them, none of the other gurgitators had eaten much that day either. That is, aside from Cookie, who was inhaling a sweating pastry he'd boosted from a passing tray. The tables around us were swamped with steaming platters: smoked fish, roasted chickens, mystery-meat patties, and what looked like some sort of eggplant-squash hybrid. All of which was off limits. The gurgitators had only a short while until the Pelmeni Championship got under way, and they'd all apparently resolved to channel their hunger into the competition.

George Shea materialized, perspiring liberally in a black tuxedo, a clipboard jammed in his armpit, his hair moist and delicately slicked back in the Pat Riley manner. He started barking instructions.

"We're going to introduce you individually! Remember when you come out to space yourselves! Don't bunch up! And make a little show for the crowd!"

From what I could gather from George's harangue, gurgitators were supposed to emerge single file through a cloud of dry ice at the top of the stage, which was set in the back of the ballroom, and then descend a short, deceptively steep flight of stairs to a narrow platform, which would maybe (maybe not) hold all twenty of them shoulder to shoulder—an imposing phalanx of whoddling flesh and bone—before they had to descend another short flight of stairs to a large U of banquet tables assembled along the periphery of a parquet floor. In other words, what sounded like a catastrophe in the making.

George wrapped things up—"Everyone backstage, pronto!"—and then sprinted off into the darkness. Gurgitators dispersed slowly, knocking back drinks and rubbing out cigarettes. I turned to Badlands and swung a crisp right hook through the air, bringing it down squarely on his wide shoulder. WHACK! He feigned injury, stumbling backwards. I went to find a seat. A few minutes later I looked over and saw him standing right where I'd left him, talking to a newspaper reporter. He'd once told me that interacting with the media used to terrify him. He'd get tongue-tied, worried about saying the wrong thing, offending someone. Now he craved the attention. Everything about contests—the cameras, the hot lights, the revolted audience—he found totally irresistible. Here, sprung from the anonymous masses, Badlands was a star, and he absolutely lived for these moments. Now he was lingering, however, and George reemerged from the shadows to give him a last pleading look to get a move-on.

Competitive eating has gained a small measure of notoriety in recent years almost entirely because of George Shea and his younger brother Rich, who together comprise the IFOCE, which they formed in 1997 to promote eating contests, half tongue-in-cheek, as "the sport of the new millennium." Today the IFOCE oversees more than 150 events a year and has over 3,000 registered gurgitators. The sport's pinnacle is the Nathan's Famous Hot Dog Eating Contest held on Coney Island every July Fourth, which is attended by thousands and carried live on ESPN. The five-time Nathan's champ and undisputed gurgitational hegemon is twenty-seven-year-old Takeru Kobayashi, a 132-pound Japanese eater who holds the record of 53.5 hot dogs and buns in 12 minutes and who is said to earn around $150,000 a year from contests in Japan and the United States.

Badlands, by comparison, is the number-five-ranked gurgitator in the world, with major victories in burritos (15 in 8:00 minutes), corned beef hash (4 pounds in 1:58 minutes), peas (9.5 one-pound bowls in 12:00 minutes), onions (8.5 ounces in 1:00 minute), and hamantaschen (50 traditional Purim cookies in 6:00 minutes), among others. While his winnings are nowhere near Kobayashi's, he earns enough from contests to make occasionally lavish upgrades to his home entertainment center. The pelmeni cash prize would help in this regard, and the three-foot-high trophy would be a welcome addition to the glinting metropolis of gurgitating honors already buckling his mantelpiece.

The Oceana was jammed to fire-hazard capacity that night, mostly with Russians from the surrounding Brighton Beach neighborhood, which is just down the road from Coney Island. Everybody looked related, or at least as though they shared a tailor. The men all wore Soviet-era double-breasted suits and had moustaches like fat caterpillars, while the women labored under mountains of hair and wore sequined evening gowns, all thighs and wilting cleavage. It was like a politburo reunion from the class of 1979. The fifty-dollar cover bought you a Pantagruelian smorgasbord and several stage performances, of which the pelmeni contest was the finale. There was way too much food, an unfathomable amount of food, in fact, and whole tables of it went untouched.

After the cabaret acts, George and Rich Shea appeared onstage. Rich is a half-foot shorter than George, his hair almost reflective, like George's, from the generous application of hair products, and his bottom lip is held permanently in a subtle pout. Together they gave their standard carnival barker introduction, expounding on the illustrious history of competitive eating and extolling the sport's "physical poetry." Then, as Guns 'n' Roses' "Welcome to the Jungle" rumbled out of the PA system, gurgitators began plodding through the dry-ice fog at the top of the stage. There was confusion at first as the blinding luminescence of the strobe lights immobilized them. A cluster of eaters crowded at the precipice, toeing the shadowy top stair and shielding their eyes as George waited expectantly below. At last, a cooperative leap of faith was made, and those in front started gingerly down, arms outstretched, fear in their eyes. The rest soon followed, and free of the stairs, they swaggered and chest-thumped one another onstage as though they were part of a college bowl game introduction.

Oleg the Russian had come first (given pole position as defending champ), followed by Cookie, Hungry, Krazy Kev, Crazy Legs, Sabatino, Dale "The Mouth from the South" Boone (who claimed to be a descendant of Daniel Boone), Gentleman Joe, Don "Moses" Lerman (carrying replica cardboard tablets), two guys wearing military-style ushanka hats and black leather boots who Rich said were members of the Ukrainian National Eating Team, and a few others.

Badlands came out second to last, waving a white hand towel in circles above his head, his underarm flesh wagging like a hammock. He appeared to be growling. An arc of spittle flew from his mouth and was briefly illuminated by the backlighting, flickering out like a dying sparkler. As Axl Rose squealed, "Feel my . . . my . . . my serpentine!" Badlands paused at the foot of the stage between George and Rich and, with the hand towel clenched between his teeth, flexed Mr. Universe style. The audience ate it up. When the applause reached its crescendo, Badlands's scowl vanished, and his face blazed into a quarter moon of teeth: his signature entrance.

A COUPLE OF WEEKS before the Pelmeni Championship, I met Badlands for lunch at a diner in lower Manhattan. A gray slab of sky

Badlands's second win at the Ben's Kosher Deli Annual Matzo Ball Eating Contest, January 2004. He ate 20 ¼ matzo balls in 5 minutes, 25 seconds. (John O'Connor)

hung over the city. Rain was coming down like sprayed buckshot and created little rivers that spilled along the curbs, overflowing the drainage grates at the corners and forcing people to leap over the sprawling puddles. Despite the weather, Badlands was in a good mood, and before we'd even sat down, he launched into a monologue on his favorite topic: the future of competitive eating in the United States.

"It's a sport. I definitely think it's going to be in the Olympics one day, if not as a main event then as an exhibition sport. I mean look, right now you got ballroom dancing as an exhibition sport. What the hell is that? Some guys twirling ladies around? C'mon, man! The thing is, everyone can relate to eating. There's a fascination there. Rich Shea calls competitive eating 'the sport of the everyman,' because in America we're big eaters, and everyone likes to pig out once in a while. Eating contests have the same things that people look for in other sports. Mainly, they're fun to watch, and they also make you wonder, how can that guy or girl eat so much, so fast?"

Badlands looked formidable across the small Formica table. I imagined it was how Gulliver appeared to the Lilliputians, and I wasn't inclined to disagree with him just then. Besides, his logic sort of made sense. Americans do like to pig out. I could personally attest to that. Plus, adding ballroom dancing to the Olympic pantheon did seem to widen the criteria for how you defined "sport." Chess was an exhibition event at the 2000 Sydney Olympics, and the mind-numbing Japanese board game Go was being promoted as a possible addition to the 2012 games. Where, after all, do you draw the line with this sort of thing?

Our waitress arrived, and Badlands ordered the ten-ounce "Colossal" hamburger with onion rings and a Sprite. Not wanting to seem abstemious, I got the Colossal too, with bacon and cheese, plus fries and a Coke. Badlands flipped open his wallet and pulled out a wrinkled photo of himself and his wife, Gina, on their wedding day. They got married right out of high school and now have three sons, ages eleven, fourteen, and seventeen (the oldest is from Gina's previous marriage). In the photo Gina is wearing a cream colored gown and holding a bouquet, her hair in a spire of curls that tilts slightly over her forehead. Badlands is in a black tux with a white corsage, a high-top fade and a thin goatee cut around his lips. He's thinner by probably 150 pounds.

When our waitress returned, she dropped our plates on the table with a heavy clunk. My Colossal, which stood a little taller than my soda glass, looked as if it had been buffed and polished. Gleaming curls of bacon jabbed from its sides, the twisted fat resembling entrails. The burger leaned against an arc of fries that seemed to have been strategically positioned to prevent it from tipping over and spilling its contents on the table.

Before we dug in, I asked Badlands if he ever worried what effect, if any, his hobby might have on his health.

"My doctor says as long as I don't eat too much during the off-season I'll be okay,"' he said.

"When is the off-season?"

"Whenever there's no contest."

As we laid siege to our Colossals, I was tempted to ask whether he considered today part of the off-season, but I chickened out.

"There's a theory that says the skinnier you are the more food you can eat," Badlands went on, "because your stomach can stretch more." He held his hands out in front of his stomach to illustrate this. "I want to see if that's true. I'm planning on losing some weight. It sounds crazy, but you really have to be in shape to be competitive in these contests. I mean, I want to be around for my kids, too, you know? But secondly, I want to be in top form for contests."

With an onion ring poised to slither through his lips, Badlands said he'd been trying to cut red meat and fried food out of his diet.

I let Badlands ramble as we ate, and ramble he did, a great meandering tangent that eventually wound back, as most things do with him, to competitive eating.

Born in 1969 in Jamaica, Queens, Badlands attended high school in Brooklyn, where he played basketball and football and got decent grades. Later, he dreamed of making it as a rapper, and in the early 1990s he recorded a rap album in a friend's basement. Nothing came of that, but in December 2004 Badlands self-released the album *Hungry & Focused*, his autobiographical ode to competitive eating.

"I wanted to do something positive and with a competitive eating theme, like the Fat Boys," Badlands explained. "But more about what I do and how I got into this and where I am in the sport."

Twelve years ago, Badlands landed a job as a subway conductor with the Metropolitan Transit Authority. Five nights a week he rides the Number Seven train its twenty-one stops from Flushing, Queens—

one stop past Shea Stadium—to Times Square and back again, three round-trips total. He has to stand the entire shift crammed into the conductor's booth, a coffin-like space in the center of the train from which he flips a switch to open and close the doors. Seeing Badlands's haunches roll off his chair in the diner, I guessed that the conductor's booth couldn't be too cozy—all 420 pounds of him stuffed into that airless, shuddering closet, hurtling under the East River and through the bowels of Queens and Manhattan in near pitch blackness, inhaling the tunnels' horrid stench while the squeal of the train's brakes broke his eardrums apart.

I started to ask him if he ever got tired of his job, but he didn't want to talk about work.

"In Japan, competitive eating is huge," he said. "It's like baseball or hockey is here, and the eaters make a pretty good living from it. Look at Kobayashi. It'll be like that here eventually. Just watch." Badlands jabbed the tabletop with his finger for emphasis, rattling the ice in our glasses. "It'll get to the point where the type of money that's available to Japanese eaters will become available to us. It's just a matter of time."

In the past few months Badlands had competed in practically every eating contest in New York City and a few others around the country, he said. Pickles, matzoh balls, cannoli, corned beef hash, doughnuts, and cheesecake. The pelmeni would be his third in three weeks.

"How do all of these contests affect you digestively?" I asked.

"I used to feel the aftereffects when I first started," Badlands said. "Basically, a lot of gas and stuff, but my body has gotten used to the rigors of the sport. Now I feel like a person after a big Thanksgiving meal. I get back into shape by taking a laxative the night after a contest, and I'm back to normal by morning."

He amended an apologetic smile to the end of this sentence and then ripped away another bite, his jaws opening menacingly and clamping down on his Colossal like Jaws on Robert Shaw.

"Why put yourself through this?" I asked. "Why compete in these contests for other people's amusement and for little or sometimes no pay?"

Badlands paused, eyes skyward and head askew, as if considering this question for the first time. "I just loved it from the first day I tried it," he said. "Just being able to know that I can eat this food faster than anyone in the world, it's a great feeling."

This wasn't exactly the response I was after, but it would have to do for now. We'd finished our Colossals, and Badlands had to go.

As we were getting ready to pay, a boy of about thirteen approached, and said he recognized Badlands from the Nathan's contest, which he'd seen on TV. He asked for an autograph. After the kid scurried off, Badlands said to me, "That happens more and more. People recognize me in the subway, in the street, wherever. When they appreciate what you do, it's really something. And you gotta show them love."

The pulse at the Pelmeni Championship had flat-lined through the cabaret acts, but by the time the contest rolled around, most people were out of their seats and swarming around the parquet floor, armed with DV recorders.

Gurgitators were spread out along the U of banquet tables with large white oval plates of pelmenis in front of them, waiting for the start whistle. Badlands was seated in the middle of the U. He'd draped dishtowels across his lap and tucked a few in his jersey and even laid them under his chair. He was doing some precontest rituals: neck rotations, arm and jaw stretches, a massive cracking of knuckles. This routine varies depending on the circumstances. At Nathan's, for instance, where gurgitators stood at waist-high tables, he warmed up by pumping his arms like a sprinter, arcing invisible hot dogs into his mouth in mock eating motion. Tonight, he would use his hands to shovel the pelmenis into his mouth, and when he'd finished his warm-ups, he sat with his face inches away from his plate, his hands twitching beside it like a gunslinger.

His mental approach is always the same, though. "What I do is I try to get a rhythm going and not worry too much about my speed or what other eaters are doing," he'd told me. "You've got to stay focused. If you let yourself get distracted and start worrying about the guy next to you, you're in trouble. The main thing is to concentrate." To help him concentrate, Badlands listens to his MP3 player during contests. The style of music varies, though recently he'd been leaning toward techno.

From my seat I caught sight of Rich Shea on the other side of the tables, waving for me to come forward. When I'd snaked through the crowd to Rich, he said he'd volunteered me, along with three others, as a judge for the contest. With the lights from DV recorders winking at us, Rich had us raise our right hands and swear to uphold the rules and regulations of the IFOCE, so help us God. We'd be responsible for counting the empty plates of pelmenis as they left the tables, he explained, and for monitoring the gurgitators to ensure there was no cheating.

"Be especially vigilant with urges contrary to swallowing," he said, employing his euphemism for puking. "That's an automatic disqualification."

Onstage, George was itching to go. He bobbed back and forth on his toes, pursing his lips and lobbing a microphone from hand to hand. Then suddenly he screamed, "Gentlemen! Start your engines!" And before I knew it, they were off.

Right away, Rich started jogging among the tables, delivering color commentary with one hand held aloft, an index finger pointing to the rafters, screeching into his microphone.

"Ladies and gentlemen! Oleg Zhornitskiy has just finished his first plate!" "Ladies and gentlemen! Dale Boone is positively RAGING!"

I'd been assigned a table with Hungry Charles and the two guys from the Ukrainian National Eating Team. The Ukrainians started strong but slowed about midway through their second plates. Hungry lost steam around his third. I've dubbed Hungry's eating style the

"Crouching Tiger, Hidden Cram," because he bends his body over and folds his arms around his plate, almost concealing it completely, and then shoves the food into his mouth hand-over-fist until he is spent. Occasionally, this is a deadly technique, and early in his career it earned Hungry a string of impressive victories. But tonight he'd reached his limit far before the rest of the field, and he looked devastated, leaning with his elbows on the table and shaking his cornrowed head, his gold crucifix dangling in his plate.

A couple of tables away, Dale the Mouth and Badlands were setting the pace. A mass of crazed Russian youth mobbed their table, shrieking and waving their arms, and a few leaned over to shout encouragement/obscenities at the two gurgitators. One commented to Dale the Mouth, who had his face mashed into a plate of pelmenis, his jaws pumping like pistons, that he was eating like a mad dog.

Badlands's eating rhythm was predictably cadenced as he nodded along to his music and swayed his body laterally. He didn't seem to notice the swarm across the table or Dale frothing next to him. He ate deliberately, not particularly rushed, pausing occasionally to take sips of water. Yet by the looks of it, he was consuming a staggering amount of pelmenis.

Finally, George blew the whistle and called for the gurgitators to cease and desist. As the turmoil subsided, the audience members lowered their cameras and gazed blankly about. The crowd had worked itself into a frenzy during the contest, yowling, thrashing, dispensing with any pretense of restraint. But everyone quickly recovered themselves and began filing sheepishly back to their tables.

Once the dust had settled, a sobering scene emerged on the parquet floor. Twenty panting, corpulent men, slathered jowl to jowl in butter and pasta fragments, stumbled around in a daze. The Shea brothers scurried from table to table, sifting through plates, sorting leftovers, hurrying to count the remaining pelmenis and declare a winner. The Pelmeni Championship has a history of controversy. Almost every year

someone demands a recount or alleges fraud or protests a disqualification. So George and Rich were anxious to have the results decided
as quickly as possible before things got ugly. We judges stood aside as
the Sheas did all of the tallying, scribbling on scraps of paper and con-
ferring with one another at the foot of the stage.

Then George trod up the stage steps and, a little hoarsely, declared
Dale the Mouth the winner with a total of 274 pelmenis. Badlands was
second with 271, and Oleg the Russian, with 267, was third. Sure
enough, Oleg's brother, Alex, who bore a striking resemblance to Peja
Stoyakovich of the Sacramento Kings, pulled George aside to argue
for a recount. But after a long night, George wasn't having it, and the
results stood.

Dale the Mouth, clad in a coonskin cap and denim overalls, received
his winning trophy onstage, a delicate dribble of pelmeni stuck in the
corner of his mouth. Overcome with emotion, he grabbed the microphone out of George's hand and screamed, "This is for the victims of
September 11 and for New York City!" George wrenched the microphone back and, with just the slightest touch of irony, said, "Ladies
and Gentleman, we are in the midst of competitive eating's best. And
Dale Boone, my friends, is a true athlete."

Badlands received a trophy, a bouquet of pink roses, and a check for
one thousand dollars. A horde of kids and little old ladies converged
on him, clamoring for autographs and pictures, to which he happily
obliged. A few days earlier he'd confided to me that there were a lot of
big egos in competitive eating but that he wasn't one of them.

"I know the same way I got these fans I can lose 'em," he'd said. "If
you don't sign an autograph for somebody and treat 'em like you
don't have the time, it's the same thing like if you're a musician, and
they're not gonna buy your record. Besides, I'm not like that. I'm not
conceited. I just try to stay grounded and be myself."

'Mbriago

LOUISE DeSALVO

Louise DeSalvo tells not only her grandfather's story (her grand-father is 'Mbriago, "the Drunk"), but also that of Southern Italy, where field workers' labor was fueled by wine, cheaper and more plentiful than water. Memoir is often criticized for "navel-gazing," but here DeSalvo looks outward—far beyond her grandfather in both space and time. This essay first appeared in Our Roots Are Deep with Passion, *Issue 30 of* Creative Nonfiction.

A Knock at the Door

It would happen like this. A knock on the crackled glass of the door to our tenement apartment in Hoboken, New Jersey. My mother, not expecting a visitor, opening it as she would for anyone who troubled to climb the four steep flights of stairs. She had nothing to fear. She knew that if the visitor was a stranger, by the time he got to our door, he would have been stopped, thoroughly checked out, and granted passage up to our apartment by one of the young men hang-

ing out on the corner of Fourth and Adams in front of Albini's Drug-
store, by the old woman leaning out the window on the first floor of
our building, or by the old man sitting in the sun on our front stoop.

So because there was nothing to fear from a knock on the door
(World War II was over, my father back home unharmed, at work a
few blocks away), my mother would put down her mending, or turn
away from her ironing board, or pull a pot off the coal stove and open
the door, hoping, perhaps, that it was my father home from work early
or Argie from down the block—the only friend who could lure her
away from the punishing rounds of her daily household chores.

Outside the door, not my father, nor Argie, but an old Italian man.
Short, stooped, ruddy-faced from years of work in the sun, wearing a
cap like my grandfather's. Surprise on his face. Then, shame. A slight
bow, as he took off his cap. "*Mi dispiace proprio,*" he'd say. "I'm very
sorry." He hadn't known a woman would open the door.

"'*Mbriago?*" he'd ask. '*Mbriago*, the drunk. My grandfather's nickname. The man had come to see him. He would be a distant relative
from Vieste, my grandfather's village in Puglia, or a crony from his
railroad days in upstate New York, or a pal from his years of working
on the docks in New York City. And he would be needing a loan.

Ours was a neighborhood of nasty nicknames—"Joey the Fat,"
"Jimmy Goose Face," "Bobby Snot Eater." Even mine—"Miss Prim,"
"Miss-too-big-for-your-britches," or "Miss Smarty Pants"—given me
by my father, were far from endearing, revealing my father's disgust at
what he called my holier-than-thou attitude. So my mother never
recoiled at her father's being called '*Mbriago*. There were many old
Italian men like my grandfather, who worked all day, drank wine all
day to fortify themselves for work, staggered home drunk, washed
themselves at the sink, changed their clothes, poured themselves a
little glass of wine to restore their spirits while they waited for their
suppers, poured themselves a large tumbler of wine to accompany
their meals, poured themselves a little glass of *digestif* so they would

sleep all night. They, too, were called *'Mbriago*. And even the ones who weren't called *'Mbriago* were drunk much of the time.

"Next door," my mother tells the visitor, pointing. She knows that anyone who comes to see her father, comes for a loan, the bargain sealed by a few glasses of my grandfather's homemade wine. My mother, worrying about how my grandfather will support himself when he retires if he gives money to everyone who comes to his door, and because she embraces the American doctrine of self-reliance, slams the door on the old man, shakes her head, and grumbles her way back to her work.

The Table

In all the photographs, in all the moving pictures of my grandparents' table, there is always bread, just enough food for satiety, and always a flask of wine. But there is never water. Not a pitcher of water, nor a glass of water. My grandfather, so far as I know, never drank water. Nor did my grandmother, much. A little glass of water for her on hottest of days is all I can remember.

When I am young, I never notice that my grandfather does not drink water, that he drinks only wine. And his nickname, *'Mbriago*, tells me nothing more about him than if he were called something else. For his drinking wine instead of water when he was thirsty was not something I questioned or remarked upon. It was as natural to me as the verdant green of the trees in the park around the corner in springtime, the sweat of summer, the melancholy falling leaves of autumn, or the death of the soul in wintertime.

Home Movie

In one moving picture, taken by my father, my grandfather is standing behind his kitchen table, miming drinking down an entire flask of wine. My grandmother looks annoyed, tries to take the flask from him. He pulls it away from her, mimes drinking the entire flask of wine again. She becomes annoyed again, grabs his arm, tries to take the flask away again. But he turns away from her. He is the hero in his son-in-law's home movie; he is enjoying playing the drunk that he is.

My mother sits at the table, looks away, cups her face in her hand, a gesture that I have come to understand indicates her displeasure at what is going on. There is an antipasto on the table. Another flask of wine. A cup of milk for me. But no water.

Water, Water

My grandfather began to work in the fields of Puglia when he was seven years old. When he worked in the fields, he was not given water to drink by the landowners or their overseers. Water was scarce; water was needed for the crops, water was needed for animals, who were viewed as more valuable than farmworkers who could more easily be replaced if they sickened and died.

In the fields of Puglia, as in fields all across the South of Italy, people working in the fields drank wine to quench their thirst, not water. Wine was abundant; wine was cheaper; wine was safer to drink, at least that's what the farmworkers believed. Even now, if you travel to the South, if you see a group of farmworkers stopping their work for a few moments to rest, you will see them passing a flask of wine among them, you will see each man or woman wiping the mouth of the flask before passing it on to a comrade. "Passing the saint," they call it.

And so, my grandfather began "passing the saint" when he was seven years old each day as he worked in the fields; he "passed the saint" each day of his farm work in Puglia until he left for America. And one of the reasons he left for America—one of the reasons many people of the South left for America—is because the South was arid, the South was drought-stricken, and because of this lack of water, farmworkers did not earn what they needed to support themselves during bad years. So, at the beginning of the twentieth century, when there was a series of droughts that left many unemployed, America beckoned. And by the time my grandfather left Puglia, the habit of drinking wine, not water, to quench your thirst was ingrained. Water was dangerous, he believed (and it often was); wine was safe (even though drinking wine longterm would kill you, but this he did not know).

If my grandfather had lived in Puglia until 1939, if my grandfather had not emigrated to America very early in the 20th century, he would have witnessed the completion of the great aqueduct that now delivers water to Puglia, albeit inadequately. It was begun in 1906 and encompasses 213 kilometers of subterranean tunnels built by 11,000 workmen. During the Roman Empire, eleven aqueducts served the imperial city. But the Pugliese people had to wait until almost the middle of the twentieth century for water to be brought to their arid land.

Perhaps my grandfather would have been one of the men building that aqueduct. But he was not. He lived in Puglia when water was scarce; when whatever potable water was available was sold to the poor at exorbitant prices, when much of the water of Puglia was tainted and undrinkable; when much of the water of Puglia was standing water, which bred mosquitoes, which gave the people of Puglia malaria, which killed the people of Puglia in astonishing numbers, especially the children and the old and the weak, who were especially vulnerable.

But the South of Italy was not always an arid land. The aridness of the South and the lack of safe drinking water in the South when my grandfather lived there was caused by human beings and rooted in history and racism—the history of conquest, exploitation of the land

and its people, and the refusal of the governments of the North to provide the South with the water it needed to sustain life.

The Englishman Norman Douglas travelled through Puglia and Calabria, to see how the modern South compared to descriptions of the region in ancient texts, such as those in the odes of Roman poet Horace (65–8 BCE), who was born in Puglia, and the *Iter Venusinum* of Lupoli, and the texts of Virgil, Martial, Statius, Propertius, Strabo, Pliny, Varro, and Columella. He wrote about what he discovered in *Old Calabria*, originally published in 1915. Everywhere he went, Douglas looked for rivers, or streams, or springs mentioned in these ancient texts, and he discovered that virtually all of them had disappeared. He remarked upon how waterless the modern South is. How in the South, unlike the North, rains come during the winter when nothing is growing—in spring and summer, instead of rain, there is hot dry air, which makes it essential for the government to provide a system whereby water is captured when it's plentiful and distributed when it is not, only this isn't done. How the only water to be had is water bottled from mineral springs and sold by vendors. How peasants and farmworkers drink wine, not water; how they're often drunk by midday.

But in Horace's time, the South was "covered with forests," and the forests were full of "hares, rabbits, foxes, roe deer, wild boars, martens, porcupines, hedgehogs, tortoises, and wolves," virtually none of which survive now because the forests have been cut down or burned by invading armies. For Douglas, the South's poverty was linked to how despoiled the land had become; he attributes the lack of water to deforestation; he attributes the diseases that have plagued the South—cholera and malaria—to what has happened to the water in the South because of deforestation.

He tells of the "noisome" waters that exist in this generally "waterless land" of the South, of how little the government has done to drain the swamplands that breed mosquitoes. He writes about how preva-

lent malaria is in the South, how taking doses of quinine is necessary
to prevent malaria, but how the poor can't afford quinine.

"I dare say," writes Douglas, "the deforestation of the country,
which prevented the downflow of the rivers—choking up their beds
with detritus and producing stagnant pools favourable to the breeding of the mosquito—has helped to spread the plague [of malaria]."
He writes how cholera is increasing, and how the government's not
providing adequate sanitation in the South has made the spread of
cholera inevitable. He tells how, because of deforestation, there are
more frequent landslides, and how, after landslides, the threat of
cholera becomes greater.

Centuries of invasion left their mark as well. Invading Turks
burned down everything they encountered—towns, cities,
forests—as they rampaged through the South. Spanish viceroys and
Bourbons and Arab invaders destroyed the land. The Adriatic sea-
coast was depopulated during the Arab invasion, and villages and
towns were destroyed, everything in the path of the invading army
was burnt to the ground, and "the richly cultivated land became a
desert."

And what the foreign invaders began, the government in the North
completed. Northern and German industrialists acquired rights to the
timber of the South, and Douglas saw the slopes of existing forests
felled during his journey. To denude hillsides of trees in countries with
abundant rainfall was one thing. But to do so in a country with insuf-
ficient rainfall was "the beginning of the end."

Douglas believed that politicians and industrialists were greedy,
and did not care that their practices would lead to disaster for the
economy of the South in the future. Once hillsides were denuded,
rainfall washed the soil away, exposing the rocks beneath, making
reforestation impossible. But why should they care? They did not live
there. The immense profits gained from these destructive practices
went north, went out of the country, and often the workers that cut

down trees were imported. So the people of the South did not profit from their country's abuse.

Centuries of conquest coupled with the ravages of exploitative capitalism left the South devoid of two important natural resources—forests and water—and turned the South into the arid land my grandfather left. These acts changed the character of the people of the South. It led to the kind of "bestialization" and "anguished poverty" that Douglas had observed; until the 1880s, the poor sold their children by officially sanctioned contracts.

Douglas tells how haggard the people are, and how "distraught" from hunger and thirst. He believed that it was because the land could not feed its people, could not provide employment for its people, could not quench the thirst of its people, that the great emigration of the people of the South to America occurred.

Later in the 20th century, Carlo Levi's observations were essentially the same as Douglas's. Levi spent time in Lucania, the desolate region between Puglia and Calabria, as a political prisoner. In *Christ Stopped at Eboli*, Levi describes the state of the region when he lived there.

Hills of clay had become its most prevalent geographic feature. Wondering how they have been formed, Levi asks a local and is told that the trees have long since disappeared and the once fertile topsoil has eroded, leaving clay. Now, because there are no trees to hold the clay during the rainfalls of winter, there are frequent landslides. "The clay," he is told, "simply melts and pours down like a rushing stream, carrying everything with it. . . . When it rains, the ground gives way and starts to slide, and the houses fall down. . . ."

Because the earth can't support agriculture, many of the men of the region emigrated to America, destroying the family structure of the region. "For a year, or even two, he writes to her, then he drops out of her ken . . . ; in any case he disappears and never comes back." The women form new attachments, but they cannot divorce, so that many of the children are illegitimate. But the children die young, or "turn yellow and melancholy with malaria."

Levi believed that the South became poor because "the land has been gradually impoverished: the forests have been cut down, the rivers have been reduced to mountain streams that often run dry, and livestock has become scarce. Instead of cultivating trees and pasture lands there has been an unfortunate attempt to raise wheat in soil that does not favor it. . . . [M]alaria is everywhere."

For Levi, the effect of chronic malaria has been inscribed into the character of the people of the region. Malaria has robbed the people of the South of their ability to work and to find pleasure in the world.

Luxury Travel

When I take my husband to Sicily for his sixtieth birthday, we stay in a fancy hotel in Agrigento, overlooking the famous Greek temples.

At the end of the day, I take a long, hot bath. It is the time of the winds that blow up from the Sahara. There is grit on my body, in my hair, on my clothes.

Later, in early evening, I take a solitary walk into a village. I hear old women complaining to each other about how, for yet another day, there has been no water. A thousand yards down the road, in our hotel, there is an ocean of water. Here, none. Why?

When I return home, I ask a Sicilian friend. He laughs at my ignorance. "The Mafia," he says. "They control the water." He tells me to read Mary Taylor Simeti's *On Persephone's Island*. There I learn that in Sicily's interior, very often there is water only once every five or ten days. This is not the fault of nature, says Simeti. For Sicily is "rich in water that flows to the sea unexploited" because of government neglect, and because the Mafia "controls the major wells and springs that tap subterranean water layers, and . . . sells its water at high prices"

and interferes with any attempts to ensure a cheap, safe water supply
for the people.

Working on the Railroad

My grandfather came to America when he was a young man. He came
for a better life, yes. But he came, too, because he was afraid that if he
stayed in Puglia he would die. Die from a bullet to the chest during the
worker's rebellions. Die from thirst. Die from starvation. Die from
malaria. Die from cholera. Or die for no reason at all.

And regardless of the stories we have been told of the people of the
South leaving because they wanted a better life in America, it was terror, more than anything else, that propelled him and the scores of
others like him up the gangplank to the ship that would take him to
America. Terror, and, yes, a job promised him by a boss recruiting
men from his village to build a railroad line in upper New York State.
The deal was simple, one even my grandfather could understand. If
you put your mark on a piece of paper, you'd get free passage to America. When you got there, you worked until you paid off your passage.
Until then, the railroad would take care of you. There would be nothing for you to worry about.

And so my grandfather came to America, and worked on the railroad, and slept in his filthy work clothes—there was no place to wash,
no water to wash with—on vermin-infested bags of straw, covering
himself with a discarded horse blanket, eight men to a roach-infested,
windowless boxcar. He awakened at three in the morning, just like in
Italy, and walked the line to the day's worksite, and worked from five
to twelve without stopping. For lunch, there was bread, and sometimes there was water, but not always, because fresh water was in
short supply. In a 1916 essay called "The 'Wop' in the Track Gang,"
Dominic T. Ciolli reported how the *padrone* of a gang like my grand-

father's complained to him because the laborers complained that they had no fresh water, had had no fresh water to drink or to wash with for weeks, and how the *padrone* said, "These dagoes are never satisfied. . . . They should be starved to death. . . . They don't belong here."

But, like in Italy, my grandfather said, there was wine, there was always wine for the workers to drink. Wine: antidote to rebellion. Wine: pacifier of those plagued by injustice. Wine: quencher of the rage. By the time my grandfather paid off his passage, and moved to Hoboken to work on the docks, he was an alcoholic. But that word does not describe who my grandfather had become: a wounded man who had lost whatever hope he'd managed to salvage from the rubble of his life.

When my grandfather talked about his days on the railroad, there was a rage in his eyes, a rage that could pummel a wife, that could start a riot, that could burn down a building, that could kill a *padrone*, but that did not. And so. He'd take a glass, pour himself some wine, and then some more wine. After his third glass, he looked for the rage, but it was no longer there. After his third glass, he'd miss his mother, his father, his *paisani*.

Last Supper

"The day your grandfather dies," my father says, "he's digging out the basement in the house of one of your grandmother's relatives. And it's hot down there, and it's hard work because he's got to put all the dirt he digs into a sack, and carry it up the stairs, and out to the back yard, and your grandfather is doing this to make a few extra bucks because his pension isn't enough to live on and because he's always giving his money away to anyone who comes to his door, and this pisses off your mother and your grandmother, but they can't do anything to stop it.

"And this day, he isn't feeling so good. He's tired and dizzy even before he starts working, and after a couple of hours, he wants to stop working, but they tell him a deal's a deal, and that he has to keep working. And to keep him working, those bastards gave your grandfather wine to drink. And, you know your grandfather, there wasn't a glass of wine he would ever refuse. So he takes the wine, quenches his thirst, forgets he's tired, and keeps right on working until mid-afternoon when the job is done. Keeps working through the heat of the day. Keeps working even though he's hot and tired and dizzy and feels like he can't breathe."

The rest of the day goes like this.

My grandfather comes home, washes himself at the sink, changes into a clean set of clothes, has a glass of wine and a bite to eat with my grandmother. After he finishes his meal, he pours himself another glass of wine, gets the spiral notebook that lists the money people owe him, sits down at the kitchen table, starts tallying his accounts using a system of his own devising—he's never gone to school, never learned arithmetic. He's scribbling away, getting angry, because it's a year later, and his wife's relatives in Long Island still haven't paid their debt, and he's tallying how much they owe him when he falls to the floor. He's had a massive heart attack.

A few hours later, my mother, my sister, and I come back home. My mother knocks on her father's door to ask for help. We've been shopping; she's tired of being with us; she wants him to take care of us while she puts her groceries away.

He doesn't answer. She panics: He's supposed to be home. She struggles my sister and me into our apartment. Tells me to climb through the open window out onto our fire escape. Tells me to climb through my grandparents' open window, tells me to unlock their door.

I do as I'm told. I've done this before when my grandfather's forgotten his keys. So this is why I'm the one who finds my grandfather dead.

Last Rites

At the wake, I go up to the casket to see my grandfather's body. He is wearing his one good suit, the one he wears to my First Communion. There is the smell of flowers from a few commemorative wreaths surrounding him, the smell of mothballs emanating from his suit, the smell of death.

"That doesn't look like Grandpa," I say. "And it doesn't smell like him, either." A neighbor stands behind me. She is watching me, listening to me, awaiting her turn to view my grandfather's body.

I am kneeling down, as I have been told to kneel by my father. I am supposed to be paying my last respects to my grandfather, as he has told me I must do. I don't know what last respects are, just like I don't know what first respects are, so I don't know what I'm supposed to do. But I have watched the stream of visitors go up to the coffin, kneel down, touch my grandfather's hands frozen in prayer, make a hasty Sign of the Cross, kiss their fingers, and move on. My mother kneels in silence next to me. She hasn't said much since the day her father died; she will say even less in the years to come. Sometimes it will seem that she has followed him to wherever he has gone.

Everyone in the funeral parlor cares about how she is "taking it." No one is concerned about how I am "taking it." My grandfather, the man who took care of me whenever he could, who sang me songs, who told me stories I couldn't comprehend, of a land where wild seas drowned fishermen, where rainfalls were so powerful they made the land slide away, rainfalls so relentless that they washed away all the good earth and made it impossible to grow anything to eat, of a land where wolves ruled the night, and men and women walked to the fields in the dark and worked in the blaze of day without a tree to shade them during their precious few moments of rest.

"And what did your grandpa smell like?" my neighbor asks.

I remember my grandfather, at his table, drinking wine. I remember my grandfather at our table, drinking wine. I remember my grandfather crushing grapes in the basement, stomping on them with feet that would stay purple until late summer. I remember my grandfather drinking wine when he took care of me, drinking it, sometimes, right out of the bottle. I remember my grandfather giving me watered wine to drink when he took care of me when I told him I was thirsty. I remember my mother being angry at my grandfather when she came back home and found me drunk, asleep on my grandparents' bed, under the giant cross on the wall with Jesus Christ bleeding.

(In high school, I am the girl who drinks too much at parties. The girl who is always thirsty but who never drinks water when she is thirsty, only booze. The girl who drinks so much she can't remember how she gets home. The girl who drinks so much that she passesout on the way home, once, in the middle of a four lane highway.)

"And what did your grandfather smell like?" the woman asks again, for I have not answered her.

"Like wine," I say.

The woman laughs. "'*Mbriago,*" she says. "That's who your grandfather was: '*Mbriago.*"

"No," I say. "That isn't who he was. He was my grandfather. Salvatore Calabrese."

Transubstantiation

In Pier Paolo Pasolini's 1966 film *Uccellacci e Uccellini* (*The Hawks and the Sparrows*), a contemporary Italian father and his son travel into the past, to the time of Saint Francis of Assisi, and become monks. The father, Brother Ciccillo, prays for a miracle. He prays that all the wine in the world be turned into water. He prays that there be no more wine in Italy. He prays that there be enough water in Italy so that those who have become drunks because they have had no water to drink will drink water, for they will no longer need to drink wine.

I read about Pasolini. Learn of his belief that the workers of the world, like my grandfather, will save the world. Learn that his father, like my grandfather, was alcoholic. Learn that his father, like my grandfather, died because he drank.

Brother Ciccillo's hoped-for miracle: wine into water, not water into wine.

Chores

DEBRA MARQUART

Debra Marquart originally planned to be a rock star, until a truck fire destroyed all of her road band's equipment. Following the loss, Marquart turned to writing. "I hope there's still evidence of singing in my writing," she says. "And I hope there's evidence of fire, a feeling that my sentences burned to be written—that they are forged from the strongest materials."

This excerpt from Marquart's memoir, The Horizontal World: Growing Up in the Middle of Nowhere, *originally appeared in* Orion.

There is a gravel road about a quarter-mile long leading out of my parents' farm in North Dakota that leads to another gravel road about a half-mile long, which eventually meets up with Highway 3, the two-lane blacktop that runs through my hometown. When I was a kid, I sat for hours in my brother's bedroom facing the highway, and I kept a running tally of how many cars and trucks passed our farm—

their color, make, model, and whether the vehicle was traveling north or south. I yearned for movement back then, for escape.

I spent a lot of time walking—restless, aimless pacing, down the gravel road, along the section lines, always kicking stones, walking with my head down, searching for some evidence that something had happened on this barren strip of land.

I drew maps with large Xs on them, marking the spot where surely treasure would be found. I looked for chipped arrowheads, a stone carving, an agate, an unusual rock formation—anything to prove that someone or something, a nomadic tribe or an ancient glacier, had passed through before me.

"You can't get there from here," my father used to say when I spoke too long or enthusiastically about the cities I planned to someday run away to. I had consulted maps; I thought I knew otherwise. Did he mean to imply that our gravel road was not connected to other roads and highways, and that those freeways had not been paved and multi-laned in preparation for my flight?

My three older sisters had made their rapid getaways after high school—the two oldest to college, the third to marriage and children in town. One by one, their belongings were packed into cars that disappeared down the gravel road. Their old bedrooms became my pick of bedrooms. Pretty soon I had the top floor of the house to myself, and I was left alone with my parents on that farm with so many chickens to feed, so many cows to milk, and so much land to work.

From sunup to sundown, my parents ran frantically from place to place trying to perform all the chores that kept the farm afloat. Because I was a teenager, and none of this had been my idea, I determined to make myself as useless as possible. The most my father could do was assign me small jobs from season to season.

One of my early chores was running the DeLaval cream separator, a machine that worked its transforming magic in a cozy closet off the milk room. In this sanctum sanctorum ordinary milk was poured into a large stainless-steel bowl on top of the whirring, spinning separator. By some alchemy, the liquid filtered through the layers of the machine. After a great deal of noise and centrifugal gyration, the separator brought forth cream that flowed like gold from one of the spigots below.

From the second spigot appeared the now-skimmed milk, which was quickly mixed back in with the whole milk in the pot-bellied bulk cooler. Every few days, a driver arrived in our yard with a refrigerated tanker truck capable of siphoning from the cooler the many gallons of milk we extracted from our cows. This was taken to Wishek Cheese, a factory in a town about twenty-five miles to the southeast.

But the cream had choicer destinations. It was collected in pint and quart jars, each marked with the names of people in town who had ordered fresh farm cream. Mother hand-delivered the jars the next day.

Of all the chores I had to do on the farm, I liked running the separator the best. The milk room was warmer than the rest of the barn, and my primary responsibility was to keep the cats away from the cream. I took a book and read as the noisy machine churned and shook the life from the milk. Around me, things were filled and emptied; cream poured from spouts; jars were whisked away; and I was left to read my book hunched over in the dim light.

At my feet, tabbies and tomcats, tuxedos and calicos, milled and meowed. They craned their necks and howled with tortured voices. They tried to scale my pant legs, their claws out, just to get a quick paw, a stretched tongue, anything, into that golden stream. I would shoo and bat them away, absorbed in thought, clutching my book and reading all the while about all the strange places and marvelous people in the outside world.

————

PERHAPS SEPARATION became my special talent, because at thirteen my father put me in charge of separating the calves from the cows when it was time to wean them from their mothers' milk.

On this day, the cows are herded into the barn, their udders heavy with milk. As usual, they file in and put their necks through the stanchions lining the barn. The slats are closed around their necks to hold them in place during milking. But as they enter the barn, their calves are culled away and taken by me to a separate pen I have prepared for them with fresh straw in another part of the barn.

At first the cows don't realize what's happening. They move through the enclosures and gates in their docile way. They eat the oats put in place for them inside the stanchions. But once outside the barn, after milking, they begin to look around, to sniff, as if trying to recall something they've forgotten. They turn their long necks; they swish their tails. Nothing.

Then they begin to call out, low mooing, until the calves answer. The cows moo and moo in the direction of the calves' voices, and the calves bleat back. This goes on for hours. The crying becomes unbearable. The calves look so small in their holding pen. They stick their heads through the fence, their bodies shaking as they wail. They push their hungry voices toward their mothers' frantic calling: "Where are you? Where are you?"

"Here I am. Here I am."

The separation of an offspring from a parent. It's the most unnatural event. You feel cruel when you're the one enforcing it. On those days, I will myself not to think about it. I only know that it's my job to feed them. I step into the holding pen with buckets of the warm milk I've mixed from powder. Our farm depends upon the real milk the mothers produce. I must convince the calves to accept the substitute.

One by one I take the bawling face of a calf into my hands; I dip my fingertips in the milky liquid in the bucket that rests hard-edged and shiny silver between my legs; I slip my wet fingers into the mouth of the crying calf. One by one they begin to suck, from exhaustion and hunger and instinct—the soft sandpaper tongue, the little pricks of new teeth on my fingertips, the slurping as they finally dip their snouts into the bucket of milk.

As they drink, the calves cry and hiccough. I stroke the curls on their soft foreheads. One by one they lie down in their new straw beds, stretch their long downy necks, and sleep.

They quiet this way, one after the other, until all is silent in the calf shed, but the crying in the mothers' holding pen doesn't stop. It goes on through the night and into the next day, sometimes for hours, sometimes for days.

Growing up on a farm, you see and do things you later wish you hadn't. I have castrated, for example—or rather, I have sat on top of a high, narrow corral, pressed tight the heaving flank of a bull calf with all the strength my legs could muster, looped and yanked his thick tail high in the air and to the side so that my father could come in and castrate.

I've seen the long-handled pincers at work, seen the Rocky Mountain oysters roll in the dirt like two dislodged eyeballs, glossy as pearl onions. I've known people who fry up these delicacies, sauté them in butter, and eat them like tender scallops. I've also known people who eat those turkey gizzards that float in pickling juices in five-gallon jars on the counters of backwater bars, although I have not been one of those people.

If you stay in the Midwest long enough and you go to the right places, you'll encounter all kinds of stuff. I've seen manure, for example, in an amazing variety of colors and consistencies. I have sprayed it with a hose, swept it into gutters, scraped it, buried it, burned it, and shoveled it. I've been up to my bootstraps in it, shit threatening to suck me down as I tried to step through it, spreading straw with a pitchfork so that the cows could lie one more day in it.

I've seen it in pastures—huge cow pies sprouting mushrooms, amazing droppage buzzing with flies, full of grass, seeds, and maggots, or dried flat as a Frisbee along the trail. There's a certain shade of it, an orangish, mustardy yellow with an almost fluorescent glow, called scours, which is a signal that you probably have a very sick calf on your hands. Clothing designers have embraced this color, reproducing it lately by some unnatural combination of dyes, and when I see it in stores in the shapes of fashionable blouses, sweaters, and pants, I can't help but think of my father standing in the calf shed, pointing to the troubling pile and then scanning the pen for the calf that's on its back, the calf with the scruffy coat, the calf with the emaciated, curving ribs.

In the milk barn, I have seen Holsteins go on happily eating their oats as they raise their tails and let loose shit with such force, shoot it like projectile vomit across the aisle of the barn, nailing another cow or some unlucky person who may be walking through the barn at that moment. To be around for cleanup after something like this has happened is to understand what chores are.

CHORES—EVEN THE word registers a feeling for the task at hand: "I've gotta go home and do chores." Never singular, always plural, a job that interrupts some fun you're having, then grows and grows like polyps in an intestine. One syllable quickly spat out or yelled up creaky stairs, the word *chores* describes a job so unsavory that to spend the energy using two syllables means you'd probably never get around to doing it.

It's best to turn away from chores, pretend you didn't hear the call, hope someone else will do them, better to turn back to the softness and warmth of your own bed, back to the brush of cotton and the sweet downy smell of sheets, than to skitter across cold wood floor in the dark, pull on old clothes and worn smelly shoes, and go out into the drafty, shit-smeared places where chores are done.

I have been pulled from my bed in my white nightgown after I've disregarded my mother's first and second calls, my father's third call for chores. I have been taken down to the big backyard near the chicken coop to help with butchering the hens.

My mother has already started. She is cutting necks. My grandmother kneels beside her, also cutting. Between them is a growing pile of chicken heads, wall-eyed, astonished open beaks, the stunned crop of white feathers against the pink wavy flesh of fading combs.

My oldest sister, Kate, is galloping around the yard like the cloaked angel of death, snaring chickens with a long wire leg-catcher. When she traps them by the ankle, they squawk wildly, trying to catch the ground with the other leg and run away until she lifts them in the air and hands them, wings flapping, feathers flying loose, over to the neck cutters. In this way, my sister is god today.

My second-oldest sister, Elizabeth, is retrieving the chickens from the headless places they have flown to. Around and around she runs, looking for the vivid sprays that will signal a chicken is nearby—blood rising in fountains on the white stucco walls of the chicken coop, blood bucking up against the trunks of cottonwoods, blood in soaked patches on the grass, the red-iron smell of oxidization strewn across the dewy green lawn.

As the youngest girl, I stand on the edge of this slaughter, guarding the three loads of laundry my mother has risen early to wash, the whites now flapping on the line. My mother is quick with the knife; her blade is sharp. She places the chicken on the ground, pulls its wings back, and severs the neck with one quick motion. Without turning to look up, she throws the bird into the air as if to separate herself from the act, then she grabs another live chicken.

My grandmother kneels beside her, moving more slowly. She cuts off the head, then holds her hand around the chicken's neck, tilting it like a wine bottle she means to pour down to nothing. Under her knee, the chicken bumps and claws until all the electrical impulses that drive its muscles are finished. Beside her is a large red pool running down the hill. And so, it seems, there are at least two ways to butcher a chicken.

The water is already boiling in tubs up the hill in the barn where we go to pluck the feathers. Sitting in a circle, we grasp the upturned claws and dip the chickens in steaming water. The feathers come off in clumps and drop into another tub between us. The smell is complex—water meets wool meets vinegar meets dirt— like wet fur, like bad feet.

We pluck the strong wing feathers with their deep roots and peel away the body's blanket of feathers. Then we rub the skin for the downy layer and pick away the tiny pinfeathers nestling inside the deep pockets of skin.

ACROSS THE YARD, Mother is in the milk house with the burning candle. She is the fire woman singeing the plucked bodies as she passes them over the flame. The room smells of sulfur, the deep-caked odor of burnt hair and flesh. Grandmother sits beside her, on a stool in front of the sink. She is the last one to receive the bodies.

She places the chicken on its back before her and opens the bird's legs, looking for the soft spot unprotected by bone. "The pooper," she says, "the last part to go over the fence." She repeats these words all day again and again to keep us from fainting.

She draws a sharp blade across the film of skin between the legs. A world of steaming darkness spills out into which she must thrust her hand, extracting the long weave of intestines, the soft gray lungs, the heart, the liver, the tiny green row of developing egg yolks, the brown gizzard, all swimming in a gelatinous ooze. Carefully she finds the small sac of bile, the green-black poison that, if ruptured, will ruin the meat of the bird, and she cuts it away.

Only she knows how to distinguish the edible from the throwaway parts. She crops the feet from the body with a hard crunch of her knife and trims away the claws, the dirt still packed tight under the nails from the chicken's constant scratching for food. We recoil when she places the trimmed yellow feet on the edible pile. She'll take them home in a bag to Grandpa at the end of the day, and we have no idea what they do with them.

And when she holds the gizzard in her palm like a warm bun and draws a blade along the edge, turning the sac inside out to show us the chicken's last supper, I expect to see bottle caps, shiny pennies, diamond rings inside, but I find only an undigested clump of oats, a few tiny bits of gravel.

At the end of the day, we tuck in the wings and legs, slipping the naked birds into the dozens of water-filled milk cartons my mother has been saving all year for freezing the meat. She sets aside four of the biggest birds for frying that night.

"Mmm, girls," she says, "just think—fresh chicken."

"Ughh," I say to Grandmother as we walk the red wheelbarrow to the dump ground to bury the parts, the metallic tinge of blood still in my mouth.

"Do I really have to eat it?" I ask.

I could use a few days for amnesia to set in. But Grandmother tells me I must. I must learn to know the taste of what my hands have done on my tongue.

Cold Autumn

WAITERRANT.NET

It's Saturday night. Beth and I are drinking dirty martinis at Istanbul, a Turkish restaurant with a fun bar and live music. I'm keen on seeing some belly dancers.

"Did you ever smoke a hookah?" Beth asks me, motioning to the ornate water pipes standing at attention behind the bar.

"Yes," I reply. "But only the ones with tobacco in it."

"C'mon," Beth says. "You're talking to me, remember?"

"No, seriously," I say. "I went to this Arab restaurant once and smoked a hookah with some friends."

"Nothing else?" Beth asks, her voice betraying a note of suspicion.

"I only smoked pot once, Beth," I say. "And that was a long time ago."

"How can you smoke pot once?"

"Never did anything for me," I reply. "But I did enough stupid things with booze to make up for it."

"OK," Beth says, unconvinced.

"You don't believe me?"

Beth just laughs and chases the last olive in her martini glass with a swizzle stick.

"Fine," I say. "Don't believe me, then."

I drain the last of my drink and set the glass down on the bar. Suddenly I feel a finger tap me on the shoulder. I turn around. The finger's attached to a cute blonde. Things are looking up.

"Remember me?" the girl asks.

I look at the young woman. She looks about 25 years old. I wait a moment and let the connections spiderweb in my mind. Suddenly I remember. This girl worked as a hostess at the Bistro seven years ago.

"Alice," I say, snapping my fingers. "My God, how long has it been?"

"Almost seven years," she says.

"How old are you now?" I ask, looking at her incredulously.

"Twenty-six."

"Wow."

Seven years ago Alice was an innocent looking young girl. Now she's a shapely young woman. Seven years ago my thirty-one-year-old self wouldn't have given Alice the time of day. But now? Things are different. My pulse quickens.

"So what are you up to?" I ask. "Finished with school?"

"Not yet," Alice says. "I'm tending bar over at Club Expo while I earn my Master's at NYU."

"Good luck," I reply. "What are you studying?"

"Social work."

"That's great."

"You look really good," Alice says. "You've lost a lot of weight."

"Thanks," I say. "Been going to the gym and stuff."

"It's working."

"I'm trying," I say, mildly flattered. A girl hasn't complimented my appearance in a long time.

"So," Alice asks, "what are you doing with yourself?"

"I'm still over at the Bistro with Fluvio," I say.

A funny look passes across Alice's face.

"Wow," she says softly. "Has it been that long?"

"Can you believe it?" I say. "It's been almost seven years."

There's an awkward pause. While I'm wondering why there's an awkward pause, someone calls Alice's name.

"Well," Alice says, "my friends are calling me over. Nice to have seen you."

"Nice to see you too, Alice."

"Bye."

Alice disappears into the crowd. I begin to think about the look Alice gave me, why she went from giving me compliments to running away. Then it hits me.

Alice thinks I'm a loser.

"Goddammit," I mutter.

I pick up my empty martini glass. Suddenly I need another drink. The bartender's too busy looking cool to notice me. A violent pressure builds up inside me. The martini glass I'm holding threatens to break in my grasp. I put the glass back down on the zinc bar and take a deep breath.

"What's the matter?" Beth asks, putting her hand on my arm. "You look upset."

I can't tell Beth a girl looked at me like I was some kind of loser. How can I be sure that was the sentiment behind the look? And why do I give a shit what a 26-year-old girl thinks of me?

"I'm fine, Beth," I say. "Something just pissed me off."

"What?" Beth says. "Tell me what happened."

I'm not sure what happened myself. Maybe I'm projecting my own loneliness and frustration into the encounter. Experience tells me that if I don't understand what I'm feeling—say nothing.

"Forget it, Beth," I say. "It's nothing important."

"If you say so."

I put some money on the bar and grab my coat. "I'm done for the night," I say.

"You're leaving already?" Beth asks.

"I'm not in a drinking mood," I say. "I just want to get home."

"OK," Beth says. "I'll see you next week."

"Your boyfriend coming to get you?" I ask.

"He'll be here soon."

"OK then," I say, feeling old and out of place. "See ya."

"Be careful going home," Beth says.

"I will."

I walk out the door. In the brisk night air I realize I'm breathing heavily. I'm intensely angry. Being fighting mad with two martinis in your system can be a dangerous thing.

So instead of going home, I walk around trying to process what I'm feeling. I know I'm angry because I feel frustrated. Sexual frustration and loneliness are part of it, sure. But if I'm honest, I'm really frustrated because I didn't tell Alice I have a book deal and I'm trying to become a writer.

Why didn't I say that? Why didn't I tell her I've got other things going on? My anonymity? Please, I'm not that schizoid. Why do I even feel the need to tell anyone I've got "other things going on?" That sounds like pretentious horseshit. I've never used my blog as a pickup line. And I'm not about to start telling women, "Hey, babe, I've got a book deal." Besides, being a waiter at thirty-eight's an honorable profession.

Isn't it?

It's a cold autumn night. An easterly wind sends leaves scuttling across the pavement, choking storm grates with red, orange, and gold. Ahead of me a young couple walk arm in arm. I step into the street to bypass them. I notice the girl has long thick black hair. I speed up, hop back onto the sidewalk, and continue on my way.

I catch my reflection in the store windows as I walk along the avenue. My reflection looks tired—like he needs a vacation, like he needs to get laid, like he needs an entirely new life.

Disgusted, I stuff my hands in my pockets and stare at the pavement as it treadmills beneath my feet. Suddenly I start shivering. I draw the sensation around me like a cloak.

It's a cold I know all too well.

Consumption

*Like other pieces collected in this anthology, "Consumption"—
which first appeared in* Isotope*—is written as a kind of montage,
a style also called segmented, snapshot, or collage writing. It is
immediately recognizable on the page: Sections of writing, often
very short, are separated one from the next by asterisks, numbers,
or, as in this case, white space.*

> We are a hundred thousand years beyond insanity.
> Plato does not speak of this.
>
> —RUMI

On the New Jersey beach as a small child he saw armies of beached
jellyfish pieces glistening in the midday sun and edged in sand
like chicken breasts coated with Shake-n-Bake. The jellyfish and their
various lost pieces stung. They showed up in hot, primary-colored
plastic buckets, or they rubbed up against him in the soupy green sea.

Their marmalade parts could be found flung far on shore. All over the beach, brown-baked children crouched around the jellyfish, poking them with twigs or driftwood, sometimes throwing them at each other, or dropping pieces into someone else's bathing suit. Often he couldn't see the jellyfish but he knew they were there. He would come out of the water prickling with pins and needles in the midday sun and his mouth would taste like metal and salt for hours. If he drank enough Lime Rickys that day, his pee would be bright green by the time he got home.

TODAY HE IS forty years old. He lives with his wife in a house that is hours away from the shore. He finds himself still waiting for summer, but the summers now are shorter and more humid, the seasons no longer reliable. When they drive to the beach for the weekend, he can no longer just watch the waves. He looks at the ocean and he sees back in time a million years, watches 4,000 centuries of rain rock the basins, water shifting its way from atmospheric top to bottom like a lava lamp. Then he sees forward as the oceans boil into vapors as the sun rides on empty and then eats itself, a starving core seething through one element after another with a hysterical and inefficient metabolism.

SOMETIMES HE WISHES he didn't know this, how all roads lead to extinction.

HE ONCE BELIEVED in a final core, the one center, the smallest unit, a beginning and an end. He did not yet know that nothing in space is greater than what it bridges, molecules light-years apart, a universe harsh, unpredictable, violent, silent, empty. He once thought that unification would be like knowing the tune and also the words.

He believed in the discrete division of surfaces. He believed every day that the sun would rise, bridges would stand as he crossed them, his atoms would stay stuck together, the jellyfish sting would soon go away. Now his not-knowing is enormous, he feels so temporary, so small, living the narrowly probable life of a soft and edible machine, or an animate, leaky canteen. He obsesses over the decadence of toilets flushed with water. His life span will be the shortest distance between two points.

THIS IS WHY he cannot watch the waves. He knows that to live here on Earth means that he must accept the randomness and possibility of sudden catastrophic weather, earthquake or volcano, flood, famine and drought, microbial plague, animals that bite, insects that sting and plants that can poison you, the possibility of impact, of quicksand, of a bus suddenly careening in your direction, that someone might murder you, molest your child or leave you because they don't love you anymore. That one day there might be a blast that will melt his gelatinous eyes, and the skin from his outstretched arms will drip like the hot cheese that hangs off a slice of pizza. That the universe is flesh-eating. That the universe is cannibal. That most of what surrounds him cannot be detected and cannot be seen.

BUT THEN, FOR a moment, this happens.

ON THE WAY to his car to retrieve his glasses at dusk, he suddenly sees a swollen green seed-casing drop from the tree in his front yard. It carves an invisible helix into the air as it falls, and there with the driveway gravel grating the bottom of his sneakers and the keys clanging dully together in his hand, it all comes back to him: the beauty of cordata's flowering backbone splaying its evolution of budding bone-shoots from his spine, the sexiness of spoons, the viper jaws of printer cables sucking at the splitter box, the greedy cohesion of water, the greedy cohesion of fingers, the screen of sky flickering stars now dead, the biological genius of love and hunger, the ash-strewn and hand-hewn steps of Pompeii split open and now leading nowhere, the plastic of his steering wheel molded to mimic mammalian skin, the word AIR BAG stamped in the center like a cattle brand, the existence of someone who was paid to design these synthetic wrinkles for this wheel, a person who was born and ate food and studied post-modern art, who finds consolation at night by saying *but at least I still create.*

THEN HE IS TWELVE billion years old, his bones a thesaurus of carbon, hydrogen, nitrogen, oxygen, phosphorous, sulfur. He languishes in the hugeness and smallness of things, though now he no longer believes in *things*; he sees instead webs of events masquerading as motion in three crude dimensions. For the moment on Earth, on this still-burning ember, he stands on a thin crust of soil that's been poorly corseted with asphalt, and he watches while the day declines into itself taut, dilates until it breaks and collapses, becomes a lingering hemorrhage spun out and slow, its perishable verges sizzling. A billion-year-old light struggles to his eyes, gasps of light smuggling their pure shards under cloaks. He stands steeped in a Higgs field, which quivers, trembles, pulsates, throbs, and the universe thrums its voluptuous entropy.

THEN HE REMEMBERS that the sky is riddled with poison. He remembers that he does not believe in these fairy-tale words, *never* or *forever,* anymore. He barely believes in *time* and *place,* and now the sand has gotten into his shoes.

_____

As A CHILD HE could not look at sand without seeing infinity.

THE BUNDLE UNDER the blanket next to him moves a bit. Beyond her he sees patches of light seep through the curtains and slick themselves against the wall near their bed. The light could just as well be car headlights or the torches of body-collectors during the plague, the birth of a star, or bodies of phosphorescent creatures in the Arctic waters, sun flares ruining the radio signals, an asteroid falling, a bomb falling, an airplane falling, anything that radiates and is called back to Earth. On his nightstand there is:

a cell phone

a telephone

a Palm Pilot

a remote control

because he is still entranced by shiny things and the glory of his prehensile thumbs. The feel of plastic buttons is as sightlessly familiar to his fingers as soil or thread must have been for his ancestors. *Louder. Softer. Up. Down. Off. On.* But still he loves blizzards, blackouts and strikes, when machines become ridiculous, events that send people running to buy water and batteries or carrion compressed into cans. *Water, energy, food,* the things always measured by *too much* and *not enough.*

TOO MUCH. NOT enough. When they still smoked, he would open a brand-new pack and beam at the wealth of tightly packed tubes. They were both always shocked when, later, they would find only one cigarette left in the box. They had smoked them all with the assumption of the box's inexhaustibility. The empty box made him sad, desperate, disappointed and surprised. This has happened a million times, a strange and startled response to the emptiness of things once full—the refrigerator, the gas tank, the medicine bottle, the belly. Like all humans, he is learning-disabled when it comes to *empty*. He will always be surprised.

HE KNOWS HE has passed the point of no return.

IT'S ALL RIGHT. Here is another.

WHEN THEY BOUGHT their first house, he hated the bathroom, which was done up in metallic black and green wallpaper and scrubbed-but-still-stained linoleum. The bottom of the linoleum had been buttered with thick black asbestos. When he remodeled the bathroom and tore up the floor, the asbestos was brittle and broke into a fine powder whenever he touched it, and someone said *put something in there, like a time capsule, before you lay the new boards*. He found an empty Tupperware container and then realized he had no idea what should go inside, which objects could represent this time and generation. A silicone breast, a prescription bottle, several worn-out TV remotes, porn of all kinds, plastic shopping bags, a bottle of iced tea? All of the things that even in their excesses are unable to satisfy? How would he represent this, living on the very cusp of the beginning of the fall of an empire? Which small pimple of land on the tectonic plates would become the next capital of excess and brute force to dictate the trends of humanity?

HE PUT THE Tupperware container away.

———

IN THE FOSSIL record, only those beings with hard parts are remembered.

WHEN HE WAS young he touched jellyfish that had already been dead for hours and then ate sandwiches without first washing his hands. He was ignorant of germs. He did not know that all warfare was biological. What does he know now? There is nothing he can be certain of now, except maybe this: he loves his wife, he will suffer and die, all that he sees will soon disappear.

This is the last time.
There it goes.
Have another.
The universe wants to fatten him up.

For a moment again he can see this now, how generous the universe is with him. It is showering him with moments the way Greek gods once showered mortals with gold in order to seduce them. The seductions always worked. Nothing persuades *Homo sapiens sapiens* quite like excess, abundance, the promise of more. There is a lust that's built in, a perpetual-need war between mouth and groin. Out loud he whispers *the universe is generous*, but his wife does not stir. He congratulates himself for being so enlightened. He is knee-deep in the old husks of spent moments. He is the wealthiest man alive.

ONCE HE ATE sandwiches by the waves and he did not care about these things, not even the germs, not even the stray grains of sand in the bread. He did not know that this small star would someday soon begin sputtering out, flailing its desperate flares against a dark falling no one would see. What was it he saw, staring out at the water while his small feet were sucked into black holes of sand? His lips were so dry with salt that the skin felt tight, drum-like. He could feel his heartbeat resonate through them.

HE CHEWED HIS sandwich pensively. The sound of water painted him. A red-faced man carrying a sweaty white ice-box dragged his feet through the beach and called *Creamsicles Fudgesicles cold Italian ices* with a voice as gritty and dry as the sand while the seagulls grazed and rejected cigarette butts and peanut shells gone spongy. Everything was beautiful.

THE JELLYFISH WERE beautiful. He was beautiful, too, because his body was brand new and it still belonged to him. His flesh was the only thing holding him in. He was as exposed as the jellyfish, but he had no idea what it meant to be exposed. He had no idea that he had no idea. He had never heard of Darwin, he already knew that he was part fish. He watched the water absently, teasing its foamy apron with his toes, and there was nothing he did not understand.

The Pain Scale

Eula Biss

"The essay, with its tremendous capacity for facts and figures, is capable of offering us a meaningful arrangement of information," says Eula Biss. *"In my experience, there is plenty of information in the world, but very little sense made of it."*

In "The Pain Scale," which first appeared in Seneca Review, *Biss arranges her experience with chronic pain along the ten-point scale by which pain is commonly assessed—as it turns out, a deceptively simple structure.*

$$0 \longrightarrow$$
No Pain

The concept of Christ is considerably older than the concept of zero. Both are problematic—both have their fallacies and their immaculate conceptions. But the problem of zero troubles me significantly more than the problem of Christ.

I AM SITTING in the exam room of a hospital entertaining the idea that absolutely no pain is not possible. Despite the commercials, I suspect that pain cannot be eliminated. And this may be the fallacy on which we have based all our calculations and all our excesses. All our sins are for zero.

ZERO IS NOT a number. Or at least it does not behave like a number. It does not add, subtract, or multiply like other numbers. Zero is a number in the way that Christ was a man.

ARISTOTLE, FOR ONE, did not believe in Zero.

IF NO PAIN is possible, then, another question—is no pain desirable? Does the absence of pain equal the absence of everything?

SOME VERY complicated mathematical problems cannot be solved without the concept of zero. But zero makes some very simple problems impossible to solve. For example, the value of zero divided by zero is unknown.

I AM NOT a mathematician. I am sitting in a hospital trying to measure my pain on a scale from zero to ten. For this purpose, I need a zero. A scale of any sort needs fixed points.

THE UPPER FIXED point on the Fahrenheit scale, ninety-six, is based on a slightly inaccurate measure of normal body temperature.

The lower fixed point, zero, is the coldest temperature at which a mixture of salt and water can still remain liquid. I myself am a mixture of salt and water. I strive to remain liquid.

ZERO, ON THE Celsius scale, is the point at which water freezes. And one hundred is the point at which water boils. But Anders Celsius, who introduced the scale in 1741, originally fixed zero as the point at which water boiled, and one hundred as the point at which water froze. These fixed points were reversed only after his death.

THE DEEPEST CIRCLE of Dante's *Inferno* does not burn. It is frozen. In his last glimpse of Hell, Dante looks back and sees Satan upside down through the ice.

THERE IS ONLY one fixed point on the Kelvin scale—absolute zero. Absolute zero is 273 degrees Celsius colder than the temperature at which water freezes. There are zeroes beneath zeroes. Absolute zero is the temperature at which molecules and atoms are moving as slowly as possible. But even at absolute zero, their motion does not stop completely. Even the absolute is not absolute. This is comforting, but it does not give me faith in zero.

AT NIGHT, I ice my pain. My mind descends into a strange sinking calm. Any number multiplied by zero is zero. And so with ice and me. I am nullified. I wake up to melted ice and the warm throb of my pain returning.

———

GRAB A CHICKEN by its neck or body—it squawks and flaps and pecks and thrashes like mad. But grab a chicken by its feet and turn it upside down, and it just hangs there blinking in a waking trance. Zeroed. My mother and I once hung the chickens like this on the barn door for their necks to be slit. I like to imagine that a chicken at zero feels no pain.

⟵————— 1 —————⟶

Where does pain worth measuring begin? With a hangnail? With a stubbed toe? A sore throat? A needle prick? A razor cut?

MY FATHER IS a physician. He treats patients with cancer, who often suffer extreme pain. My father raised me to believe that most pain is minor. He was never impressed by my bleeding cuts or even my weeping sores. In retrospect, neither am I.

MY FATHER ONCE told me that an itch is just very mild pain. Both sensations simply signal, he told me, irritated or damaged tissue.

BUT A NASTY itch, I observed, can be much more excruciating than a paper cut, which is also mild pain. Digging at an itch until it bleeds and is transformed into pure pain can bring a kind of relief.

WHEN I COMPLAINED of pain as a child, my father would ask, "What kind of pain?" Wearily, he would list for me some of the different kinds of pain, "Burning, stabbing, throbbing, prickling, dull, sharp, deep, shallow. . . ."

HOSPICE NURSES ARE trained to identify five types of pain: physical, emotional, spiritual, social, and financial.

THE PAIN OF feeling, the pain of caring, the pain of doubting, the pain of parting, the pain of paying.

BUT THEN THERE is also the pain of longing, the pain of desire, the pain of sore muscles, which I find pleasurable. . . .

THE PAIN OF learning, and the pain of reading.

THE PAIN OF trying.

THE PAIN OF living.

THERE IS A mathematical proof that zero equals one. Which, of course, it doesn't.

←——— 2 ———→

The set of whole numbers is also known as "God's numbers."

THE DEVIL IS in the fractions.

ALTHOUGH THE DISTANCE between one and two is finite, it contains infinite fractions. This could also be said of the distance between my mind and my body. My one and my two. My whole and its parts.

THE SENSATIONS OF my own body may be the only subject on which I am qualified to claim expertise. Sad and terrible, then, how little I know. "How do you feel?" the doctor asks, and I cannot answer. Not accurately. "Does this hurt?" he asks. Again, I'm not sure. "Do you have more or less pain than the last time I saw you?" Hard to say. I begin to lie to protect my reputation. I try to act certain.

THE PHYSICAL THERAPIST raises my arm above my head. "Any pain with this?" she asks. Does she mean any pain in addition to the pain I already feel, or does she mean any pain at all? She is annoyed by my question. "Does this cause you pain?" she asks curtly. No. She bends my neck forward. "Any pain with this?" No. "Any pain with this?" No. It feels like a lie every time.

ON OCCASION, AN extraordinary pain swells like a wave under the hands of the doctor, or the chiropractor, or the massage therapist, and floods my body. Sometimes I hear my throat make a sound. Sometimes I see spots. I consider this the pain of treatment, and I have come to find it deeply pleasurable. I long for it.

THE INTERNATIONAL ASSOCIATION for the Study of Pain is very clear on this point—pain must be unpleasant. "Experiences which resemble pain but are not unpleasant," reads their definition of pain, "should not be called pain."

———

IN THE SECOND circle of Dante's *Inferno*, the adulterous lovers cling to each other, whirling eternally, caught in an endless wind. My next-door neighbor, who loves Chagall, does not think this sounds like Hell. I think it depends on the wind.

WIND, LIKE PAIN, is difficult to capture. The poor wind sock is always striving, and always falling short.

IT TOOK SAILORS more than two hundred years to develop a standardized numerical scale for the measure of wind. The result, the Beaufort scale, provides twelve categories for everything from "Calm" to "Hurricane." The scale offers not just a number, but a term for the wind, a range of speed, and a brief description.

A FORCE 2 wind on the Beaufort scale, for example, is a "Light Breeze" moving between four and seven miles per hour. On land, it is specified as "wind felt on face; leaves rustle; ordinary vanes moved by wind."

⟵ ——— 3 ——— ⟶

Left alone in the exam room I stare at the pain scale, a simple number line complicated by only two phrases. Under zero: "no pain." Under ten: "the worst pain imaginable."

THE WORST PAIN imaginable. . . . Skinned alive? Impaled with hundreds of nails? Dragged over gravel behind a fast truck?

———————

DETERMINING THE INTENSITY of my own pain is a blind calculation. On my first attempt, I assigned the value of ten to a theoretical experience—burning alive. Then I tried to determine what percentage of the pain of burning alive I was feeling.

I CHOSE THIRTY percent—three. Which seemed, at the time, quite substantial.

THREE. MAIL REMAINS unopened. Thoughts are rarely followed to their conclusions. Sitting still becomes unbearable after one hour. Nausea sets in. Quiet desperation descends.

"THREE IS NOTHING," my father tells me now. "Three is go home and take two aspirin."

IT WOULD BE helpful, I tell him, if that could be noted on the scale.

THE FOUR VITAL signs used to determine the health of a patient are blood pressure, temperature, breath, and pulse. Recently, it has been suggested that pain be considered a fifth vital sign. But pain presents a unique problem in terms of measurement, and a unique cruelty in terms of suffering—it is entirely subjective.

ASSIGNING A VALUE to my own pain has never ceased to feel like a political act. I am a citizen of a country that ranks our comfort above any other concern. People suffer, I know, so that I may eat bananas in February. And then there is history. . . . I struggle to consider my pain in proportion to the pain of a napalmed Vietnamese girl whose skin is slowly melting off as she walks naked in the sun. This exercise itself is painful.

"YOU ARE NOT meant to be rating world suffering," my friend in Honduras advises. "This scale applies only to you and your experience."

AT FIRST, THIS thought is tremendously relieving. It unburdens me of factoring the continent of Africa into my calculations. But I hate the knowledge that I am isolated in this skin—alone with my pain and my own fallibility.

⟵———— 4 ————⟶

The Wong-Baker Faces scale was developed to help young children rate their pain.

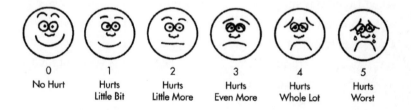

| 0 | 1 | 2 | 3 | 4 | 5 |
| No Hurt | Hurts Little Bit | Hurts Little More | Hurts Even More | Hurts Whole Lot | Hurts Worst |

The face I remember, always, was on the front page of a local newspaper in an Arizona gas station. The man's face was horrifyingly distorted in an open-mouthed cry of raw pain. His house, the caption explained, had just been destroyed in a wildfire. But the man himself, the article revealed, had not been hurt.

SEVERAL STUDIES HAVE suggested that children using the Wong-Baker scale tend to conflate emotional pain and physical pain. A child who is not in physical pain but is very frightened of surgery, for example, might choose the crying face. One researcher observed that "hurting" and "feeling" seemed to be synonymous to some children. I myself am puzzled by the distinction at times. And, after all, pain is defined as a "sensory and emotional experience." In an attempt to rate only the physical pain of children, a more emotionally "neutral" scale was developed.

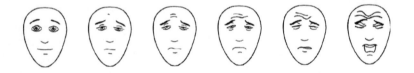

A group of adult patients favored the Wong-Baker scale in a study comparing several different types of pain scales. The patients were asked to identify the easiest scale to use by rating all the scales on a scale from zero: "not easy" to six: "easiest ever seen." The patients were then asked to rate how well the scales represented pain on a scale from zero: "not good" to six: "best ever seen." The patients were not invited to rate the experience of rating.

I STARE AT a newspaper photo of an Israeli boy with a bloodstained cloth wrapped around his forehead. His face is impassive.

———

I STARE AT a newspaper photo of an Iraqi prisoner standing delicately balanced with electrodes attached to his body, his head covered
with a hood.

NO FACE, NO pain?

A CRYING BABY, to me, always seems to be in the worst pain imaginable. But when my aunt became a nurse twenty-five years ago, it was
not unusual for surgery to be done on infants without any pain medication. Babies, it was believed, did not have the fully developed nervous systems necessary to feel pain. Medical evidence that infants
experience pain in response to anything that would cause an adult
pain has only recently emerged.

THERE IS NO evidence of pain on my body. No marks. No swelling.
No terrible tumor. The X-rays revealed nothing. Two MRIs of my
brain and spine revealed nothing. Nothing was infected and festering,
as I had suspected and feared. There was no ghastly huge white cloud
on the film. There was nothing to illustrate my pain except a number,
which I was told to choose from between zero and ten. My proof.

⟵———— 5 ————⟶

"The problem with scales from zero to ten," my father tells me, "is
the tyranny of the mean."

OVERWHELMINGLY, PATIENTS tend to rate their pain as a five,
unless they are in excruciating pain. At best, this renders the scale far

less sensitive to gradations in pain. At worst, it renders the scale useless.

I UNDERSTAND THE desire to be average only when I am in pain. To be normal is to be okay in a fundamental way—to be chosen numerically by God.

WHEN I COULD no longer sleep at night because of my pain, my father reminded me that a great many people suffer from both insomnia and pain. "In fact," he told me, "neck and back pain is so common that it is a cliché—a pain in the neck!"

THE FACT THAT 50 million Americans suffer from chronic pain does not comfort me. Rather, it confounds me. "This is not normal," I keep thinking. A thought invariably followed by a doubt, "Is this normal?"

THE DISTINCTION between test results that are normal or abnormal is often determined by how far the results deviate from the mean. My X-rays did not reveal a cause for my pain, but they did reveal an abnormality. "See this," the doctor pointed to the string of vertebrae hanging down from the base of my skull like a loose line finding plumb. "Your spine," he told me, "is abnormally straight."

←——— 6 ———→

A force 6 wind on the Beaufort scale, a "Strong Breeze," is characterized by "large branches in motion; telegraph wires whistle; umbrellas used with difficulty."

OVER A CENTURY before preliminary scales were developed to quantify the wind, serious efforts were made to produce an accurate map of Hell. Infernal cartography was considered an important undertaking for the architects and mathematicians of the Renaissance, who based their calculations on the distances and proportions described by Dante. The exact depth and circumference of Hell inspired intense debates, despite the fact that all calculations, no matter how sophisticated, were based on a work of fiction.

GALILEO GALILEI delivered extensive lectures on the mapping of Hell. He applied recent advances in geometry to determine the exact location of the entrance to the underworld and then figured the dimensions that would be necessary to maintain the structural integrity of Hell's interior.

IT WAS THE age of the golden rectangle—the divine proportion. Mathematics revealed God's plan. But the very use of numbers required a religious faith, because one could drop off the edge of the earth at any point. The boundaries of the maps at that time faded into oceans full of monsters.

IMAGINATION IS treacherous. It erases distant continents, it builds a Hell so real that the ceiling is vulnerable to collapse.

TO BE SAFE, I think I should only map my pain in proportion to pain I have already felt. But my nerves have short memories. My mind remembers crashing my bicycle as a teenager, but my body does not. I

cannot seem to conjure the sensation of lost skin without actually losing skin. My nerves cannot, or will not, imagine past pain—and this,
I think, is for the best. Nerves simply register, they do not invent.

BUT AFTER A year of pain, I realized that I could no longer remember what it felt like not to be in pain. I was left anchorless. For a while,
I tended to think of the time before the pain as easier and brighter, but
then I began to suspect myself of fantasy and nostalgia.

EVENTUALLY, I discovered that with some effort I could imagine
the sensation of pain as heat, which brought a kind of relief.

PERHAPS, WITH A stronger mind, I could imagine the heat as
warmth, and then the warmth as nothing at all.

7

I accidentally left a burner on the stove going for two and a half
days—a small blue flame, burning, burning, burning. . . . The duration
terrified me. How incredibly dangerous, so many hours of fire.

WHEN I CRY from it, I cry over the idea of it lasting forever, not over
the pain itself. The psychologist, in her rational way, suggests that I do
not let myself imagine it lasting forever. "Choose an amount of time
that you know you can endure," she suggests, "and then challenge
yourself only to make it through that time." I make it through the
night, and then sob through half the morning.

THE PAIN SCALE measures only the intensity of pain, not the duration. This may be its greatest flaw. A measure of pain, I believe, requires at least two dimensions. The suffering of Hell is terrifying not because of any specific torture, but because it is eternal.

THE SQUARE ROOT of seven results in a decimal that repeats randomly into infinity. The exact figure cannot be known, only a close approximation. Rounding a number to the nearest significant figure is a tool designed for the purpose of making measurements. The practicality of rounding is something my mind can fully embrace. No measurement is ever exact, of course.

SEVEN IS THE largest prime number between zero and ten. Out of all the numbers, the very largest primes are unknown. Still, every year, the largest known prime is larger. Euclid proved the number of primes to be infinite, but the infinity of primes may be slightly smaller than the infinity of the rest of the numbers. It is here, exactly at this point, that my ability to comprehend begins to fail.

$$\longleftarrow \quad 8 \quad \longrightarrow$$

Although all the numbers follow each other in a predictable line, many unknown quantities exist.

EXPERTS DO NOT know why some pain resolves and other pain becomes chronic. One theory is that the body begins to react to its own reaction, trapping itself in a cycle of its own pain response. This can go on indefinitely, twisting like the figure eight of infinity.

MY FATHER TELLS me that when he broke his collarbone it didn't hurt. I would like to believe this, but I am suspicious of my father's assessment of his own pain.

THE PROBLEM WITH pain is that I cannot feel my father's, and he cannot feel mine. This, I suppose, is also the essential mercy of pain.

SEVERAL RECENT studies have suggested that women feel pain differently than men. Further studies have suggested that pain medications act differently on women than they do on men. I am suspicious of these studies, so favored by *Newsweek*, and so heaped upon waiting room tables. I dislike the idea that our flesh is so essentially unique that it does not even register pain as a man's flesh does—a fact that renders our bodies, again, objects of supreme mystery.

BUT I AM comforted, oddly, by the possibility that you cannot compare my pain to yours. And, for that reason, cannot prove it insignificant.

THE MEDICAL definition of pain specifies the "presence or potential of tissue damage." Pain that does not signal tissue damage is not, technically, pain.

"THIS IS A pathology," the doctor assured me when he informed me that there was no definitive cause of my pain, no effective treatment for it, and very probably no end to it. "This is not in your head."

———

IT WOULD NOT have occurred to me to think that I was imagining the pain. But the longer the pain persisted, and the harder it became for me to imagine what it was like not to be in pain, the more seriously I considered the disturbing possibility that perhaps I was not, in fact, in pain.

ANOTHER THEORY OF chronic pain is that it is a faulty message sent by malfunctioning nerves. "For example," the Mayo Clinic suggests, "your pain could be similar to the phantom pain some amputees feel in their amputated limbs."

I WALKED OUT of a lecture on chronic pain after too many repetitions of the phrase, "We have reason to believe that you are in pain, even if there is no physical evidence of your pain." I had not realized that the fact that I believed myself to be in pain was not reason enough.

WE HAVE REASON to believe in infinity, but everything we know ends.

$$\longleftarrow \quad 9 \quad \longrightarrow$$

"I have a very high pain threshold," my mother mentions casually. This is undoubtedly true. I stand by uselessly and cover my ears as my mother, a very small woman, lifts the blunt end of a pick axe over her head and slams it down on a metal pipe she is driving into the frozen ground.

————

"I BREATHE, I have a heartbeat, I have pain . . ." I repeat to myself as I lie in bed at night. I am striving to adopt the pain as a vital sensation. My mother, I am sure, mastered this exercise long ago.

ONCE, FOR A study of chronic pain, I was asked to rate not just my pain, but also my suffering. I rated my pain as a three. Having been sleepless for nearly a week, I rated my suffering as a seven.

"PAIN IS THE hurt, either physical or emotional, that we experience," writes the Reverend James Chase. "Suffering is the story we tell ourselves of our pain."

YES, SUFFERING IS the story we tell ourselves.

"IF WE COME to the point where we have no place for suffering," Reverend Chase writes, "to what lengths will we go to eradicate it? Will we go so far as to inflict suffering to end it?"

CHRISTIANITY IS NOT mine. I do not know it and I cannot claim it. But I have seen the sacred heart ringed with thorns, the gaping wound in Christ's side, the weeping virgin, the blood, the nails, the cross to bear. . . . Pain is holy, I understand. Suffering is divine.

IN MY WORST pain, I can remember thinking, "This is not beautiful." I can remember being disgusted by the very idea.

———

BUT IN MY worst pain, I also found myself secretly cherishing the phrase, "This too shall pass." The longer the pain lasted, the more beautiful and impossible and absolutely holy this phrase became.

$\xleftarrow{\hspace{4cm}}$ 10
The Worst Pain Imaginable

Through a failure of my imagination, or of myself, I have discovered that the pain I am in is always the worst pain imaginable.

BUT I WOULD like to believe that there is an upper limit to pain. That there is a maximum intensity nerves can register.

THERE IS NO tenth circle to Dante's Hell.

THE DIGIT TEN depends on the digit zero, in our current number system. In 1994 Robert Forslund developed an Alternative Number System. "This system," he wrote with triumph, "eliminates the need for the digit zero, and hence all digits behave the same."

"ONE OF THE functions of the pain scale," my father explains, "is to protect doctors—to spare them some emotional pain. Hearing someone describe their pain as a ten is much easier than hearing them describe it as a hot poker driven through their eyeball into their brain."

A BETTER SCALE, my father thinks, might rate what patients would be willing to do to relieve their pain. "Would you," he suggests, "visit

five specialists and take three prescription narcotics?" I laugh because
I have done just that. "Would you," I offer, "give up a limb?" I would
not. "Would you surrender your sense of sight for the next ten years?"
my father asks. I would not. "Would you accept a shorter life span?" I
might. We are laughing, having fun with this game. But later, reading
statements collected by the American Pain Foundation, I am alarmed
by the number of references to suicide.

THE DESCRIPTION OF hurricane force winds on the Beaufort scale
is simply, "devastation occurs."

BRINGING US, of course, back to zero.

Full Gospel

J. D. Schraffenberger

"A poem is more likely to take a snapshot of the world, but nonfiction keeps the camera rolling, resists the urge to say Cut!" says J. D. Schraffenberger. "As Fellini said of cinema, 'Nessun altro mestiere consente di creare un mondo che assomiglia così da vicino a quello che conosci,' No other literary form, for my money, allows you to create a world that comes so close to the one we know."

This essay first appeared in Brevity, *an online journal of concise nonfiction.*

1.

What I see as a child on my way to church with my grandparents: dead barns, CHEW MAIL POUCH TOBACCO faded into the gray wood. Also: Southern Indiana hills, knobs, knolls, ancient ripples where glaciers halted at the Ohio. What I see at my grandparents' church: an Appalachian diaspora. Millions fled the mountains mid-century during the so-called Great Migration, headed north—to Cincinnati, Pittsburgh, Detroit, and Chicago, big industrial Midwest cities holding out the promise of employment. My grandpa, one among the millions, moved his family to Louisville, where he worked for General Electric until he retired. Now he's a preacher: Full Gospel.

Whole Appalachian suburbs dot the north, pockets of mountain folk finding each other far from home. The church voices of old people here: like banjos now as they praise the lord.

The church itself shines—a great geodesic dome Grandpa helped click together from a kit, piece by piece—skylights placed to catch the sun in shafts and beams that touch the sheen of his polished podium.

The congregation: serene old people bow their heads, quiet. But when Grandpa gets excited and the shafts of light scream, these old people get up, they dance, my grandma weeping, red-faced, waving her hand above her like a confused, grievous beauty queen. This is the most frightening thing I've ever seen.

2.

When my brother Jonathan is hospitalized at 14 years old, Grandma believes it's the devil inside him, demons in the rap music he listens to. She calls the devil Old Scratch, a mountain name. The congregation prays for him.

3.

On holidays, Grandpa says grace before we eat. We stand in a circle, hold hands, aunts and uncles—alcoholics, drug addicts, long-lapsed Christians—my rough-and-tumble cousins putting on their straight pious faces, my mom cozy in her Touched-By-an-Angel theology, her Thomas-Kincaid-printed dreams.

My dad, who grew up in the city across the river, taught my brothers and me how to be ironic about God: being Catholic, this came easy to him. But his face in prayer is serious and quiet, too.

Grandpa begins grace with a deep bass *Lord*, and Grandma sprinkles a high lonesome *Jesus* here and there into the prayer: the name lisps, *Jesus*, a whisper, *Jesus*, the name on her teeth cutting through all irony. *Jesus. Thank you, Jesus.*

I learned quite young to make my brothers laugh by imitating Grandma. We played video games, and when I won, I whispered the same sincere *Jesus. Thank you, Jesus.* Now during grace I look up at Jonathan, who is red-faced, eyes clenched tight.

4.

When my cousin David dies, we try to make each other laugh. It's our way of dealing with the death of someone so young. My aunt takes pills, my uncle starts drinking again, my mother makes food nobody eats.

And there at the funeral home, I say it, my father and brothers and me gathered in a small circle in the corner: *Jesus. Thank you, Jesus.* Jonathan, who has been released from the hospital to attend the funeral, laughs loud and can't stop, a frenzied laughter, worried laughter, his eyes frightened and begging me. He clenches his fists, pounds his thighs.

When the others look at us, huddled in our safe corner, I put my hand on Jonathan's shoulder, think *I'm sorry*, say *Shh*, think, *David, this isn't happiness, I swear*, say *It's okay*, think *These are our tears*.

The Truth about Cops and Dogs

REBECCA SKLOOT

When Rebecca Skloot's dog, Bonny, was attacked by a pack of wild dogs in Manhattan, Skloot turned the inquisitive spirit that makes her a successful freelance writer for many national magazines toward navigating an alphabet soup of city agencies to find out how to keep the dogs from doing the same thing to another dog, or even a person. The resulting story, a shorter version of which first appeared in New York *magazine, was named Best Personal Essay of the Year by the American Society of Journalists and Authors.*

Eight months ago, if you'd told me I'd be obsessed with a little old Greek guy and fantasizing about killing his dogs, I'd have said you were nuts. If you'd said a little old Greek guy's pack of eight junkyard dogs had been roaming the streets of mid-town Manhattan for years attacking people and tearing apart their dogs while city officials said, Sorry, that's not *our* problem, I'd have called you a conspiracy theorist. A pack of wild dogs? In Manhattan? Never happen. Boy would I have been wrong.

Here's how I know: The Sunday before Christmas, I woke up to my friend Elizabeth pounding frantically on my door. She was staying at my apartment—that morning, as I slept, she'd taken my dog Bonny for a walk. When I opened the door, Elizabeth stood clutching Bonny's empty, bloody collar, screaming, "Something awful happened!" I bolted into the hallway wearing nothing but underwear, heading toward the snow and ice to find my dog. Elizabeth grabbed my shoulder: "It's cold out." I spun around, grabbed a blanket, cell phone, and credit card, threw a long down coat over my underwear, then ran barefoot out the door.

My doorman looked to the ground whispering, "I'm sorry" over and over; Ralphie, my maintenance man, pointed toward a small courtyard behind the building. "A pack of dogs," he whispered as I ran past. "Huge dogs." That's when I saw the first puddle of blood and the fist-sized chunk of Bonny's muscle on the sidewalk. "They eat her," Ralphie yelled after me. "Don't look."

I was a veterinary technician for ten years. I started off vaccinating and X-raying people's pets, but eventually left general practice for a vet school, where I worked in the morgue performing daily autopsies, then became an adrenaline-pumped emergency room tech who did CPR on dying dogs and used words like CODE RED and STAT. I'd seen animals bigger than Bonny literally torn in half by packs; I'd seen missing limbs and decapitations, I'd done autopsies on dogs who'd eaten children and I'd documented the contents of their stomachs for police reports. Which is all to say, when I heard the phrase "pack of dogs," I had clear visuals of what I was about to find.

I ran into the courtyard, yelling Bonny's name, trying not to look at the blood-smeared walkway. I heard her crying before I saw her, quivering in a pool of blood behind a small bush, eyes wide, intestines hanging through a hole in her side. She screamed as I scooped her up, wrapped her in the blanket and lowered her on a picnic table. That's when vet-tech in me took over. I didn't feel emotions or my bare feet in the snow. I just lifted the blanket, checked her heart rate, pupils and the color of her gums. I thought clinical terms like lacerations, puncture wounds, and decreased capillary refill time, but the reality was, they'd bitten her so many times it looked like she'd been sprayed with machine gun fire. They crushed her pelvis and ripped her body open from hip to armpit on both sides. They slit her throat so deep I could see her jugular vein. They sank their teeth into each of her thighs and pulled her legs in opposite directions, detaching her muscles from her bones. They ripped and tore until Ralphie heard the screams, grabbed a two-by-four, and ran outside swinging. When he got there, Bonny had the biggest dog by the throat, but its jaws were twice the size of hers, and wrapped around her neck. The others were going for Bonny's intestines. No mistake: They were going to eat her.

A FEW MONTHS before my seventeenth birthday, my best friend and I went to a grocery store for some coffee and eggs and came home with Bonny instead. We adopted her in the parking lot, straight from a cardboard box in the trunk of a rusted-out Chevy with a sign that said "FREE PUPS." Her littermates squealed and climbed over each other, but Bonny just stared at us, eyes locked, knowing full well she was supposed to go home with us, just waiting for us to figure it out. She was maybe three pounds, with ears so huge and pointy they met in the middle of her head, like one giant ear. We named her after the remote hill outside Portland, Oregon, where we lived—Bonny Slope. With time, as her ears continued to grow, we'd call her "Radar," "Satellite Dish" or "Bat Dog," and she'd answer to each one.

Now, Bonny looks like a jackal, with a lean body built for running through endless nights. She's a 35-pound lap dog who refuses to go out in the rain and tip-toes around mud puddles, but loves full-contact wrestling, scaling trees after squirrels, and running commando through the woods. She's lithe and graceful as a greyhound, even at 15. She was all black until about seven years ago when her muzzle started to grey, then her chest, then feet. She's part border collie—a dog bred for keeping its herd safe, riding on the backs of sheep and weaving between the hooves of stampeding cattle, nipping heels to keep everyone running straight. Border collies are known for having eyes so intense they can lock onto a stray bull and maneuver it back into a herd. Bonny's got that stare. She's turned it on me many times: When my house caught on fire, when a man tried jimmying the lock of my hotel room. She uses it at least once a week when we walk the streets: Locking those chestnut eyes on mine like, don't ask questions, just follow, then pressing her body against me, putting herself between me and whatever she doesn't like and steering me home, sometimes using streets she's never walked.

Bonny is a worrier: eyebrows always wrinkled, ears in constant motion. And I'm her biggest worry: In the last year we'd moved from one city to the next; we'd gone from 3-bedroom house to tiny apartment, divorced my husband, and cried together as my other fifteen-year-old dog, Sereno, died in my arms. Which is to say, I'd become Bonny's entire herd, and she'd become mine.

MINUTES AFTER the attack, I held Bonny in the back seat of Elizabeth's car and screamed at her to ignore the one-way signs and red lights. After crawling through 46 blocks of gridlocked Christmas-week traffic to the only hospital open on Sundays, and after Bonny went into the surgery doctors said she probably wouldn't wake up from, I did two things: I looked down at my blood-covered self, still barefoot and naked except for a coat, and I actually laughed. It was a deep, disturbed, this-isn't-really-happening kind of laugh. Then I lost it.

The next thing I remember is Elizabeth saying we should call the police, and me thinking, *Damn right.* She called 911. "Sorry," the dispatcher told her, "We don't handle dog-on-dog complaints. We can't do anything unless they bite a person. Call Animal Control."

So she did. "Dog-on-dog attacks aren't our jurisdiction," they told her, "call the ASPCA."

So she did. "We don't handle dog versus dog attacks," they said. "Call animal control."

Elizabeth laughed: "They just told me to call you." "Okay, then call your police precinct."

Elizabeth got the 10th precinct on the phone and said she'd like to file a complaint. "Sorry," he told her, "we only take human complaints, you can't file a complaint for a dog. Call the Department of Health."

So she did, and guess what they said: "We don't handle dog-on-dog complaints. You should call 911."

Elizabeth sat down next to me and stared at her phone like it'd just done the craziest thing. "What'd they say?" I asked. "They said you should call back on Monday," she told me after a long pause. "The weekend people are clueless."

That night, with Bonny still unconscious after hours of touch-and-go surgery, I walked into the lobby of my apartment and overheard two neighbors talking. See the blood on the sidewalk, they said. Harry's pack did it again. This time they killed some dog named Bonny. Ate her alive.

I stopped. "Excuse me," I said, "did you say Harry's dogs?"

"Yeah," one woman said, shaking her head, "that homeless asshole's crazy pack of dogs has attacked a bunch of people and mauled, what, a dozen dogs?"

The other neighbor nodded. "At least."

"They've been attacking people for years," my doorman said. "The city won't do anything about it."

I asked if anyone had called the police and they laughed like, yeah right. The woman, who insisted I not use her name, whispered: "You want my advice? Throw rat poison into the lot. That's the only way you're gonna get results. While you're at it, throw some poison in for Harry, it's his fault they're like this."

HARRY THEODORE WAS born Theocharas Paleologos on a Macedonian goat farm and raised in Greece, where he trained Doberman Pinschers to hunt and kill wild boar. He came to America at 18 with dreams of becoming an engineer, then went from factory job to long-shoreman to hot-dog vendor. Business never did take off because his cart was always surrounded by a pack of German Shorthaired Pointers. Harry started breeding them in the 60s, when a friend gave him two dogs that he bred and in-bred until, at one point, he had more than 50.

Harry's in his late sixties now, five feet five inches tall, with a leathery face covered in gray stubble. He and his dogs live on 36th Street just east of Eleventh Avenue, a few blocks from my apartment, in a junkyard full of rusted hot-dog carts and car parts, scraps of rotting linoleum, mildewed blankets, rats, and piles of garbage Harry scrounges from neighborhood markets to feed his dogs. The lot was part of a shantytown until the city cleared it in 1997; Harry moved in later that year, when he got kicked out of an abandoned house on the East Side. He used to sleep in a plywood shack in the back of the lot, but it burned down a few years ago. After that, neighbors say, he started sleeping in a gutted van. They also say Harry subsidizes his social security checks by selling puppies, but that he doesn't sell to police officers—they get dogs for free.

I've never talked to Harry—I kept myself anonymous so I could sit across the street from his lot on a loading dock, watching him and his dogs. Which is what I did the night Bonny was attacked, right after my neighbors told me where he lived. I expected I'd want to kill those dogs when I finally saw them, but I didn't. I wanted to stop Harry. His dogs were covered in sores and scars; one had a huge tumor on its lip, others had what looked like a broken leg, a dislocated or malformed jaw, hugely swollen joints, maybe from arthritis, maybe just from generations of inbreeding. Their coats were dingy and thin, like they'd been malnourished and riddled with mange or mites for years. Two males fought over a piece of bread crust. A female cowered as I walked up to the gate, then scooted away, barely lifting her hips from the ground because her arthritis hurt too bad to stand.

I went home, typed "Harry Theodore" into a few search engines, and couldn't believe what I found: A feature-length profile the *New York Times* ran in 1994, and a small news story in the *New York Daily News*. These were not stories about a man with a dangerous pack of dogs—they were about Harry, a colorful and quintessentially New York character, a poor homeless man who could barely feed himself, yet opened his heart to the countless dogs he kept happy, healthy, and walking leashless throughout the city, like a "shepherd . . . watching his flock."

THE MORNING AFTER the attack, I sat down with my phone and notebook and started what would become months' worth of calls to the same string of organizations: The NYPD, Department of Health, Animal Control, ASPCA and Mayor's Office. The Health Department knew all about Harry's dogs—they'd recently taken a report of his dogs biting a man. I told the story to Officer Baldino at the NYPD's 10th precinct and he said, "Oh yeah, I know who you're talking about. Those dogs are really bad—I don't know why they don't stop them."

Who's they, I asked. Aren't you they?

"No," he said, "Call the ASPCA again. I'm surprised they're not helping you."

So I talked to Giselle at the ASPCA's animal law division. "Oh right," she said, "we get complaints about him all the time." Turns out, an ASPCA officer was at the lot in response to another complaint just days before Bonny was attacked. He found no evidence of a problem. "It's embarrassing," one ASPCA operator told me, "but the city has no law against dogs mutilating other dogs."

I simply didn't believe that. So I started studying dog law. Dangerous dogs (i.e., dogs that should be contained or confiscated) are defined in the New York City administrative code as "any dog with a known propensity, tendency or disposition to attack when unprovoked, to cause injury or to otherwise endanger the safety of human beings or domestic animals." Sounds straightforward. But the problem is, not all relevant city and state laws list biting domestic animals as an offense. Even if they did, dogs don't qualify as domestic animals in New York—they're considered property. The inconsistent laws and that definition of domestic animal—a holdover many states did away with years ago—in effect create a loophole city organizations can point to and say, See, there's no law against dog-on-dog attacks. The truth is, the city could tackle dog-on-dog crime under any number of laws. But it doesn't.

I talked to animal law experts from all over the country, like David Favre, a law professor at Michigan State University who runs the Animal Legal and Historical Center. "I'm shocked that New York animal law is as backwards as it is," he told me. But regardless of that loophole, he said, "if the city wanted to do something they could. The dogs are clearly a nuisance—they've bitten people, and even if they hadn't, New York law says 'any police or peace officer shall seize any dog which poses a threat to public safety.' And these dogs do."

When I explained the situation to Marie Mar, an attorney with the

BAR Association's Committee on Legal Issues Pertaining to Animals, she said, "What you're dealing with is selective law enforcement." She rattled off some of the many reasons Harry's dogs should be confiscated: leash laws, public nuisance, destruction of private property, imminent threat to humans. "They'll come get these dogs in a second when they kill a person, but it shouldn't have to get that far."

Kenneth Phillips, an attorney and author of the books *Dog Bite Law* and *What to Do If Your Dog Is Injured or Killed*, nearly threw the phone in disgust when he heard about Harry's dogs. "Canine behaviorists have shown time and time again that dog packs hone their hunting skills in a series of escalating attacks that start with other animals, then often turn to humans, which means this could easily result in a dead adult or child, and probably will."

MY NEIGHBOR, Andrew Lauffer, was attacked only a month before Bonny. "There were so many of them I couldn't see the ground around me," he told me. "They were all biting me, biting my dogs." Harry's pack cornered Bob Lee on an icy sidewalk and ripped pieces out of his dog's flank. And they surrounded 67-year-old Richard Foster on his stoop: "Fourteen of them came out of nowhere," he told me. "They knocked me over and pinned me down so I couldn't move." Then they went after his dog, tearing several holes in its side.

Five years ago, in response to the attacks, Bob, Richard, and at least ten other neighbors formed a group called The Neighbors Concerned With the Dog Pack Attacks. They spent two and a half years fighting to get Harry's dogs taken away. They complained to the city and testified at community-board hearings in front of the Health Department (and Harry)—one man even testified that he'd seen Harry beat his dogs with large metal poles. The community board asked Harry to keep his dogs confined. And that was it. Harry didn't comply, no one made him, and eventually The Neighbors gave up.

ONE MORNING AFTER Bonny came home from the hospital—
after 87 stitches, more than a week in intensive care and $7,000 in
vet bills—my doorman called and said, "Don't come downstairs,
Rebecca, Harry's dogs are pacing out front." I grabbed my cell phone
and a carving knife, in case they came after me, then ran downstairs.
But they were gone. I called animal control.

"Where are the dogs now?" the dispatcher asked.

"I don't know, but they can't be far," I said. "They're probably
headed for the lot."

"Sorry," he said, "we can't come pick up the dogs unless they're
loose and you know where they are."

That's when I snapped: Bonny was covered neck to tail in bandages
and bruises, she couldn't walk and no one knew if she ever would, my
neighbors were afraid to let their children outside, but no one would
do a damn thing about the dogs. So I ran back to my apartment and
did something most people can't do. I called press offices and said,
"Hi, I'm a reporter writing an article about a pack of dangerous dogs
that's been roaming the streets attacking people and dogs for years.
Numerous people have filed complaints with your organization, and
I'd like to find out why nothing has been done."

Suddenly, they started paying attention. Well, sort of. Mainly, they
made excuses: Budget problems. Not enough officers. Not our jurisdiction. When I called Ed Boyce, the head of the Veterinary Branch of
the Department of Health, I read him the relevant law.

"I'm aware of it," he told me. "I can only tell you that dog-to-dog
attacks are not enforced by the Department of Health."

Who does enforce them?

After a long pause he said, "No one enforces dog-to-dog laws."

"Wait a minute," I said. "So you're telling me there is a law against
what this pack is doing but no one enforces it?"

His response: "That's correct."

Okay, I said, so how about going after the dogs because they bite people? Nope, he told me: The people they bite don't count because they were with dogs—the pack was probably going after their dogs and the people just got in the way.

"So you're saying you'd rather wait until they maul a person?"

"That's what you're saying," he told me. "That's not what I'm saying."

ELIZABETH COULDN'T talk about the attack until weeks after it happened. She and Bonny had been walking down 36th Street when three of Harry's big brown-and-white hound dogs pushed open their junkyard's gate and charged. One grabbed Bonny by the head and lifted her off the sidewalk; the others took her hind legs and pulled in opposite directions. Elizabeth kicked the dogs and pounded their faces, yelling, "Somebody help—they're ripping her in half!" No one responded. Five other dogs ran from the junkyard and latched onto Bonny's face, tail, stomach, and throat. Harry eventually hobbled from behind the fence saying, "Don't make trouble for me, I have a bad heart." Somehow Bonny slipped away, flying up 36th Street toward home, her body torn open and bleeding, with eight dogs on her tail. That's when she ran into the courtyard, where the pack cornered her until Ralphie came along with the two-by-four.

I replayed that scene in my head for weeks as I watched Harry's lot, hoping his dogs would get loose so I could call 911 like everyone said I should. But it didn't happen. So instead, I called Channel 2, the local CBS affiliate. That night, the evening news showed pictures of Bonny after the attack and me lamenting the city's inaction. It showed the rickety latch on the junkyard gate and Harry saying the reason his dogs attacked Bonny was because "somebody opened the gate." Most importantly, it showed Harry, standing in front of his lot, smirking, and saying this: "If somebody opens the gate by mistake, they might attack somebody else."

Still nothing changed. As Bonny began healing and needing to go outside four or five times a day, I walked the streets of Manhattan carrying a carving knife—exactly the kind I used to perform autopsies on dogs in the morgue. I clutched the handle, blade hardly hidden in my pocket, and walked the streets of mid-town knowing that any second 600 pounds of dog could come running around a corner ready to kill us. I walked along reviewing my dog anatomy and planned my routes based on where I could hide Bonny when the dogs came: This convenience store, that dumpster, the entryways of those apartment buildings.

I called the mayor's office again, the community board, the city council, you name it. They told me they'd look into it and call back. They never did. People started saying I should sue Harry. But for what? His rusted hot-dog carts? An injunction that would take years to get, and that he'd probably ignore?

So Harry's pack is still going strong. A few weeks ago, a neighbor told me the dogs cornered a group of children playing in front of the Javits Center. They barked and lunged until people heard screams and ran them off. A few days later, they tore apart another dog and attacked its owner, Hal Caplin, who ended up in the emergency room with twelve stitches in his face. He called the Health Department and the police and got the same old story. As have others. The *Times* recently ran an article about a group of neighbors on the East Side who've seen their dogs attacked and beheaded by two Rottweilers, but the city gives them the same we-don't-do-dog-on-dog line they gave me. Maybe I'll call this group next, to see about challenging the city together.

So yes, I'm still obsessed with Harry and his dogs. I'm furious about what they did to Bonny, but this is about more than my dog. It's about the city needing to fix a law—and a law-enforcement—

problem. It's also about an autopsy I did ten years ago—an autopsy that still haunts me. It was a Rottweiler who mauled and killed a young girl as she played on her swing set. During the autopsy, I had to sort through that dog's stomach and take inventory: One long blond braid with scalp attached. One child's ear. That dog had a history of mauling other dogs. Just like the Florida pack that killed 81-year-old Alice Broom in her front yard days before Bonny's attack. They'd terrorized Alice's neighborhood for months, attacking people, mauling other dogs. Neighbors complained endlessly to authorities but got nowhere.

A few weeks ago, as Bonny and I walked up Ninth Avenue with my friend David, I saw four of Harry's dogs trotting toward us. They were two blocks away, weaving through pedestrians during rush hour. Harry was a good half-block behind the dogs. Bonny didn't see them; if she had, she'd have been gone. Because here's the thing: After almost a year of nursing, she walks and runs just fine. She may never regain full use of one hind leg, but other than that she's okay, physically. Mentally is another story: She recently started wrestling with me again, but full contact terrifies her. Dog barks send her into a panic— she screams and flails, struggles to escape her collar or bite through her leash to run home. So when I saw Harry's dogs coming toward us, I handed David the leash. "Those are the dogs," I said. "Take her across the street."

As David and Bonny crossed Ninth Avenue, I stood in the middle of the sidewalk, facing Harry's dogs, watching them run toward me. And I did what every city official said to do when I saw them loose: I called 911.

"Are they attacking anyone right now?" the dispatcher asked.

"No."

"Sorry," she told me. "Try Animal Control." I called Animal Control, the Health Department, and the Mayor's Office. I talked to a traffic cop, then called 911 again. Guess what they said: "Are they attacking anyone right now?"

"No," I said, as Harry's dogs ran past me toward the junkyard. "Would you rather wait until they do?"

_____

In response to this story and the outpouring of reader responses that followed, the Mayor's Office of New York City condemned the lot where Harry lived, spayed and neutered all his dogs, and sent all but two of them to a shelter in Pennsylvania. They moved Harry into public housing in The Bronx, where he now lives with two of the eight dogs that attacked Bonny.

Double Take

OPINIONISTAS.COM

Nothing drives home the viral power of American culture like seeing it on the other side of the world. Step off a bus on the South China Sea coast, snap a picture of jutting cliffs stretching into lush forests, turn around to nab an action shot of the rustic seaside village and BAM! There's Mariah Carey writhing across a 20-foot billboard, her airbrushed cheekbones towering over roadside vendors peddling pork buns and cuttlefish balls. "In Hong Kong for One Night, Her Only Concert In Asia!" screams the English headline beneath her pillowy breasts. Walk into a Wan Chai pharmacy and you'll hear Justin Timberlake squawking and thumping over the loudspeakers. Turn on the TV and see MTV Asia's gelled veejays gushing over Leo's latest look and Paris Hilton's love life—"Does she still love Stavros? Or has she moved on?" It's enough to turn one mid-afternoon Tsingtao into a three-digit bar tab (in Hong Kong dollars, of course). Nine thousand miles of travel to new continents, and here it is, the same old saccharine carbonated crap shoved down our gullets. Though I'll admit, there's something transcendent about watching a pasty British pop star in a plaid jumpsuit blurt, "Right, let's pimp my ride, shall we?"

At last we reach Vietnam, where the culture and halcyon landscape are still untouched by KFCs and Body Shops. We're in a car heading south to Cu Chi, and I sigh with relief, safe at last from Pepsi and Lancome and Tag Hauer and the cagey emptiness of pop culture ubiquity. After two hours of cruising along a dirt road, we pull through a village consisting of a few aluminum-topped houses, a crafts shop leaning heavily to one side and an open-air restaurant. A handful of patrons lounge on stools just shy of the road, drinking black coffee in clear glasses.

I gaze out the car window wishing I could freeze frame moments, giving me time to absorb it all; barefoot children waving and giggling at our Western faces pressed against the windows; a small but muscular man whizzing by on a motor scooter with four feet of sugar cane packed behind his seat, all held in place with twine; rice fields stretching for miles, broken up by occasional ponds where boys gather to fish with bamboo rods; stray dogs, bored cows and mud-coated water buffalos wandering along the side of the road, oblivious to the scooters and occasional car. It's different and perfect; finally, a place that exists without the More-Is-More doctrine worshipped so unequivocally in Western culture.

I rub my eyes, watery from the lash-singeing sunlight that doesn't seem to bother anyone but Westerners. When I open them, I see an older man (though it's impossible to guess his age—he could be 40 or 70) squatting on a patch of grass, his feet just clear of a mud puddle. He's extending an arm to point out his wares: portraits of faces on rough parchment, done in stunning detail. "LOW PRISES" boasts a cardboard sign nailed to a wooden stake. I glance at the row of pictures depicting smiling babies, local children, farmers, a few sweating tourists, and . . . wait, what the hell?

"Hey, guys, stop the car a sec. Look at that!" I point to the largest portrait, propped up against a bush in a prominent position. "You have got to be kidding me."

We sit gaping for a second at the unmistakable image—blond hair, carefully lined blue eyes, pert ski-slope nose, a set of culture-embodying features branded into our gray matter: Britney Spears.

"Holy crap, that's either hilarious or really sad," says one travel companion. "Please don't let that be the only example these people have of American culture."

"Why shouldn't it be? I'd say it's pretty accurate," I respond as he restarts the car. "Deeply and incurably depressing, maybe, but still accurate."

Trapeze Lessons

Marie Carter

"To what extent can you be creative with the narrative and still call it nonfiction?" Marie Carter wonders. "At what point does it become fiction? The boundaries have always been murky to me as a reader but more especially to me as a writer who works with fiction and nonfiction. As I've tried to recollect memories exactly as they happened and have had friends and family members read it and say, 'No, that's not it,' and then argued with them about who's in the right, I see that it's not the history of the matter that's most important but rather making the narrative work. Working in creative nonfiction gives a writer that extra bit of flexibility to make the narrative more interesting."

This story first appeared in Hanging Loose.

It Begins . . .

The lyra artist caught the hoop beautifully every time, sometimes with her feet, sometimes with her arms, and a couple of times with her head. She projected long shadows against the wall of the tent. She took risks. There were many times in her sequence when I thought she might fall and break her neck, but she didn't.

When I got home, I couldn't stop thinking about her. I was so touched by the way she defied everything human in herself. I tried to imagine what it would be like to be her: unafraid of heights, flexible, strong, and defiant.

At night, I dreamt shadows were dancing above me. I awoke to my own shuddering because I thought I was falling from a trapeze.

Mortality

The older I get, the more I become aware of my own mortality: my father died of a sudden heart attack five years ago and a colleague of mine recently died of pancreatic cancer. My mother has MS and when she comes to visit, she has to hold on to my arm wherever we walk. When I take the bus home at night, I dream the bus crashes and I break my arm and crush my hip.

I have been reading Edward Abbey's *Desert Solitaire*. He writes, "The fear of death follows from the fear of life. A man who lives fully is prepared to die at anytime."

During my lunch break I walk to the Westside Highway and watch people taking lessons at the trapeze school. I watch enviously, as strong flexible people glide through the air and hang upside down by their knees. They jump off the net, their faces red with exhilaration.

I tell a friend of mine in his fifties what I've been doing with my lunch break. He tells me to learn trapeze while I'm still young.

The Nervous Child

I was not an adventurous kid. One day, when I was ten years old, it was snowing and my mother said she wanted to get me out of the house.

She was tired of my antisocial activities, nesting in my room, reading a book. She decided she would take me sledding the next day to a small hill near the back of our house where other children went sledding, threw snowballs, and made snowmen.

That night, I had nightmares. In one dream, I lost a leg. In another, I died colliding with someone else in a sledding accident. I couldn't envision how the experience might turn out well. I was incredibly nervous on my first day but once I got into it, I stopped worrying. I even became quite adept at the activity once I lost my fear.

But still, I was always cautious about everything I did. From flying in an airplane to rollerskating to riding my bike to camping, I always lived in fear of adventurous activities.

I always believed I would hurt myself.

No Religion

My therapist asks if I believe in the afterlife.

"I don't believe in anything. I'm an atheist," I say.

She nods. "I'm not suggesting you adopt a religion," she says, "but some people find it a helpful tool in understanding and coping with death."

"My father was an atheist, too," I say.

Once our session is over, she recommends a book for me to read. It's called *Your Loved One Lives On Within You.*

From the back cover, I read, "[This book] will show how your untapped imagination can lead to a new beginning with the person you considered lost to you forever.

It is true that the old relationship has come to an end. You will never again be in the physical presence of the person. However, death need not cut you off from those you love. An inner relationship with the person who has died continues on after death."

My Father in the Bedroom

My father sits at the edge of my bed in the morning, examining the pictures on my wall. He squints at them and points.

"That one's crooked," he says, getting up from the bed to set the frame right again.

I say nothing. I've barely slept all night in anticipation of my first trapeze class.

My father continues to observe the room and when he is not, he is fixing things: the cracked plaster on my wall, the wobbly chair, and the doorknob that comes apart in my hands.

I curl back under the covers and doze. When I wake again to check my watch it is 5:30 in the morning. My father is wiping the dirt off my blinds.

Discipline

I keep thinking about the iron yoga, bodybuilding instructor I'd read about in *Outside* magazine. When he was twenty-one, his friends knew him as a taco-eating pig. When one of them took him to the gym, he could barely do two squats. Now he's known as one of the toughest, most disciplined teachers in Colorado.

This man gives me faith. If a taco-eating pig from Colorado who couldn't do one squat is now a bodybuilding yoga teacher, then I can become an aerialist.

My First Handstand

Everyone in the class is doing handstands against the wall to warm up for the trapeze class. They split their legs wide apart and with control tumble upside down against the wall, arms pressed against the brick.

I've never done anything like this before; even when I was a child and supposedly more flexible, I couldn't do handstands. I walk my feet up the wall and try to bring my hands in, but they rest a good two feet from the wall. The feeling in my arms is agony. My breath is erratic.

From my upside-down position, I notice the trapeze teacher, Diana, watching me, smiling encouragingly. My gaze lowers to the floor. I feel foolish. I'm the only one who's had to walk her way into a handstand. My father is watching me from the corner of the room: he is nervously picking at the skin around his fingernails.

A Lesson

I jump into a half-assed handstand and feel myself instantly coming back down when Susan grabs my legs and sends me over. There's a shaking sensation in my arms, blood rushes to my head, and I feel disoriented. I let out a little yelp, more because I'm scared, not because I'm in pain. My legs pivot back down to the floor so I'm upright.

"You did it," Susan says, smiling.

When I arrived at Susan's apartment earlier, I told her I couldn't do handstands. As a former gymnast, she decided to teach me this basic trick by spotting me into a handstand against the wall.

"Even when I was a kid, I couldn't do it," I told her.

Now that I was able to go over with help, I needed to learn to do it by myself. Susan spots me four more times. On the fifth try, she pulls away from me.

"Try it on your own now," she says.

So I try by myself. To my surprise, my whole body tumbles over and I'm in this strong, upside-down shape, my feet pressed against the door.

Amazement

The ad on TV for the fitness center has a slogan that reads "The Power to Amaze Yourself."

An Apology

Diana is trying to position me into an ankle hang in which I am upside down and gripping the ropes with my ankles, but my feet keep sliding and I become nervous. My head inches toward the floor and in reaction I sit back up and take hold of the bar with my hands, push my legs into a knee hang, then take my feet off the bar, one at a time.

"Nice," Diana says.

But for me, it is not enough.

"Sorry," I say to her.

"Don't apologize to me," she says.

Later, I realize I am apologizing to myself.

My Father Laughs

I am watching Charlie Chaplin's *The Circus*. My father is sitting in his favorite rocking chair, chortling loudly and slapping his thighs.

I remember when I was a child my father would take me to the cinema and it was always embarrassing when people would laugh at him laughing. In all the photographs I have of my father, he is pulling a funny face. He didn't like to be serious.

At the beginning of *The Circus*, a trapeze artist is swinging from the rafters. After her performance at the circus, her father slaps her across the face and chastises her for a poor performance and the trapeze artist begs for her father's mercy. She was "trying."

Earlier in the evening I had been practicing handstands, belly to the wall. I'd been trying to hold them for a minute, then walk my hands back out. Instead, my legs fell away from the wall, so I landed in an awkward backbend. My father rolled up laughing.

Obsession

It is snowing heavily and as I walk to trapeze class my hair gets damper. It must be love if I'm prepared to walk to class on a cold snowy night like this. I feel like a teenager with a silly crush. At work when I am bored or stressed, I simply have to notice the calluses on my hands and I smile. At night I dream that I haul myself into a pike on the bar, two hands grasping the bar, my body folded in half and my nose pressing to my belly, legs straight. Sometimes I dream that people are standing on my shoulders.

The other night I practiced the crucifix, a trick that involves locking myself into the bar with only my outspread arms and arched back. Dark purple bruises have appeared on my arms. At work, they have been joking that I must be into some kinky sexual practice.

Lately, my cats have been tightrope-walking across my bed-frame.

Lopsided

Diana has called in sick today and in her place is another woman. The idea of having a new teacher discombobulates me. Trapeze requires so much trust, especially when novices like me are involved. But I'm not such a novice anymore. I've been taking lessons for six months and I still can't do an arrow. With one leg at 90 degrees facing the wall and the other leg gripping the rope, and the head dangling toward the floor, the lock is held in the hips. Often, I can't find the right place to rest the hips; it's always my bone that comes to rest on the bar and it hurts like hell.

I still haul myself to standing from sitting. You'd think I'd have learned these tricks by now.

Today, I've been thinking about why I like trapeze so much.

I used to do Egyptian dance, but I didn't go to class regularly and didn't practice the moves very often. I picked it up so easily I didn't feel I had to work at it and thus my passion was never terribly excited. But trapeze is different. It's precisely because it's difficult that I need to work hard at it, that I'm fascinated by it.

The substitute teacher asks me to do ten knee beats, hanging from the bar by my knees and throwing my upper body toward the floor, then up using my abs to bring my head back up to my knees. I can't do knee beats. I am scared the teacher will let go of my feet. But I didn't trust Diana at first, either.

Even my father seems put out. He's examining the trapeze closest to the bathroom.

"This thing is crooked," he says when I approach him.

My Father Nitpicks

My father was such a perfectionist. He was always straightening pictures around the house and fixing tiny anomalies. After I left home, I would occasionally visit on the odd weekend. At night, when everyone was asleep, I would go around the apartment and make all the pictures crooked. When my father woke, I would hear him yelp at the bottom of the stairs. Several hours later, he'd still be straightening things.

Our Injuries

Someone in class is talking about the time she took a flying trapeze class and knocked heads with her catcher.

"We were both out, unconscious for several minutes," she says. "But they made me get back out there and throw the same trick with the catcher again. I had a black eye and I had to get up at ten the next day for another class. When I threw the trick again, I could barely let go of the bar."

I have heard of trapeze artists having serious accidents: everything from a black eye to death. So far, all I've gotten are some nasty bruises on my arms. I am waiting for the worst to happen.

One day, Diana said, "I keep chipping my teeth."

Pain

The neurologist tells me the needle will hurt.

"Are you chicken or are you quite good with pain?" she asks.

"Chicken," I say.

She tells me she'll be gentle and that I can look the other way if that will make it easier.

She inserts the needle and I don't even flinch.

After the test is over, she says, "You're not chicken at all. You didn't even say a word. I had a police officer in here earlier who did the same test and he was screaming."

Sometimes I wonder whether I talk myself into believing I'm cowardly.

Sometimes, I think I fear the concept of pain rather than the pain itself.

Skin-the-Cat

Diana is demonstrating "skin-the-cat." With her hands gripping the bar, body folded in half at the waist in pike position, she lowers her feet to the ground so her shoulders and upper arms twist. Once her feet hit the ground she releases her grip from the bar to stand.

I decide I can't do it. I don't think I'll be able to hold my weight. It looks painful on the shoulders.

"Try it on a low bar," Diana suggests.

But I'm still afraid. I push myself, though, and I'm amazed to find the movement does not hurt. In fact, it's surprisingly easy and doesn't hurt my shoulders at all.

The Family Heart

My mother is always reminding me I am from a family of men with weak hearts. All of them have died at a young age of heart attacks. I don't need to worry about things like cancer or strokes because there's no history of such a thing in my family, but she doesn't like it when I'm stressed out or afraid. "Watch your heart," she is always telling me, even though I'm still in my twenties.

I can be the same way with her. She orders a burger with fries at McDonald's and I scold her, saying, "I don't know how you can eat that shit. Didn't you watch *Supersize Me*? Didn't you read *Fast Food Nation*? You should be careful with your heart."

She asks the vendor to supersize her order.

At trapeze class, I try to maneuver myself into an arrow but my hips are having a hard time rolling over the bar and when I finally come into the position, I scare myself by almost falling out of it again. And even though Diana has caught me, a little voice in my head whispers, "Watch your heart."

What Heaven Looks Like

I'm an atheist and I don't believe in heaven but I like the concept of it. Sometimes, I like to imagine what my father would do in that place called "heaven." He'd eat peaches and ice cream for dessert every day, smoke cigarettes, and watch football. He'd have access to all the socks and handkerchiefs he could ever want. For me, heaven is full of aerialists, dangling limply from hoops, fabric silks, and trapeze bars. In heaven, I will be strong and supple.

Sometimes, when I go to trapeze class, I think, "I want to die here."

Notes on Frey

Daniel Nester

Daniel Nester profiled James Frey for Poets & Writers Magazine *in 2005, when the "memoirist" was still a best-selling, up-and-coming young writer (before his name became shorthand for deception). In this piece from* Creative Nonfiction, *Nester looks back on the scandal and his experience with Frey, and tries to make sense of it all.*

How does one begin to defend James Frey, the infamous lying memoirist? By asking readers to imagine a future in which memoirists write and sign affidavits when they hand in their manuscripts? Who will check their facts? Will it be editorial assistants? Computer programs? Psychic profilers? *Quis custodiet ipsos custodes?* Who shall Google the guards?

Still another suggestion: Ask readers to ponder whether the James Frey Affair marks the end of a time when writers who wish to record how they perceive their own lives may do so rather than stick to what

is on public record? Judging by the media fallout and Oprah's indig-
nation, many would applaud such a development. But there are other
ways of looking at the Frey fallout. Whole wings of psychotherapy
await their debunking; whole shelves of memoirs, from Harriette Wil-
son to Primo Levi, wait for their warning stickers. The next Hunter S.
Thompson, if there will ever be one, should expect knocks on the door
by the Authenticity Police, asking him if he really took that many tabs
of acid that weekend in Vegas.

How does one begin to defend James Frey? I can't. I can, however,
try to tell you some stories, confess my own sins, and ask how others
deal with theirs.

HERE'S A STORY. On the afternoon of April 12, 2005, I spent an
hour with James Frey at Nan A. Talese's Doubleday office in the
Saatchi & Saatchi building on 375 Hudson Street. That lower-
Manhattan building's shiny, postmodern curves show up in exterior
shots on the sitcom *Seinfeld* to set up scenes at Elaine's publishing
office.

I was assigned to write a profile of the memoirist for *Poets & Writers*, a magazine that goes out to 60,000 aspiring creative writers
nationwide. I had just read both of Frey's books—*A Million Little
Pieces* and the sequel, *My Friend Leonard*—in rapid succession. Along
with review copies of these books, I held two tape recorders (one dig-
ital, one analog), pads of yellow legal paper, a box of black uni-ball
ultrafine pens and a printout of my questions in my shoulder bag.

When I mention my Frey story to people, that I met him and all,
many think it was after he was picked for Oprah Winfrey's book club.
People forget or don't realize that *A Million Little Pieces* had a life of its
own before then. His raw account of rehabilitation was, in fact, Ama-
zon.com's best-selling book of 2003 and a *New York Times* best seller,
and it had garnered a huge following. Frey got the one-two punch

from the *Times* that only big-time books get: a review in *The New York Times Sunday Book Review* and a "Books of *The Times*" article, in which Janet Maslin called attention to the fact that the book was sent around as fiction, then as a memoir.

Back then, however, I knew of Frey only from the now infamous article by Joe Hagan for *The New York Observer* in February 2003, in which Frey talked shit about Dave Eggers' 2000 memoir, *A Heart-breaking Work of Staggering Genius*: "[A] book that I thought was mediocre was being hailed as the best book written by the best writer of my generation," he said. "Fuck that. And fuck him and fuck any-body that says that. I don't give a fuck what they think of me. I'm going to try to write the best book of my generation, and I'm going to try to be the best writer."

In "Writing Personal Essays: On the Necessity of Turning Oneself into a Character," Phillip Lopate writes that to make an essay success-ful and interesting, "we need to *dramatize* ourselves" [italics his] and that as part of that character-inventing process, we "maximize that pitiful set of quirks, those small differences that seem to set us apart from others, and project them theatrically, the way actors work with singularities in their physical appearances or voice textures."

Frey certainly presented himself theatrically, both in his books and to the media. He seemed like a total badass. A famous image at that time was a black-and-white photo of Frey with buzzed hair and no shirt, staring at the camera, crouched on a futon bed. One of his many tattoos is an inspirational acronym: *FTBSITTTD* (Fuck The Bullshit It's Time To Throw Down).

HERE'S A CONFESSION: I have never, ever wholly believed dialogue in a memoir. Especially in a coming-of-age memoir. It rarely reads as real to me.

Maybe that's because it isn't. When I was a teenager, I thought the opposite: Writers had these photographic memories for every word ever said. But since then, I have become well aware that the arbiters of creative nonfiction, essay, autobiography, memoir, and lyrical whatchamacallits have all convened somewhere and given "quoted dialogue" a free pass on the authenticity highway. But let's speak plainly here: It is a lie. As we all know, in memoir, dialogue usually comprises representative snatches of what might have been said; it's an emblematic device to remind us that This Important Discussion took place, refracted through the author's subjective, often faulty memory. Set aside that bad writers crutch on dialogue in every genre; even the great memoir with dialogue rubs me the wrong way. In bad memoirs, I find myself skipping through these made-up, composite conversations.

Part of the blame rests on my 12 years of Catholic catechism, where I was taught, among other things, that sins are subdivided into those of thought, word or deed (*cordis, oris, operis*). Thought and word and deed are not only all the same thing, but any combination of this unholy trinity not only reinforces but compounds the sin. Comedian George Carlin sums up the compounding of sin on his 1972 album *Class Clown*:

> It was a sin to wanna feel up Ellen; it was a sin for you to plan to feel up Ellen; it was a sin for you to figure out a place to feel up Ellen; it was a sin to take her to the place to feel her up; it was a sin to try to feel her up; and it was a sin to feel her up—it was six sins in one feel, man!

When I read dialogue in a memoir, then, I can't help but have my Catholic thought-word-deed sin-detector go off. The writer is vouching for these people's words and has gone and placed them inside "quotation marks," those most authoritative punctuation marks of the journalist and researcher. Memoir dialogue, to me, is three sins in one: The writer not only lies about what is said but also provides the exact words for that lie and then writes down whatever is accounted as gospel truth. How easy for the memoirist to enfold event and detail inside these conversations! And the memoirist who embellishes an event, is he or she more or less guilty of sin?

APRIL 12, 2005, WAS a beautiful spring day, a perfect 61 degrees. I sat at the head of a long table, and James Frey sat about four feet away. He was not a psycho badass motherfucker. He was a nice guy. He was calm and comfortable. He did not smile. He wore flip-flops and drank Diet Coke. His Tribeca loft, according to one of the publicists, was a couple of blocks away. "Should we get you a limo for the ride home?" the publicist joked to him.

I slid both tape recorders toward him. There was no need: His voice was loud, much louder and confident and easygoing than it would be in his television appearances months later on *Larry King Live* and *The Oprah Winfrey Show*.

> ME: I find it amazing when my novelist friends lash out at me and say, "You don't know what it's like, how much work is involved in this." I know people who have been working on their novels for six to seven years, and I sometimes think, "Shit or get off the pot."
>
> JAMES FREY: I hear those stories, too. I feel like I work with a lot of confidence. I never doubt myself at the beginning of the day, that I'm not going to do what I set out to do. I never worry that I'm not going to get my work done. I don't self-edit. I don't read what I write. I start something, and I just keep going forward. I don't think I'm the best judge of my work, so I just keep going forward and let someone else take a look at it.
>
> ME: That's a gift. I mean, that's a gift to have that kind of confidence as you write. I know so many people who don't.

JAMES FREY: Well, I think part of what holds people up is a fear of failure or a fear of criticism. And neither of those things scares me at all. If I fail, I fail. I give it my best shot every day. I work really hard. And I think if anything, that's my gift. It's the ability to work really hard, very, very consistently. Now I know a lot of people who are smarter than me or who are probably more talented than me or more naturally gifted than me. But what I can do that they cannot do is go back every day for eight to 10 hours a day and work. And it seems to be working for me.

Under the klieg lights of Oprah's Book Club, it didn't take long for reporters to reveal that the hard-working and super-confident James Frey had lied, had over-dramatized himself. In January 2006, The Smoking Gun Web site published "A Million Little Lies: Exposing James Frey's Fiction Addiction," a 13,000-word exposé on the inconsistencies between Frey's book and what is public record. "Frey appears to have fictionalized his past to propel and sweeten the book's already melodramatic narrative and to help convince readers of his malevolence," the story read. The Web site also found that Frey had sought to expunge what record did exist of his criminal past to build "walls" around himself.

"So why would a man who spends 430 pages," it continued, citing a page count not found in any English edition of *A Million Little Pieces*, "chronicling every grimy and repulsive detail of his formerly debased life . . . need to wall off the details of a decade-old arrest?"

HOW DO OTHERS deal with their own stories? On July 28, 2003, three months after *A Million Little Pieces* was published and two years before the James Frey Affair, writer Vivian Gornick also found herself in an authenticity bind when, speaking at a writers conference at Goucher College, she mentioned that in her critically acclaimed 1987

memoir *Fierce Attachments*, she had invented scenes and conversations, and that in a couple of pieces she wrote for *The Village Voice*
between 1969 and 1977, she had used composite characters.

Let me back up. Gornick is a hero of mine. She is the author of *The
Situation and the Story: The Art of Personal Narrative*, a standard text
in many memoir and creative nonfiction classes. In it, she emphasizes
that what happened to writers of personal narrative "is not what matters" but rather what "is achieved when the reader is working hard to
engage with the experience at hand." "These writers might not 'know'
themselves—that is, have more self-knowledge than the rest of us,"
she continues, "but in each case—and this is crucial—they 'know who
they are at the moment of writing.'" Personal essay and memoir focus
on different things to accomplish different goals; the essayist focuses
on a particular situation, while the memoirist must "deliver wisdom."

Four days after the talk at Goucher College, *Salon* published
student-journalist Terry Greene Sterling's account of the events. The
scene at the Gornick Q-and-A segment that followed, Sterling writes,
led to a "culture clash": "a sophisticated New York memoirist facing
off against a crowd that included highly regarded journalists." [Ster-
ling may be referring to herself here; one of the first Google search
results for Sterling is a reprint of "Sterling Gets Top Reward" (*Phoenix
New Times*, April 22, 1999), penned by Sterling herself, which
announces her as winner of Arizona's Journalist of the Year award, in
part for her "exhaustive investigation" into the Baptist Foundation of
Arizona.]

The Gornick story gained still more traction when book critic and
Georgetown University professor Maureen Corrigan offered her own
response on National Public Radio's "Fresh Air." Corrigan was "disheartened" and "betrayed" by the "oddly offhand admission" that
Gornick "played fast-and-loose with the truth."

"Any reader who falls in love with a work of nonfiction leaves him- or herself open to being betrayed," Corrigan said in Cassandra fashion.

HOW DO WE deal with the sinner? That the ruckus and fallout over the lies in *A Million Little Pieces* started only after its selection for Oprah's Book Club can't speak only to the popularity of a talk show. It says something about the insularity of literary culture, if such a thing even exists. But there has to be more.

Maybe it suggests that pre-Oprah readers suspended their disbelief, as I do reading dialogue, or that they were more sophisticated than post-Oprah readers, who not only sought wisdom from the book but looked to it for a pragmatic, utilitarian, self-help function. Or maybe it speaks to the fact that every writer does what Frey did, though he had the misfortune of choosing to embellish verifiable facts rather than inner states of being, torn-down buildings, dead people's accounts of events. Or maybe it's simply that success always breeds a smackdown.

Or is it the unseemliness of a writer entering the public realm and being on television at all? "The writer on a television talk show," Richard R. Lingeman wrote in his essay "Writers As Show-Biz" for *The New York Times Sunday Book Review* in 1971, "is a little like a minister touting his next sermon at a kootch show, while being frequently interrupted by the barker's spiel."

HERE'S ANOTHER story. I am a tragically hip, middle-aged professor with a dusty record collection. I am reading the June 2006 issue of the English music magazine *Mojo* and its cover story on Joe Strummer, the rhythm guitarist, singer and main songwriter for The Clash. Reading Pat Gilbert's story, "The Man Who Wasn't There," I learn for the first time that Strummer, far from being a man-of-the-people who sang such manifesto-anthems as "London Calling," "White Riot" and "I'm So Bored with the U.S.A.," was actually the son of a junior-level English foreign diplomat and had lived in Turkey, Egypt, Germany and Mexico before he was sent off to boarding school at 9 years old. At 17, he went to Buckingham Palace to see his dad become a Member of the Most Excellent Order of the British Empire for services to Queen and country. Yet the former John Graham Mellor rarely addressed his middle-class background when he played in The Clash. Instead, he helped other Clash camp members "act working class" and talked to reporters about "slitting people with flick-knives."

IT WOULD BE fair to say that Strummer lied, to a certain degree, all his life. Had I found out about Strummer's past as a 14-year-old punk rocker, I would have stopped listening to The Clash and denounced them, no questions asked.

My reaction now? I wouldn't question Strummer's punk status, and I'll still listen to "London Calling," but for me the question remains: Why did Strummer/Mellor do this? Why didn't he present himself as a middle-class kid sympathetic to working-class causes rather than present himself as a character who had dramatized himself?

Maybe those post-Oprah readers and critics of Frey are the equivalent of 14-year-old punk rockers who denounce their heroes when they find out they don't get their clothes from the gutter. Frey's book, with its tale of overcoming addiction that inspired so many of Oprah's viewers, was especially ripe for this kind of backlash.

FREY'S CONFESSION, "a note to the reader," was posted on River-head's Web site in January 2006. Frey lied and exaggerated, he explains, because he "wanted the stories in the book to ebb and flow, to have dramatic arcs, to have the tension that all great stories require." He also changed details, he says, to protect other people's anonymity. He had outlined a couple of these on his second visit to *The Oprah Winfrey Show*; for instance, Frey admitted that his girlfriend, called Lilly in the book, had killed herself not by hanging but by "cutting her wrists."

He writes that he spent three months in jail. That, too, was a lie; it was more like "several hours." There are other "embellishments" in the book as well. "I made other alterations in my portrayal of myself, most of which portrayed me in ways that made me tougher and more daring and more aggressive than in reality I was or I am," he writes. When I read this, I think back to Frey's dented-in boxer's nose as I talked to him. It clearly had been broken, and every time he spoke, there was a clear whistle from his septum. People's "skewed perception of themselves," he writes, helps them "overcome" problems, "do things they thought they couldn't do before."

"My mistake," he writes, "and it is one I deeply regret, is writing about the person I created in my mind to help me cope and not the person who went through the experience."

GORNICK DIDN'T OFFER up a confession. She didn't feel the need to. In her response to Corrigan on August 11, 2003, she sounded angry, like my sister scolding one of her sons in stern staccato. She called "Fresh Air" from the Yaddo artist colony and said:

> A memoir is a story taken directly from the raw material of a writer's own life and shaped into a piece of experience that can hold meaning for the disinterested reader. What actually happened is only material; what the writer makes of what happened is everything. To state the case briefly: Memoirs belong to the

category of literature, not of journalism. It is a misunderstand-
ing to read a memoir as though the writer owes the reader the
same record of factual accuracy that is owed in newspaper
reporting or literary journalism. What *is* owed [by the mem-
oirist] is only the ability to persuade that the narrator is honestly
trying to get down to the bottom of the experience at hand.

Just as Oprah gets the last word with Frey, so Corrigan is given the
chance to comment yet again. In her first commentary piece, Corrigan had spoken of an "Autobiographer's Pledge," which each writer
implicitly recites when taking an "accounting" of one's life, as well as
an "Autobiographer's Contract." To those of the more academic per-
suasion, these terms, *pledge* and *contract*, might recall French literary
theorist Philippe Lejeune's 1973 essay, "The Autobiographical Pact"
("*Le Pacte autobiographique*"). Unlike Corrigan, Lejeune does not
map out a doomed, litigious writer-reader relationship, nor does he
assert the lack of any relationship at all, as Roland Barthes does in his
1977 essay "The Death of the Author." Instead, Lejeune describes a
middle path where the author connects the "world-beyond-text and
the text."

"An author is not a person," he writes. He is "defined as simultaneously a socially responsible real person and the producer of a discourse. For the reader, who does not know the real person, all the
while believing in his existence, the author is defined as the person
capable of producing this discourse, and so he imagines what he is like
from what he produced." Paul John Eakin, a scholar in life writing
studies and a professor at Indiana University, writes that "Lejeune's
position resides in his willingness to concede the fictive status of the
self and then to proceed with its functioning as experiential fact."

But what's perhaps the most maddening to me about Corrigan's
second commentary, her response to Gornick's response, is the inter-
changing of the words *memoir* and *autobiography*. In her 359-word

commentary, forms of the word *autobiography* are used nine times; *memoir*, four times. The difference between memoir and autobiography, to many writers, is a crucial one. Gore Vidal goes to great pains to point out the difference in the introduction to his memoir, *Palimpsest*. A memoir, he writes, "is how one remembers one's own life, while an autobiography is history, requiring research, dates, facts double-checked." "[I]n a memoir," Vidal continues, "there are many rubbings-out and puttings-in."

HOW SHOULD WE deal with such sins and sinners? I don't think it's an accident that while Frey embellished his stories consciously to punch up his narrative, many of his fellow memoirists who gathered in the town square to cast stones were, by and large, ones who—whether they want to admit it or not—embellish their own work unconsciously and punch up their own unverifiable, emotional truths, for which there are no notes, no Smoking Guns, nothing but a conscience to fact-check them.

Take, for instance, memoirist Mary Karr's op-ed piece, "His So-Called Life," written for *The New York Times*, in which she calls Frey a "skunk" who broke the "cardinal rule" of memoirs: You don't "make stuff up." The key phrase that Karr, whose classic 1995 memoir, *The Liar's Club*, recalls chunks of her childhood with remarkable detail, uses to explain why she doesn't "make stuff up"—she tells how she declined her publisher's request to make up a happy ending to her memoir—is "God is in the truth." Had she found out Helen Keller was "merely nearsighted, not deaf, blind and mute," she writes, her "bubble might have popped."

Perhaps a more apt comparison of Frey with Keller, however, would be if Frey were merely a problem drinker, not a drug addict. Or if the author of *The Story of My Life* embellished the set of circumstances that led to her condition and situation, as Frey did with a made-up criminal past that led to his stint in rehab. Keller, you may recall, became deaf and blind at 19 months, an age for which, most neurologists and psychologists agree, humans have few if any memories. Here's what Keller claims to remember:

> I fancy I still have confused recollections of that illness. I especially remember the tenderness with which my mother tried to soothe me in my waking hours of fret and pain, and the agony and bewilderment with which I awoke after a tossing half sleep and turned my eyes, so dry and hot, to the wall, away from the once-loved light, which came to me dim and yet more dim each day. . . .

"[D]uring the first 19 months of my life," she continues, "I had caught glimpses of broad, green fields, a luminous sky, trees and flowers, which the darkness that followed could not wholly blot out."

Picking on Helen Keller isn't exactly playing fair, I know. I suppose what I am asking is if we should allow the existence of more than one kind of memoirist. On one end of the spectrum, there are memoirists who invoke fancy and God's will to get to the Truth. They take pledges and sign contracts. On the other end are memoirists for whom the truth is their own to name. These are the ones who do not profess an allegiance to fancy or a fictive god. They value emotional truth over public record. They do not take an oath or sign a contract. On the one end, we have faith; on the other end, will.

What I mean by *will* is that perhaps what enrages people most about James Frey is that he willfully changed the details in his life to serve the story, whereas for so many other memoirists, doing so is an unacknowledged sin. The cobbled-together childhood conversation as a major plot-point registers as less of a sin on the authenticity meter—and diminishes less a writer's capacity as truth-teller—than a tall tale of a criminal past.

"Do these members of the Goucher College audience imagine that memoirists walk around wired for conversation capture like snitching mobsters?" Tom Bissell writes about Sterling's Gornick account in *Salon*. "Do they believe that everything in nonfiction has to be exactly documented to be emotionally true? Do they not understand the huge difference between literary memoir and a newspaper article entitled 'Property Sale Raises Questions Amid Ethics Inquiry'?"

Take for Exhibit A Kenneth Goldsmith's *Soliloquy*, a 400-page book in which the author—a poet, visual artist and freeform radio DJ—transcribes everything he says in a week in 1996. Nothing is edited. Here's an excerpt of a still longer excerpt that appears in the online journal *Readme*:

> It was Rick, Aki, Mike, there was this guy also that you probably never heard of named Nick Arbatsky. Sure you never heard of Nick. He dropped out he did a Alaskan oil spill project his big claim to fame he had this big fundraiser so when the Titanic crashed out there in the waters the oil spilled all over the Valdez he went up there with canvases, right? Everybody chipped in he had a big party. He went up there with canvases to try to make like oil Valdez soaked. And he came back, man, and this. That was a good idea. And then he had a coming back party so he could show what he got. And the guy comes back with like, we figured he would have like these dripping, rich canvases, you know, like birds plastered. They were like these canvases he kind of drew on a little bit and and and. No no there was no tar. It was the most like like Helen Frankenthaler washes and it was his impressions in it and that was it for Nick, man, that was the last you ever heard of Nick. Nick was like like like pegged to be the next huge thing in those days too because of that project. And and the Village Voice might have written something about him. So, have you read the Voice since it's free? I I hate the Voice.

When did we stop reading the Voice what year? Yeah. Everybody once, yeah yeah. Well we picked it up because it was free and it's the same thing. It's like a cliche. Oh my god, yeah. Much better. We like Time Out. Yeah, the ad is good.

You get the idea. Just as Bissell proposes, Goldsmith wore a wire—a hidden, voice-activated microphone, actually, one that, Goldsmith writes to me over e-mail, tripped on and off "from the moment I woke up Monday morning till the moment I went to sleep Sunday night."

BEFORE HE WROTE his story and after he left rehab, James Frey was an aspiring screenwriter. He wanted to write something that "someone would pay me money for." His first two screenplays, he tells me, "were just awful." The third, a "very commercial romantic comedy," was readable. He sold it.

That very commercial romantic comedy was 1998's "Kissing a Fool," a box-office and critical flop that Frey co-wrote with director Doug Ellin. In an opening scene, aspiring writer Jay Murphy, played by Jason Lee (*Clerks II*, *My Name Is Earl*), has set up his best friend, the womanizing sportscaster Max Abbitt, played by David Schwimmer (*Friends*), on a blind date with his editor, Samantha "Sam" Andrews, played by Israeli actress Mili Avital. (Jay is working on a novel, by the way—a roman à clef based on his own life.)

Max bangs on Jay's door at 6:30 the next morning to complain about Sam's behavior at a fancy restaurant, where, Max says, she "drank like a fish" and "acted like a psychotic." Minutes later, Sam knocks on Jay's door. Jay hides Max in the closet. Sam complains about how Max took her to the Crazy Horse, a gentleman's club, for drinks and came onto her in his convertible Mercedes. Max rushes out of the closet and argues with Sam. Jay can't decide which conflicting account to believe. He leans toward Sam's story. Max is shocked his best friend would do this.

"I'm not taking sides," Jay says. "It's just that her story sounds a little more like you than your story sounds like her."

The whole thing, it turns out, is a ruse. Sam and Max had a great time on their date and spent the whole night together. They decided to wake up their friend and play a joke on him.

"Wow," Jay says, taken aback. "You guys really over-plotted this thing, didn't you?"

So HOW WILL we define memoir now? Is the state of the genre any better or worse after the James Frey Affair? As I write this, I have my notes from my interview with Frey and a big stack of philosophy books on my desk. I thought I'd consult the Great Thinkers to help me define words like *truth* and *memoir* and *autobiography* and *lying*. I've got the Pablo Picasso quote ready: "We all know that art is not truth. Art is a lie that makes us realize the truth." Then there's Ralph Waldo Emerson: "All history becomes subjective; in other words, there is properly no history, only biography."

Then I thought about dragging out that hoary device of using the dictionary to look up all those words, their histories. I thought better of it and went back to philosophy. "When we are disputing about the proper meaning to be attached to a particular word in a sentence, etymology is of little use," the great literary critic Owen Barfield writes in his essay "The Development of Meaning." "Only children run to the dictionary to settle an argument."

HOW DOES ONE begin to defend James Frey? I haven't even started. I haven't mentioned how Oprah made this more about herself and her own addiction to veracity. I haven't even started on the publishing industry's role, its genre relativism, its obsession with marketing authenticity. I want to point out that no quotation marks appear in either *A Million Little Pieces* or *My Friend Leonard*, that there's no attempt at made-up dialogue, re-creations for what was or was not said. Jerry Stahl, author of another extreme addiction memoir, *Permanent Midnight*, writes that Frey "stepped over standards and precedent as an impediment to Getting The Job Done. The job, in this case, being the creation of a history compatible with one's own myth." Whether Stahl means it or not, I agree with him.

In the *Poetics*, Aristotle talks about the two sources of poetry. One is our instinct for imitation, to reproduce reality, our pleasure in the artist's attempt. The other is our instinct for harmony and rhythm, our "rude improvisations." I don't think I can defend what Frey lied about as such as much as his right to imitate and harmonize, those "rude improvisations." Single-source news stories will still run on the front page and be accepted as fact. Future writers' parents will wear wires. Everything will be transcribed into a public record; nothing will be edited or crafted, and no one will be dramatized into a character. No one will be disheartened or betrayed as the drudgery of documentation continues. It might be a step forward. But writers will always have the desire to imitate and transform, not simply record, real life.

Miles to Go Before We Sleep

Jeff Gordinier

Increasingly, the Internet is a rich source of stories; surfing the Web, like browsing the shelves of a bookstore, can bring surprising rewards. This immersion piece about a ride on the Poetry Bus, snatched directly from the Web site of the Poetry Foundation, evokes the spirit of such classic road-trip stories as On the Road *and* The Electric Kool-Aid Acid Test.

> Americanos! conquerors! marches humanitarian!
> Foremost! century marches! Libertad! masses!
> For you a programme of chants.
>
> —Walt Whitman,
> "Starting from Paumanok"

Okay, so everybody on the bus knows Montana is going to be good—maybe even intense, possibly flat-out momentous—but we've got no idea how right we are until the Green Tortoise tour bus

The Poetry Bus on the road near Missoula. (Maggie Jackson/Wave Books)

starts to inch down a curled-rattlesnake driveway into the Butler Creek Ranch. The ranch lies on 23 Edenic acres a few miles outside of Missoula. It looks like a bowl—there's a house and a field ringed all around by piney slopes. People at the bottom of the bowl are grinning and jumping and waving at us, which is really nice. After a long and groggy drive from Spokane, we, the 10 passengers on the Wave Books Poetry Bus, are prepared to get stoked: *Hey, look down there! Yes! O wonderful waving and grinning and jumping people of Montana! You're freakin' hungry for it, aren't you?! Hungry for . . . poetry! Yes! Watch how we descend from the peaks of the Bitterroot Range like conquering warriors!*

Except something's off. Something isn't right.

We get the news as soon as we lumber out of the bus: chaos. Just a few minutes before our heroic entrance, a rogue guest at the party apparently went kind of bonkers. People at the ranch were watching the guy from a distance as he danced around in a black suit and a bowler hat and took swigs from a bottle of something that was most likely not Mountain Dew—and then all of a sudden the cowboy droog hopped into his mammoth white SUV, backed it straight through the ranch's fence, uprooted some posts, peeled off toward the porta-potty as if this were a monster truck rally, and burned rubber down a dirt path into the brush. There he'd collided with a tree, flipped his gas guzzler, crawled out of the wreckage, and bolted up a hill on foot.

But he's all right, the locals assure us. In fact, he's out there running around in the woods. But hey, welcome to Montana!

So the crowd is still processing all this when we arrive, because of course one does not generally attend a poetry reading expecting to see an outtake from *The Dukes of Hazzard*.

"This is very rock 'n' roll, I have to say," a bespectacled MFA student muses as cop cars, fire engines, ambulances, and tow trucks begin snaking down into the bowl and heading over to the crash site.

Giving American poetry a rock 'n' roll transfusion—well, you might say that's one of the explicit goals of the Poetry Bus as it takes wing through 50 cities this fall. And yet this particular style of merry prank—a one-man demolition derby—well, that's not at all what Joshua Beckman and Matthew Zapruder had in mind when they dreamed up the transcontinental tour. No. Here they stand only three days into their excellent adventure, and already they're overhearing whispers that the Montana reading might have to be moved to a new site, or maybe even canned altogether.

Which is a supreme bummer—by now a pig has been roasted, homemade pies and salads have been laid out on a buffet table, the parking area is filling up with cars, and our hosts have printed up a lovely program with an apt invocation, "Driving Montana," by local legend Richard Hugo.

> *. . . You are lost*
> *in miles of land without people. . . .*

Obviously a ton of work has gone into this thing. Zapruder sighs, plants himself in a portable lounge chair, and surrenders to a state of equanimity. "I feel confident somehow that we'll be able to do this," he says. "Isn't this the Big Sky country?"

Amazingly, his confidence is not misplaced. Somehow it all works out, and then it goes beyond just working out. After we wait around for a tense couple of hours, our friends in law enforcement determine that the Poetry Bus and all these word-hungry westerners are welcome to stick around, just as long as they don't smoke cigarettes near the dry grass in the middle of the fire season.

"We're on!" says poet Anthony McCann, pumping his fist. "We're staying!"

In spite of, or maybe because of, the bizarre saga of the demon SUV, the Wednesday night reading at the Butler Creek Ranch winds up feeling like something for the history books: one of those rare and genuine moments of everyone's-on-the-same-wavelength connection. The night is cool, the air is fragrant with forest-fire ash, the audience is prone to happy cheering and hooting, the podium's a stack of logs, and the sound system is so fiber-optically loud and clear that you can hear the way the readers breathe in between each line and the sound of every poem booming away in the hills.

McCann, his dark hair flopping to and fro and his jeans in a perpetual state of ass-crack free-fall, hits the dais like the life of the party, bobbing and weaving. His timing is so fluidly spot-on that he leaves the audience both awed and in stitches.

Katy Lederer's inflections are sharp, nuanced, pulsating; she treats each poem with the sort of meticulous care that a spider might bring to the task of devouring a trapped fly.

Erin Belieu gives a ferocious reading of a single poem from *Black Box*, called "Pity." ("Once I took it in my mouth, I had to / admit, pity tastes good, like the sandwiches / they make in French patisseries, the loaf smeared / with force-fed organs, crust that shreds the skin behind /

your teeth.") Then she tells the crowd that altitude sickness has made her too woozy to go on. Which, of course, feels perfect.

Oh, then there's Michael Earl Craig.

See, earlier in the day Craig happened to catch a ride to the Butler Creek Ranch in a white SUV. Yep, that white SUV. It was a friend of Craig's who went lulu and mangled it, and so after the accident it was Craig himself who had to dash over to the wreck and climb into it in order to rescue a few things: (1) travel gear for the next leg of the bus tour, (2) a bunch of books that he intended to sell along the way, and (3) a bottle of bourbon.

So, yeah: When Michael Earl Craig finally steps up to the microphone, the moment's charged up with more than a little bit of anticipation. "It's been an exciting day," he deadpans from the pile of logs. "The police officers were very kind to me."

FOR THREE DAYS in early September I was embedded on the Wave Books Poetry Bus as it traveled from Seattle to Spokane to Missoula— the first leg of a lunatic trip that will eventually wobble its way through Lincoln and Omaha, Minneapolis and Pittsburgh, Boston and Austin, Las Vegas and Santa Fe, New York and New Orleans. Based in Seattle, owned and underwritten by the wealthy arts patron Charlie Wright, and edited in a partnership between Beckman and Zapruder, Wave is an independent publishing house that's all about newness and risk and West Coast brio, and the Poetry Bus tour is ready to give those principles a high-octane road test.

I wanted to tag along because I think there's a renaissance under way in American poetry—a thrilling new movement that most of the national mass media is too clueless, navel-gazing, and Paris Hilton– fixated to recognize—and because I figured that rolling around the country in a bus full of poets sounded like a gas. And it was a gas. Now and then it even rose to the level of transcendence, as I discovered on the ranch in Montana. But that doesn't mean it was easy like Kesey. You hear about a Great American Road Trip such as this one and you can't help but think: *On the Road . . . The Electric Kool-Aid Acid Test . . . Fear and Loathing in Las Vegas . . .* Lewis & Clark . . . a squadron of like-minded and free-spirited people getting sloppy-wasted and heading out on the highway for a 13,000-mile marathon from Stagnation to Bliss!

The only problem with that utopian fantasy is that it doesn't take into account how often stuff goes haywire. It is possible to satisfy your bliss fix on the Poetry Bus, but what you automatically get in return is a fair amount of bedlam. Before we left Seattle, I admired Beckman, 34, and Zapruder, 38, for having the chutzpah to put this logistical nightmare together, but I admired them even more when we started moving and I saw that these two old friends and their unflappable 27-year-old tour manager, Travis Nichols, were facing a new wrinkle in Murphy's Law roughly every five minutes. We weren't even out of Seattle's suburban gridlock when Beckman realized that one of the bus windows was refusing to close; he grabbed it and held it in place with his hands until we pulled into a rest stop. Somewhere in the middle of Washington, poet Melanie Noel was sleeping serenely at the back of the bus when the Green Tortoise began farting and growling and she was blanketed by a freakish wind of carbon monoxide and heat. A panel inside the bus, right above the rear tires, had somehow shimmied loose and popped open, exposing everyone to baking exhaust fumes. Beckman raced back and clamped the panel shut with his own size-16 feet. We pulled into another rest stop.

Beckman and Zapruder are often asked, "So what's the *point* of this endeavor? What's the Poetry Bus *about*?"

Having traveled with them on the Green Tortoise, I would argue that this shotgun tango between bedlam and bliss *is* the point, that what we're witnessing is a tragically obscure and insular American art form getting reacquainted with the stresses and obstacles of the real world. That can only be good for the art form. If the most common beef against much of American poetry is that it's cut off from American life, well, I can't think of a better remedy than to ride out on a 40-foot bus and take poetry straight into a teeming pandemonium of Wal-Mart and crystal meth and *American Idol* and obesity and video games and Rush Limbaugh and killer gas prices. "For every atom belonging to me as good belongs to you," as Whitman said, right? Or, to put it another way, consider this moment from the trip: We'd stopped for lunch in a place that felt to me like the nexus of all abandonment—I mean, the absolute pinnacle of nowhere, just a falling-down gas station surrounded by hot dirt, hard by a burger joint whose only salvation was a badass jukebox. We got in line to order our burgers, and the bright young woman behind the counter glanced outside, saw the giant red letters that said POETRY BUS, and asked us what we were up to.

Beckman told her we were traveling all over the country, reading poems in 50 different cities.

Her eyes flashed. The signal was unmistakable: she was ready to quit her job and climb aboard.

"Fabulous!" she said.

It was indeed fabulous, whenever the bus was moving, to stare out the windows and watch the passengers in the cars and trucks alongside us. You could see it in their eyes first, and then in their scrunched brows, and then in the way they moved their lips: POETRY BUS?! *What the hell is that?* Responses on the interstate ran the gamut: confusion, suspicion, laughter, longing, euphoria. Probably a few thousand people will come into contact with the Poetry Bus through the actual readings, but hundreds of thousands of Americans will find themselves within spitting distance of those bold red letters on the freeway, and that's exactly what Beckman and Zapruder are going for.

Hey, America, if you don't think you're in the mood for poetry, you can avoid a Web site. You can avoid a radio broadcast. You can avoid a book. But you can't avoid huge red letters on the side of a bus, especially when you're bored stiff and cruise-controlling it past an alfalfa farm somewhere north of Walla Walla.

So the point of the bus is to promote poetry, sure, and to promote Wave Books, right, but it's also to promote something else—a mindset, the very possibility of considering poetry as an antidote to one's daily tedium. "I believe in changing the context for poetry," Zapruder told me. "I can't stand the way people think of poetry. Poetry is a process of being awakened to the thing you're being awakened to, and it's the same thing with this bus. We don't know what'll fuckin' happen."

The first reader was Christine Deavel, the co-owner of Seattle's Open Books, one of the only book emporiums in America devoted solely to poetry. It was Labor Day and the Poetry Bus was parked in a shady spot at Bumbershoot, the sprawling Seattle arts festival. The surrounding environment was frenzied and flesh-dense, with thousands of sun-dazed people milling about in a vortical quest for bratwurst and falafel and satay and funnel cakes while the Steve Miller Band trotted out FM-radio oldies from the main stage. Bumbershoot was loud, so instead of listening to readings outside, people climbed right into the bus, where they could presumably hear each poet without being overwhelmed by bongo drums and bagpipes. Deavel blessed the bus with an Emily Dickinson poem ("This ecstatic Nation / Seek— it is yourself") and finished 15 minutes later with Theodore Roethke's "The Waking," the last line of which could serve as a mission statement for the entire trip: "I learn by going where I have to go."

When Deavel read that, something clicked—a rush of feeling ambushed Beckman, and his eyes teared up. "It didn't occur to me," he said, "that it would be emotional like that." More and more Bumbershooters began packing the bus to catch the readings—so many that some people had to be turned away. We left Seattle at around 9:30 the next morning.

. Still, the vibe on the bus was not in any way solemn or meditative—nor even very poetic. Katy Lederer was constantly engrossed in a pile of glossy celebrity magazines. "I have to find out if Angelina's pregnant again!" Zapruder listened to the Arcade Fire and Clap Your Hands Say Yeah on his iPod, Melanie Noel talked about her day job in "edible landscaping," Erin Belieu sported an AC/DC Highway to Hell T-shirt and regaled us with a running commentary.

"I hope we go past, like, the world's biggest ball of yarn. I love that shit."

"How did we go from freezing our asses off to the desert? It's weird. Okay, where are the lizards?"

"Do we have snacks on the bus? I don't need snacks. I just get sort of panicky when there aren't any."

The poets spent a whole lot of time talking about which other poets, male and female, were sexy. They did not spend a whole lot of time gazing out the window at the pretty landscapes, although when they did, the signs along the road seemed to be throwing poems right back at them . . .

Wolf Lodge District
Women in Timber Thrift Store
100,000 Used Books
Rattlesnakes are inhabitants of this area
Don't Be a Clown. Eat with a King
Surly Staff. Poor Selection. High Prices. Terrible Quality.

They chain-smoked. They broke out the plastic cups and drank unwisely—white wine followed by port followed by Irish whiskey. "I've got to stop with the smoking after this thing," said Anthony McCann, whose hair constantly seemed to be pioneering new permutations of bedhead. "Smoking, soft drinks, liquor. When this thing is over. . . ." A few minutes later he took a swig from a bottle of Wild

Turkey (a gift from Open Books), winced, and said, "This is definitely *not* going down smooth." He picked up someone else's half-finished cup of coffee and poured a couple of ounces of Wild Turkey into it. "*There* we go."

In Idaho it was time for a supermarket run. The bus pulled into a strip mall and the poets headed into an Albertson's to stock up. Shoppers there didn't know what to make of Beckman, whose personal style might be described as part Jerry Garcia, part Hasidic scholar, and part Chewbacca. I guess Coeur d'Alene is not accustomed to seeing a guy with a thick rabbinical beard and a nimbus of bandanna-wrapped frizz ambling around the fruit section in ripped khaki cutoffs, open sandals, tinted specs, and a faded T-shirt saying "Show Me Your Text." That day Albertson's was full of religious fundamentalists decked out in 19th-century frocks. They stopped in their tracks and gazed upon Beckman as if he were a prophet just back from eating honey and locusts in the desert.

And if they thought that, they weren't entirely wrong. Beckman is the spiritual leader of the bus—its gentle sage. Most of the time he doesn't say a word, but when he does, everyone listens. It was Beckman who instigated all random acts of, well, randomness. In Idaho, as we shot by the small town of Wallace, he picked up a megaphone, switched it on, and began reading a Frank O'Hara poem out loud— "Lana Turner has collapsed!" The town of Wallace, Beckman explained when he was finished, was the birthplace of Lana Turner.

At the podium Beckman was a force. His readings managed to swing theatrically back and forth between radiance and petulance, lethargy and liturgy. He was like a slacker Moses on the mountaintop: you half-expected him to pull a couple of stone tablets out of his knapsack. Audiences were transfixed. At a Beckman reading in Spokane, a young guy wearing a black T-shirt with a flaming Aztec bird on it couldn't stay in his chair. After a couple of Beckman's poems he stood up, walked to an area behind the seats, and began furiously pacing back and forth, blurting out "yes!" whenever a line really got to him.

> *and I saw the best minds of my generation*
> *living in lofts*
> *thinking they were the best minds of their generation*
> *while the world hacked up tax breaks and jet fighters*

That night the bus pulled into the Trailer Inn RV park, and the poets slept alongside the roar of Route 90. Zapruder walked around in a pair of blue rubber sandals. "I got these so I can shower in the RV park without feeling like a disease is going to crawl up my legs," he said.

It was only the first night on the road, but already you could tell what an endurance test this thing was going to be.

WHY, YOU MIGHT wonder. *Why subject yourself to days and days of motion sickness, monotony, insomnia, halitosis, hangovers, spinal aches, bad-burrito indigestion, traffic, nasty coffee . . . ?* I think I got the most sensible answer from Bill Wesley, the driver of the Poetry Bus, when, for no reason that I could discern, we pulled over to the side of the road one afternoon in order to see some petrified gingko trees that Bill knew about. As the poets headed up a sun-broiled hill to see the petrified stumps, I turned to Bill and asked, "So why are we doing this again?"

Bill looked at the hill and said, "Why not?"

Apparently we'd learn by going.

Job No. 51—Executive Director and Job No. 52—Psychic Medium

OLIVERDAVIES.BLOGSPOT.COM

I began this afternoon by attempting to apply to be the new voice of the speaking clock—a job that is open to any UK resident by means of entering a competition at the BBC Children in Need website.

However, it seems that, even in a competition that is open to anyone, my application did not go well. I made the phone call (which costs £1.50) and gave them a sample of my best speaking clock voice before being given the chance to answer a qualifying question that would allow my entry into the competition. Given three options, I selected the correct answer—but it appears even giving the right answer won me no favours with the BBC as a female voice told me, "That is not an option. Goodbye," and immediately cut me off.

So, with my wallet £1.50 lighter and yet still no nearer to being the voice of the speaking clock, I began to browse the *Guardian* jobs site rather randomly (it is a very good site to explore, especially if you approach the process with no sense of either purpose or direction) until I found myself in a position to answer a higher calling.

There are many, many Executive Director positions advertised on a myriad of recruitment websites but very few can boast of divine inspiration; you see, this position would see me—quite literally—on a mission from God as I would be working for Churches Together in Britain and Ireland (CTBI) as an Executive Director of Operation Noah.

As the job advert said, "Climate change is humanity's biggest challenge. Help the Churches lead the way."

I think this is excellent forethought on behalf of the CTBI; after all, back in the day, Noah had to do everything himself without even the hint of a schedule or effective project managerial leadership. The initial contract is for two days per week for twelve months so I'm assuming things aren't too desperate just yet and there's plenty of time left for ark construction and animal gathering.

The position is based at the London HQ of CTBI, which, rather helpfully, is only a couple of hundred yards from the Thames—thus allowing for the ark, in times of flood, to simply clear its moorings and float down Stamford Street before bearing hard to starboard and using Hatfields to majestically sweep its way past the BBC Television Centre and into the Thames (from which point, things become far easier in terms of navigation).

I'm hoping, as Executive Director, I would be given a little leeway in animal selection this time around as this idea of taking two of every species is surely a little old now—for example, I'd rather hope we can leave the wasps behind as they seem to be of very little use. Also, I'm certain the CTBI could make an absolute bundle if it were to sell space in the ark (perhaps to celebrities and their pets?). I was sure there would be plenty of opportunity to discuss these sorts of ideas during the course of my interview but wanted my personal statement to, at least, hint at them:

> I am extremely interested in your project as I believe it is a necessity for the Church to take a lead in this area. The Church can be unfettered by the restrictions that a similar project would have in the commercial, or even governmental, arena and this means Operation Noah can be a huge success.

I have plenty of experience of managing complex technical projects against strict timescales and believe that this experience would be essential for the success of Operation Noah.

I am also creative and imaginative and would hope to be intimately involved with the decision process to ensure that we don't rely on out-dated ideas. It is vital for Operation Noah to truly represent the 21st century and I feel that there are means to develop funding streams through the course of the project—especially with regard to celebrity involvement.

I'm certain, with me at the helm, Operation Noah can be a tremendous success. I plan to give London Zoo a ring tomorrow and see if I can negotiate some kind of sponsorship deal up front to show the CTBI I mean business . . .

Job No. 52—Psychic Medium

In the past I have come across jobs that seemed interesting, I've come across jobs that looked a possible match and I've even come across the odd job that felt right—but, up until now, I'd never come across a job that was my destiny . . .

Today, while taking an afternoon stroll around the Internet, I stumbled across a vacancy for a Psychic Medium in Glasgow (on a Wednesday)—and the advert stated that "Only those who feel that working with the Tarot and the Psychic Arts is their destiny need apply." Well, I have to admit, I wasn't sure whether it was my destiny or not, so I decided that I should check by using the full spectrum of paranormal fortune-telling at my disposal.

1) First of all I tried an online tarot reading—which gave me the following answer: "*The essence of air behaving as water, such as a refreshing mist.*"

2) Then I decided that I should try out Stichomancy—which basically involves asking a question and then selecting a random passage from a book which is meant to offer insight. My tome of choice was the Yellow Pages and I

received the following answer: *"Peking Chef, Chinese Take-away, 01642 767070."*

3) Finally, I decided to consult the I-Ching, which turned up Hexagram 42 to represent the future giving me the answer. *"There will be advantage in every movement which shall be undertaken, and it will even be advantageous to cross the great stream."*

Now, this all made perfect sense to me.

First, we have two references to water—a refreshing mist (which clearly relates to the drizzle forecasted tonight in Glasgow) and a mention of "crossing the great stream," which, I'm sure you'll agree, relates to my need to cross the River Tees in order to get there . . .

But, the clincher for me was the Stichomancy reading—this was pure dynamite. Peking Chef is a Chinese restaurant and China is in the East—and Glasgow is in the West. Which would seem to be a negative but it's a Tuesday today and Peking Chef is always closed on a Tuesday! Not only that, but my favourite items on the Peking Chef menu are number 15, Singapore Style Rice Noodles, number 11, Curry Sauce and number 12, Chips . . . and, by using numerology, we can see that my favourite items equal the number 2 (1+5+1+1+1+2 = 11 = 1+1 = 2)—with the New Age definition of this number meaning *"Hidden influences at work."*

I rest my case. I am destined to take this job. I decided I should emphasise this fact within my application letter:

Dear Sir/Madam

I wish to apply for the position of Psychic Medium, as advertised on your website.

Although my working life has been spent in the field of computer game design, I have always possessed a strong psychic ability and am an expert in the field of tarot cards. I have attached a suitable reference at the base of this email who will be willing to testify to my abilities in this area.

I am especially keen on 22 card spiritual readings, but am also fully capable of performing mundane readings with a full deck. I believe in the use of Orris root and the necessity of a cleansing ritual for cards prior to use (and keep my deck wrapped in purple cloth and within a walnut box for spiritual purity).

As soon as I saw the job I felt a tangible pull to the North West and I felt certain that my destiny lay with you. However, to be on the safe side, I performed a number of rituals to see whether our auras would be properly aligned and I was delighted to find that we would form a natural balance. In my divinations, the name Sam was prominent—I'm not sure if this means anything to you?

I feel certain you will feel the same spiritual bond when you read these words and can sense that I will be hearing from you very soon. . . .
Regards,
Oliver

If ever there was a job that was a cast-iron certainty, surely this is it! Already I can sense strong positive psychic waves telling me to get ready to deliver my spiritual message to the people of Glasgow . . . on Wednesdays.

Pimp

OLIVIA CHIA-LIN LEE

Creative nonfiction, says Olivia Chia-lin Lee, lets her "trick the reader into going places she would not normally—because that is exactly how I survived and experienced my own life." This excerpt of Lee's memoir-in-progress, which first appeared in Narrative Magazine, *takes the reader into the world of high-class prostitution, a world with which the writer, formerly one of the highest-paid call girls in San Francisco, is intimately familiar.*

Eric hires children. If we are of legal age, then we are just barely that. There are times when a prodigy comes to him. Someone who is beyond the acceptable "start" age, like me—I'm twenty-two but can easily pass for seventeen. And then it is like a gift lands at his door because it will take only a matter of weeks to train me. Not the months and years required for his other girls to learn the subtle tricks of being the highest-paid escorts in San Francisco. It's matter-of-fact for him. All top-end madams think in terms of numbers. How many are in his stable? How old are they? How far-fetched, how sane, how pretty, how many clients does he have waiting to pay for her stunning attributes? It's a matter of percentages and commissions, tedious accounting work.

He catches a telescopic glimpse of me as soon as I get out of my car. Even in the gray suit I've been instructed to wear, along with black heels, pearls, and minimal makeup, he can make out the long pair of legs cradled into my five-foot-seven-inch body unfolding onto the asphalt. I step, I walk like an athlete. "Tomboy," he scribbles onto his legal pad. My bones are all structured and lined up with just enough flesh to build the shape of a nubile teenager. It's like bottled perfume—every woman's body—and Eric never releases the scent until she's ripe.

In his world of instant demand, he not only as madam but also as the mentor of sex as religion is deviously and insanely patient. Every client will eventually pay in cash for each savored moment when he withholds a girl from the clutching eyes of the market. The product he offers bears his indelible mark. From this day forward, my sex is stamped. I become one of "Eric's girls."

"You're Chinese?" is the first thing he says to me in person. I blot out his face, lest I lose my focus. Today, I'm his pony, warned by his entourage of "screeners" that if I don't compel him within the first thirty seconds by my voice, wit, poise, and beauty, then he'll excuse me from the interview.

"Taiwanese," I correct him. He invites me to slide into the leather booth across from him. The four-star bay-front restaurant is empty at three in the afternoon. The hour appointed for his exclusive use.

"An islander." He notes the mistake of one of his secretaries. His eyes pass over me. I feel him fingering me with the steady, holding gaze of a mother inspecting her new infant.

"But you could be Okinawan, Tibetan, Tahitian, Eskimo, or Burmese." He inhales and holds the air while his mind pauses.

"Most of my girls come to me because they're seduced by the lifestyle. And I mold them into the best. I sense you want something else. Why do you want to work for me?"

I search for an answer. "Curiosity."

He does a double-take. "Graduated with honors two years ago from Berkeley. What were you planning to do for a career?"

"I was about to apply to Harvard Divinity for a master's in theology." His breath skips. This is a new one. "And?" he grins.

"My dad got sick and passed away. So I changed my plans."

"Mm. So before you decided to become a first-class call girl, you were going to be . . ."

Fifteen seconds pass.

"A preacher."

His mind speeds, making all the correlations before I can even spit them out. When he asks me the next question, he watches me closely while I talk. "How will this benefit me?"

"When I was thirteen years old, an angel came into my room one night while I was praying and blinded me. I gradually lost my eyesight since then. Now I'm wearing strong contact lenses just to see your face.

"But I developed a kind of inner sight where I experience the dreams and secret longings of a person when I'm near them. I can tell you what makes them tick, what moves or touches them, even spurs them to hate. For years, I intended to be a missionary or minister. But my Church told me that God did not grant women the authority to stand at a pulpit. I never believed them until my father died. Now I'm looking for a different arena in which to practice my skills."

I look at him, not to see him. For him to see me. In my eyes is the flame of the adolescent he wants to hire. The rest, he can slowly chip away at in the coming weeks. The twenty-two year old is not important. It's who she surrenders to becoming as he bends her into his pliable arabesque. She'll be a black swan, he already decides for me. The ugly duckling no more.

"Every girl I pick is unique. She's either an ex-runway model, porn-material bombshell, disowned debutante, or fluke accident—like you with a combination of sensuality, ambition, and youth. I mold her into something notches above what she is destined to be. Normally, I start with a girl at fourteen, fifteen, sixteen. I'll go so far as nineteen. You're riveting enough at this point for me to experiment. But I don't know how well you perform until one of my 'first-timer' clients evaluates you. Each man is different. They all want something else. Damned if there is any one girl who can provide it for them across the board. The goal isn't to be the perfect woman. There is no such thing. The goal is to be as perfect a version of you as can be, and then I'll make sure they respect that."

He writes down "power? innocence?" next to my name, then pencils in something else I can't see.

"Your new name is . . ." He squints at me, waiting for the psychic revelation. "Cody. From now on, your old identity to me is lost. Do not make the mistake of referring to yourself by your birth name, especially on the phone."

I look at him and read him. Images flash chaotically through my mind. Later, I'll decipher them into paragraphs. But for now the less I know, the easier it remains for me. Eric knows it's not my looks a man's willing to pay for—not when you compare me to his other girls. Because they're mannequins, surgically enhanced and interchangeable. In fact, he will charge more than twice for me what he charges for them—doling me out like morphine or ice.

"I want them praying to you," Eric says to me three months later. "You're not their fantasy girl, you're their reality girl. You represent the reason he married his wife thirty years ago or the scandal that forces her to divorce him. You reenact or return him to that great fall in his life—into love, heroism, guilt, imminence, whatever. If he is a boy or a man at that point . . . you must be prepared to meet with either. For the client, what separates you from my mannequins is trust."

How unprepared I am for the men he sets me up with. More than a wife, mother, or mistress, I am their confessor. And what they bear to me, I charge for relentlessly. Robbing them, it seems, because they ask me to rape them and relinquish their pain.

Eventually, Eric buys me S and M manuals, tantric books, Jungian texts, and cassettes of dream interpretations to deconstruct the symbols of my sex sessions. He watches me crumble and then reinforces me with Learning Annex memberships, private healing retreats in Sonoma, journals from women's collectives. And then finally, he seeks out a psychiatrist. Not for me, but for him.

"I have an angry employee," he starts out confiding in Dr. Shrink. "She gets paid roughly ten times your salary, works only two hours a week and is a valuable asset to my company. It's just one of a few factors driving me nuts."

He returns to me with holotropic breath work. Sitting in the passenger seat of my car, he demos for me. I purposely don't smile. We're focusing on the letter B. Breathe, Eric. You breathe, because I don't need to. My tips exceed your shrink's earnings, and it isn't about money anymore. It's about faith. So Eric finally sends me to see the psychiatrist.

Little does he know how deep I dig to find something that interests me. I end up turning some of my "challenge clients" (i.e., Eric's nice boy) into guinea pigs for psychosexual exploration. When they call him back dazed and somehow addicted to more kinky forms of play, Eric wipes me off their lists as well as his shrink's. By then, the market is surging. He shuffles to fulfill the demands of johns who all seem to be asking for a onetime last-minute fix-it kind of girl who can home in on their pain and treat it head-on. Sort of an intuitive extremist.

"A specialist?" I ask Eric.

"No, more like an ER surgeon," he explains. "Even if you don't beat it out of them in one date, I don't think they want that. They just can't seem to open up to a girl unless she can see the true thing that ails them. You don't have to cure them, Cody. Just pretend you know the root of what's bothering them. Then make something up."

But I can't resist the scalpel. When the pedophile or CEO, senator or celebrity wants to do me as a way of purging his guilt—all I see, rather than status, wealth, or old age, is the first time a boy kissed his uncle or plucked fruit from an orchard, the moment he lost love or his integrity vanished in the choice he made to become himself. The greatest hurt is love. It is the ultimate female revenge, and it cuts, scars like a knife.

CLAUDIA, ERIC's assistant, shows up on my doorstep, blond and plump, looking thirty-something but with the demeanor of forty-two. A measuring tape hangs off her shoulder, and she whips the tape out to measure me and inspect for moles, dimples, scars, body hair, tattoos, cellulite, blemishes, or pimples. She photographs me wearing a business suit and then sketches me on rice paper while I pose for her in a bikini. At last, she briefly examines my pelvic area and aureoles. Her pencils shade in toffee, cocoa, sienna, and sometimes splashes of peach.

"Do you wax?" she asks. She has a collapsed nostril so that her voice squeezes through one shallow pipe. "All of it." She pats my tummy but means the downy fuzz circling my rectum and vulva.

"Thin as a rail, perfect," she notes on my sketch. "Nipples protrude three-fifths of a centimeter, a sign of maturity."

"If a mosquito bites you—if a scratch, bump, nick, bruise, or faint tan line appears, then call in sick. I'll come over to see what we can do until it heals, okay?"

Graph paper underlies her transparent sheets of anatomy diagrams, I assume to annotate for future flaws. She hands me a plastic cup. "By your glossy skin tone, I'm assuming this is unnecessary." She wants a urine sample.

"Drugs, alcohol, cigarettes, soda, fried foods, chocolate, and coffee are no longer part of your diet. The rare exceptions always occur on a date."

She gets out her cell phone and calls Eric. "She's got the health of a baby ox and the body of a preteen, Eric. She'll be fine."

Later, Eric reports, "Claudia gave you an A for looks, combined with a low-grade B for attitude. I think . . . Jacque." He pulls out an index card with the address of my first date. "Three hours for three thousand dollars." He turns to look at me.

"After three dates, you get a raise. As you progress, the client gradually names your price, which in most cases exceeds my value of you. This," he notes the amount, "is just a starter fee. Something to gauge against.

"Remember, you are a lady. This means he is to treat you as a lady. Should he try to test you on this, your magic wand is what?"

"The word no."

He sopranos, "No, no, no, uh-unh!" and wags his finger in front of my face. "I am a lady."

"I am a lady." I try to repeat the lisp he devises for me, "Pleath, thit. Thank-ths." He releases the card to me. "Have fun. Remember to smile."

I NERVOUSLY RING the doorbell of a five-story wooden mansion in the Berkeley hills. I'm in a velvet headband with my thick black hair ironed slick, curled at the ends, and a thick veneer of pink shading my lips. I'm carrying only a wallet purse cut from fabric matching my pleated gray plaid miniskirt.

"Bonjour." A Frenchman answers the door, surprised at the package waiting on his front porch. No doubt Eric described my looks as generic. The Frenchman remarks, "You are quite nice. Come in. And you are Cody?"

"Yeth."

He guides me into the back of his house to a cubby designed for casual recreation. The shelves are lined with boxes of board games and action DVDs. He offers me a glass of wine from a cabinet, carved from the trunk of a single oak, that glows with imbedded track lighting.

He pulls himself down onto the couch in front of a miniature TV set. "I was jus' relaxing right here before you came. Why don't you have a seat?"

I sit mawkishly on the edge of a dark green cushion while he leans back, keeping his eyes steady on the race cars on the TV. Their engines buzz through the wall speakers.

According to Eric's charts, this man seems to prefer company more than sex. We speak about school, his daughters, the au pair (shhh! she lives upstairs), and the kind of work he does (escrow analysis, corporate real estate). My s's form soft thhh's, sort of like the slow leak of a bicycle tire. He stares quite a bit between my knees to the triangle of my light pink panties, and he grows more reflective. He puts down his empty wineglass and asks, "Have you done this before?"

"Thith is my firth time. Didn't Eric tell you?" I wrinkle my brow. "I'm a lady."

"Oh, yes, I forgot," he says and withdraws his advance.

"Close your eyes, I'll give you a surprise," I taunt. He hides his eyes with his hands, playing peek-a-boo through the slot of his ring and middle finger. The cushion springs as I moon him and resit.

"Do it again," he asks but this time won't cover his face. I flash him with my skirt—panty, no-panty, butt, front-back twist, all snippets of apricot skin as he fixates on the yoyo-ing cotton underwear shooting down to mid-thigh and then back up like an elevator rocket. Finally, he snatches it and wrests it over my knees.

"Noooo," I whine. He tickles me to untangle it from my ankles until I am bottomless beneath the skirt. To tease him, I bend forward and blow into his ear.

"Have you ever made butt-angels?" I ask.

He looks confused.

"Here." I grab the Johnson's Baby Oil from a nearby shelf. "Now we need a powder puff."

He runs into the nursery and comes back with a ribboned parcel of scented talcum. I make him sit as I stand sideways, so that when I lean forward into spanking position, he sees the profile of my naked bottom. "Oil and poof me, pleath," I instruct. He rubs the oil ever so gently on me. Beads of moisture dot his hairline as I lithely arch for him.

"I'm going to poof you," he says tensely. I spread my legs and prepare for the dust. It showers over us like a hurricane as he sidles off his seat to reach my farthest buttock. When I look back, his face has aged with whiteness—dipped in snow or cake frosting as he licks his finger to wipe some off.

"Here we go!" I shimmy through the house, level after level—skipping the au pair's private flat—perching my oiled and talcumed butt onto stools, glass tabletops, marble counters, redwood benches, even a guitar, which he pats onto my glute like a badminton racket. Each time I wiggle onto a surface, he resprinkles me with the powder puff. After a couple hours, four floors of his home are upholstered with my butt-prints. The clearest one sits framed in a mirror he hangs in the nursery, and he pats the diaper-changing table for me to mount. I scoot up onto the padded surface as he begins to rub my thighs with baby wipes.

"I wish you would never grow up." He smiles at me. I gurgle and bite my thumb, then pop it in my mouth like a jawbreaker. As he nears my vagina with the baby wipe, I twitch away from it. "Arrrr, arrrr, Daddy," I whimper.

"Oh, ohhh," he pantomimes sorry and puckers for me, "Daddy wants to clean his baby."

He loses himself in the train of baby wipes and the dewy bald petals of my vulvic pattern. "Oh baby. . . . Mmm. You love Daddy so much, don't you?"

I fold myself up into his chest and murmur, "Daddy." His voice gets husky.

"Yeah, you like Daddy, play with Daddy, not those hotshots at work who need to criticize his portfolios, call him an aging dufus, step all over me. Mmm. . . . I'm your Daddy, huh, baby? Am I your Daddy?"

I don't even have to move at this point because I can feel him quivering. Every "what if" canoodles through his mind at gateway speed. He wants all the possibilities at the start of relationships, career, and life to be left open. As soon as he comes, those valves will expel themselves and close. His life will race before him to a finish as soon as he sees the semen on her belly. So he pushes his baby away from the front zipper of his trousers. "No, Baby, not for you." He snuggles his chin into his neck.

Before I leave, I slingshot my panties across the hall for him to keep as a handkerchief, and three minutes later, he calls Eric to deliver my grade. "A-plus!"

The Woot Files

In this piece, written for John McPhee's Creative Nonfiction class at Princeton University, Monica Hsiung Wojcik chronicles her search for the origin of the exuberant "woot," a quest undertaken primarily through AOL Instant Messenger (AIM). Wojcik's handle, "Pete7fish," dates back to the sixth grade, when she first began using AIM and had a pet fish named Pete. The resulting essay, about technology's impact on verbal communication, also demonstrates the ways in which new means of communication can affect written language.

Pete7fish: do you know what "woot" means
hmmcolor: monifca
hmmcolor: sure
Pete7fish: you spelled my name wrong
hmmcolor: i know
hmmcolor: it's spelled w00t, for starters

My "woot" age began somewhat recently—without my knowing what the term meant, where it came from, or why I decided to use it. In an online conversation with my Georgian roommate, I typed "woot" one day as a response and she, thinking it another New England-ism from me, verbalized it—beginning to use "woot" conversationally. I did, too. But its origin remained a mystery.

Pete7fish: what is 1337

CYMikeLee: lol . . . um
CYMikeLee: it's pronounced "leet"
CYMikeLee: as in a shortened form of "elite"
CYMikeLee: it comes from a language called "1337speak"
CYMikeLee: where people (mostly young, adolescent geeks) say stuff
    and think it's cool

Pete7fish: ohhh, do you ever use it?

CYMikeLee: haha, thankfully, no
CYMikeLee: i don't know, i think lots of gamers use it though

Pete7fish: what are gamers?

CYMikeLee: like people who play games online
CYMikeLee: i think i know a few other words
CYMikeLee: . . . "pwn" instead of "own"
CYMikeLee: as in "I so pwned you that game"
CYMikeLee: i guess w00t is one too

Pete7fish: woot!

Leetspeak, or "1337sp34k," emerged during the early stages of the Internet, in the mid-to-late eighties. Leet is short for "elite," the elite being hackers and online gamers—the top of the online community crop—back when those, including my parents-to-be, who were knowledgeable about this new medium truly were an elite few. These people would communicate via online "bulletin board systems." Sometimes they would converse about illegal activities: cyber-crimes like hacking or software piracy. The operator of the BBS would then create a filter to scan and remove postings containing words like "hacker," and so alternate spellings emerged to slip through the filters. Enter "h4cker," "h4ck3r," and other variations. Initially, the operators would try to censor these alternate spellings as well, but it soon became clear that the polymorphic nature of leetspeak made censorship impossible. There are no rules or conventions; 1337 evolves faster than an adenovirus in winter. Thus triumphant, leet lived on. The "gamers," or members of the online gaming community, soon adopted the nascent cipher as well. Some would translate their online names into leet to make them harder to type, thus making themselves harder to kick out of the gaming rooms by the "!kick [username]" command. Others did it because a non-leet spelling was already in use. Raptordude2003, a sophomore here at Princeton, gives a basic overview:

raptordude2003: 1337 is an adjective that the internet junkies or online gaming community use to describe something that is awesome, kool, or impressive. ie "That was a 1337 avatar" or "I am uber 1337 and untouchable at Counter-Strike"
raptordude2003: 1337 sp34k
raptordude2003: they often spell words differently, like "teh" for "the" and "pwn" for "own"

Leetists embrace the common typo. "The" often comes up "teh" by accident; "p" is near "o" on the keyboard, leading to the pwn/own translation. Other common replacements involve using numbers for letters: "3" for E, "4" for A, "2" for "R."

raptordude2003: A's are replaced with either 4s or @ symbols.

Pete7fish: hot
Pete7fish: i will pwn y0u
Pete7fish: w4tch 0u7

raptordude2003: yeah . . . so 1337 stems from the word "elite" which is used only by the best players . . . those who don't deserve the title are deemed "n00bs"

N00bs is short for "newbies," or those who are not yet leet-s4vvy. Part of the 133tist appe41 is its cryptic capability. Terms are increasingly added to make it incomprehensible to outsiders. Many derive from other languages: ub3r, from the German "uber"; b4k4, from the Japanese "baka," meaning "idiocy" or "stupidity"; and g0s\/, a variation on "gosu," the Korean word for "pro." Some additions, however, are not as logical. For example, the adding of "zor" or "xor" to phrases perhaps derives from one of the original permutations of "hackers": "haxor" (and variations).

raptordude2003: yup now, the more 1337 you are, the more often one uses "zors"
Pete7fish: such as?
raptordude2003: for example, if I am really good at CS, then I would say to everyone that "I r0x0rs"
Pete7fish: haha, like "hi danzor"
raptordude2003: lol well . . . no

Apparently I have not spent enough time in the realm of the 1337. Zors has evolved to be a diminutive ending, but only in circumstances to which I am not sensitive.

raptordude2003: it would be something like . . . "j0 F8t@14zn, @wzom killzors"
raptordude2003: "j00 b3s7 134v3 n00b"

It's a stab at me, from raptordude2003's leet alter ego, "Fatal Asian," who apparently has "awesome kills": "You best leave noob."

raptordude2003: j0 is the popular term used to hail other 1337 players
raptordude2003: "yo"
raptordude2003: the j replaces the y

Pete7fish: so can you read that pretty much fluently?

raptordude2003: yeah . . .

While raptordude learned his leetspeak from an online encyclopedia, actively seeking out new terms to add to his lexicon, a high school friend of mine named Evan learned by experience with Quake III. By Evan's era, however, leetspeak had acquired a different connotation (the wonders of Semantic Change). As the Internet mainstreamed, and n00bs became aware of leetspeak, it lost its exclusive, nether-culture appeal.

raptordude2003: (from Wikipedia) In recent years, leet has dropped out of style in some communities. Some gamers and Internet users choose not to use it as they consider it to signify weakness and immaturity rather than coolness or of "having skills/sk1LLz." However, many words from leet are now a significant part of modern Internet culture—not only "pwned," the common leet misspellings such as "teh" (73|-|)—but also the "z" at the end of words, such as "skillz." Another prominent example of a surviving leet expression is the ever-popular "woot/w00t." Also, gamers for whom using leetspeak seriously is out of style sometimes use it in an ironic sense. "h42 h42, u ar3z s00 1337" or "ph342 m\/ 1337 sk1LLz."

Pete7fish: seee
Pete7fish: i'm being ironic

raptordude2003: 2h, k00
raptordude2003: h4st4

Some say that "woot" is an alternate version of "woohoo!" Some say that it stemmed from the phrase "Wow, loot!" or "Wonderous loot!" an expression of delight during the popular role-playing game "Dungeons and Dragons": for example, when one defeats the evil sorcerer and finds a reward. It may stand for "[I] Want One Of Those," typically referring to electronic gadgets; in fact, www.woot.com is an online purveyor of bargain electronic goods. It may also stand for "We Owned [the] Other Team," again in an online gaming sense. It could even be an Elmer Fudd-like pronunciation of "root," root privileges granting one full control of a computer. In 1993 the hip hop group 95 South had a Billboard hit entitled "Whoot, There It Is," expressing pleasure at the sight of a voluptuous derrière. Definition number 16 from the online Urban Dictionary says woot is the state of being cool, and presents the delightful phrase, "when you know that the wootness flows through you like water." The German "wut" means rage. The Renaissance Italian "sprezzatura" is indefinable but indicates a state of supreme nonchalant awesomeness. Sprezzatura is woot. W00t itself is woot (w00t).

When you use it you know what it means but you can't explain; define "hooray!" define "YESSSSS!" My woots are completely ironic and thoroughly tongue-in-check (if you haven't got tongue-in-cheek, you haven't got anything). My roommate tells me she just got the lead role in the latest musical production? My sister sends me a picture of her prom dress? I just put my shoes on? "Woot!" In the beginning I put it in quotation marks to alert people that I was being ironic and hilarious. That soon dropped.

Still, I attempt to find the origin of my own personal flirtation with leetspeak.

Pete7fish: yang
Auto response from akuma2strider: dinner at the house
Pete7fish: i need to interview you

akuma2strider: hah, about what?

Pete7fish: 1337 speak

akuma2strider: 1337 speak? huh?

Pete7fish: leet
Pete7fish: like "w00t"
Pete7fish: it's right up your alley

akuma2strider: I don't understand what leet means
akuma2strider: but what are these questions you need to ask me?

Pete7fish: like, that techie computer game lingo
Pete7fish: so you don't have any experience with this
Pete7fish: i just figured you might, since you do a lot of computer
    stuff

akuma2strider: I don't use "techie computer lingo"
(Note: this from a person whose "buddy icon" is a robot.)
akuma2strider: w00t, I've never used
akuma2strider: Evan uses it all the time
akuma2strider: he seems like a better candidate

Pete7fish: hey ev
Pete7fish: can i ask you a few questions

jdubbm j: monicaaa
jdubbm j: waddup
jdubbm j: sure

Pete7fish: i need to find out about where I got woot

jdubbm j: lol ok i'm an expert
jdubbm j: so i'm a good source for you
jdubbm j: i don't know the origin of the exclamation, i was first
        exposed to it while it had already been established
jdubbm j: i was first exposed while playing computer games online
jdubbm j: after making a good play or winning a match people would
        type in "woot" or "w00t" and i would see this on the bottom of
        my screen in the text box
jdubbm j: i first observed it in quake 3, if my memory serves me
        correctly

Pete7fish: cause i think i got it from you

jdubbm j: i think that is very possible
jdubbm j: i was quite obsessed for a while
jdubbm j: all the cool kids were saying w00t
jdubbm j: i was obsessed with the phrase

jdubbm j: and quake 3 :-), but i was referring to "w00t"

Pete7fish: did you ever use any other terms?

jdubbm j: to express similar sentiments?

Pete7fish: i guess

jdubbm j: well the only one i can think of right now (it's been a while)
jdubbm j: is after you made a good play or you had a dominating performance you could say: "owned" or, in computer game terms,
"pwn3d"

Pete7fish: but i mean . . . it's not exactly easier to write that way

jdubbm j: no, . . . but it is, are you ready for this?, 133ter!

Unlike its reluctant bedmate, AOL Instant Messenger/online chat-
room lingo (to which leetists turn up their n0ses), leetspeak is not
shorthand. In fact, it takes longer to compose in 133t than to write
normally. An example is the use of exclamation points: what began
as !1!!!1!!—adding a smattering of "1"s within a series of exclamation
points, representing excitement to such a great extent that the
person is unable to hold down the shift key—soon evolved to
!!!1!!one!!!eleven!!11one! I never got that far in my 133tness, but
thanks to Evan and online chatting I did find my woot.

Pete7fish: w00t
Pete7fish: you are 1 c001 d00d

jdubbm j: h3h3
jdubbm j: 7hanks

jdubbm j: i'm gonna go to the gym and see if anyone is playng basketball now
jdubbm j is away at 10:51:12 PM.

Perhaps leetspeak has not quite affected modern language—not so
much so as other technological neologisms such as to "google" (from
the Google search engine), to "spam" (send junk email), or even to
"email" (from "electronic mail"). Furthermore, there was a time when
a "mouse" was nothing but a small, furry rodent. Now it also refers to
the external navigation tool for clicking on your computer screen.
Everyone knew about "hardware" (hammers, nuts, bolts), but now we
have "software" (Microsoft Word, Adobe Photoshop, SimCity) as
well. Many resist using terms related to technology, feeling them to be
inaccessible to those who are not tech-savvy. A family friend would
cringe and cover her ears, yelling "numbers and letters, numbers and
letters!" when my parents started talking of MP3s, DSL, PDAs, RSA,
6.4 GHz, 1.3 MB, 15 Gbps—no matter how simple these terms may
be. Thus the language of the "techie" elite—those that read the Slash-
dot website ("News for Nerds: stuff that matters") more frequently
than *The New York Times*—remains theirs, the mark of a specialized
group. And today the principle legacy of a once-trendy Internet street
slang is people like me saying "woot," without knowing for certain
what it means (though I know that my wootness flows through me
like water) and stirring up varying responses:

akuma2strider: yeah you're gonna have to knock off the "techie talk"
akuma2strider: its cute
Pete7fish: why

hmmcolor: i never use any of that shit
Pete7fish: why not
Pete7fish: you're too "c001"

hmmcolor: it's stupid
hmmcolor: go away
Pete7fish: hahaha
Pete7fish: thanks d00d
hmmcolor: uhhhuh
Pete7fish: m4d skillz

CYMikeLee: lol
CYMikeLee: i wouldn't recommend using it
Pete7fish: haha why not?
CYMikeLee: um
CYMikeLee: people might think you're weird
Pete7fish: they'll think i'm a "gamer"?
CYMikeLee: haha
CYMikeLee: prolly not
Pete7fish: they'll think i have m4d ski11z
CYMikeLee: haha
CYMikeLee: hahahahaha

Sleepy Head

HOTCOFFEEGIRL.SQUARESPACE.COM

Some of you who know me know that I am a narcoleptic. For those of you who don't, I am.

It's been a fun little problem for me for a while. My best friend Ali has some good stories to tell. She and I used to work together, and she would come into my office on numerous occasions to find me in various states of comatose. Drooling face-down on my desk was the most frequent . . . but there was the one time where I slid out of my chair and onto the floor under my desk. She actually thought I had left until she saw my purse and had to search around for me. This was before I was diagnosed, to be sure. Now when she finds me sleeping on the job, it just means I'm drunk.

The diagnosis was a long time coming. I have always seemed to need more sleep than most. I loved naps—even as a child when you were supposed to hate them. As I grew older, though, I suspected that there was something wrong. I would doze off all the time. I would feel sleepy—even after a good night's sleep. I grew a little ashamed—only really lazy slobs slept as much as I wanted to. When I was married, I would sometimes leave work early to take a nap, taking care to set the alarm for 15 minutes before he was going to be home. I would even make sure I used a satin pillow so there would be no tell-tale crease marks on my face.

I was a junkie hiding a nasty little habit. Naps.

I had what seemed like every test known to man. Blood tests for sugar, protein, all manner of levels. I had my thyroid tested. I even went and saw a shrink because everyone kept saying, "Oh, you're just depressed. That's why you sleep so much." Well, after about 4 sessions, she confirmed that I was, indeed, a whack-job . . . but not a depressed one. No help there. It finally dawned on me that if there was no other medical problem that was causing me to sleep too much . . . maybe it was the sleep itself. I scheduled an appointment at a sleep clinic.

A few weeks later, I had my bags packed for "Sleep Camp" (my name, not theirs). I was to check in in the evening, and get hooked up to a fuckton of electrodes. Then I settled in for bed with a camera trained on me (and not in the fun Paris Hilton video way) and machines quietly measuring me. (A Multiple Sleep Latency Test—or MSLT for you brainy types.) The next morning, I was woken up at 7:00 a.m. and was scheduled to take naps at 8, 10, noon, and 2. They basically say, "Go to sleep" . . . and you try. Being the over-achiever I am, in two of the "naps" I fell asleep in under 30 seconds. The other two, in under 15 seconds. I entered REM Sleep every time. Yeah, I'm that good.

The nurse informed me upon leaving that the doctor would call me within a few weeks and I would come back for a visit. To my surprise, he called the next day asking, "Um . . . how do you function?" I actually think I cried with relief at the diagnosis. It is so hard to know that there is something wrong, but not be able to name it. It makes you feel a bit nuts, to be honest. He called in a script that night for Provigil, and said that I needed to start on the medication the next morning. I did, and the change was immediate. Like many users, I thought that it wasn't working—there was no "high" . . . no buzz . . . nothing that I could feel. Until it was 6:00 that night, and I was still awake. And then at 10:00. I fought the urge to stay up later, but had no problem sleeping once I did settle in. It was amazing. I could go on in greater detail about how this diagnosis—and this expensive little drug—changed my life.

But perhaps another time. Because . . . I told you that story to tell you this story.

I got a pretty good night's sleep on Monday—turning in at a fairly early hour for me, anyhow. I woke up, drank my coffee, and even ate breakfast. As I settled in to work on a client's site, I washed my face, grabbed a Coke, and a Provigil. I was coding away when I heard from the next room the little dog that lives with me having a little dog nightmare. I went over to her, woke her up, and petted her until she calmed down. When I woke up two hours later still curled up on the bed, I was stunned. What the hell? I immediately started to worry. Maybe I am getting worse. Maybe the drug isn't working. Maybe this is all happening again. The mind reeled.

It wasn't until I walked out to the kitchen to grab another Coke that I saw the untaken pill sitting on the counter where I had left it.

I had to take another nap after that because I was exhausted from kicking my own ass. What a fucktard.

The Answer That Increasingly Appeals

ROBIN BLACK

Robin Black says: "I hate writing about myself. Yet, I write mem-oir. Why? you ask. Why do it, if you hate it? Because . . . I am driven to convince myself and who knows, maybe other people too, that life makes some kind of sense."

In this piece, from Colorado Review, *Black takes what might be considered the* Jeopardy! *approach to writing, working backward from a series of answers to figure out what questions she's really asking.*

A phenomenon that fascinates me:
Patina.

A fragment of something I wrote on that subject:
"Are we taking the patina approach?"
"Yes."
It was the only way.

I lived in fear of every scrape, of every drop of water on our new much too expensive leather chair; until he asked and I answered and we took the patina approach. We held our eyes screwed shut for just about one year, the official period of mourning in many religions (mine to name but one), until each individual scratch and every stain just disappeared, and merged into something wonderful.

A short period of endurance. In retrospect. For something so lovely. (Forgiveness itself, as I now understand.)

It takes your breath away.

A funny question:

What exactly is my religion?

9:34 a.m. Nov. 7, voice mail message left by me:

"Rabbi, hi. My name is Robin. Robin Black Goldberg. My husband Richard and I are members of the synagogue, yours, and our daughter Elizabeth is having a bat mitzvah this coming April. Becoming a bat mitzvah this April. I guess that I'm calling because I am feeling some conflict about this due in part, maybe entirely, to the fact that my father, who is dying right now, isn't Jewish. My mother is.

"Anyway, we were wondering if we could come in to talk to you about this. Just us. Not Elizabeth. I am really not looking to dump my ambivalence on her. To burden her. Our phone number is 555–1429, and if we could come in, maybe just to sort some of this through, I would really appreciate that."

9:42 a.m. Nov. 7, overstatement to my husband made by me:

"Sometimes I feel that I am the bravest person I have ever met."

9:47 a.m. Nov. 7, deceptively complex thing my brother says to me on the phone:

"There's actually a new book out called the *Half Jewish Book* that I was going to buy you for Christmas but it costs twenty-five dollars. In fact, I was wondering if maybe this Christmas we could just skip grown-up gifts altogether."

9:47 a.m. Nov. 7, my immediate response:

"Actually, I could really use some presents this year."

My most prized possession:

The hand sewn Christmas stocking my grandmother made for me. It's velvet, a deep red that I have never been able to match. Edged in green satin ribbon and covered with miniature toys. A half inch frying pan with quarter inch fried eggs. An impossibly small pair of scissors, which actually do cut. And jingle bells. There's a little baby-doll girl attached to the center of the front; and when you lay the stocking flat her eyes fall shut. But when the stocking is hung, her eyes open wide. They're blue, just like mine. I liked knowing as a child that the doll was hanging there to watch Santa Claus when he arrived. I named her Robin, after myself.

6:03 p.m. Nov. 7, snippet of conversation between my husband and me:

"The rabbi didn't return my call, by the way. I guess my spiritual crisis can just wait."

"Well, I'm not trying to excuse the guy, but generally Mondays are their day off. They work weekends, you know."

"Oh. No. I didn't know."

10:12 a.m. Nov. 8, snippet of my telephone conversation with the rabbi:

"So, I don't know, I assume, Rabbi, that this isn't uncommon. People who are mixed. Having mixed feelings. You've dealt with this kind of thing before, I assume?"

"Well, yes. Though usually it's been resolved by now."

"Oh."

"But why don't you and Richard come in and we'll see where we go from here."

"Thank you. That would be great."

Reason my father is concerned about authorizing anyone to pull the plug:

Fear of eternal damnation as a result of assisting in his own suicide, which is a mortal sin.

Helpful Hint from me to you:

The proportions on the Manischevitz Matzo Meal Box are wrong. In their Matzo Ball recipe. You want to put in a lot more liquid than they say. Twice as much. And you want to let the mixture get back up to room temperature after you have refrigerated it. And you want to refrigerate it for longer than they say. And sometimes, for reasons I will never understand, you may have to let them cook for up to three times as long as you think. Even if you have done absolutely everything else right.

4:32 p.m. Nov. 8, statement made by me to Elizabeth that documents my ambivalence about not burdening Elizabeth with my ambivalence:

"We're going to meet with the rabbi on Friday to discuss my feelings about your bat mitzvah."

Something about Elizabeth that started when she was ten, the meaning of which I do not understand:
She won't eat pork.

Way she handled this when we were in Italy where just about every sauce contains pork:
Asked her parents loudly at every meal: "Is this pig?"

Something that I like about myself:
Despite enormous temptation, born of tremendous inconvenience (not to mention irritation), I have never misled Elizabeth about whether something we were eating was or was not pig. And never will.

Precise cost, tax excluded, of The Half Jewish Book, A Celebration:
U.S.A. $22.95
Canada $32.95

A request for advice:
To Whom It May Concern,
I have a question. I am in need of some advice.

I am meeting with my rabbi this coming Friday to discuss with him the ambivalence I feel as a half-Jew/half-Southern Methodist in having my daughter bat mitzvahed this coming Spring. In having her become a bat mitzvah, that is. My husband will also be at this meeting. I do not know the rabbi at all, but he is about our age, either side of forty. I assume that he is a spiritual person, at least I hope that he is, and I hope that he is an intelligent person as well. Because I think that the problem I am struggling with is a complex one, quicksilver, a matter of balance and of shades of identity.

I have chosen to raise my daughter as a Jew for two reasons. The first is that it is important to my husband that she be raised that way—though to be fair, he would be fair. He's not a bully on matters like this. Or anything, in fact. Not at all. But I like giving him this. The second reason is that I want her to have somewhere to turn in times of loss. I want her to have a spiritual home to come home to. When life hurts her. If she chooses to. I don't have a home like that, and when I have been hit hard, hit with grief, I have longed for that. I have felt at sea.

I think that it's too late for me, but this is a gift of sorts that I want to give to her.

So my question is, on Friday, for this meeting, what should I wear? Seriously. This isn't the punch line. I don't know what the right thing is to wear. I've never met with a rabbi before.

Question Elizabeth will ask when my father dies:
Am I allowed to say kadish for Grandfather even though he wasn't Jewish?

Authority with which I will say "Of course":

Circa 1975, my mother on the subject of organized religion:
"It's all horseshit."

Throughout my childhood, my father on the subject of organized religion:
"If I really wanted to be rich, filthy rich, wealthy beyond all dreams of avarice, and did not believe in the Lord, Jesus Christ, which I most

certainly do, I would make up a religion and just watch the money come pouring in."

After her heart attack, my mother, again, on the subject of religion:
   "I know it's all horseshit, but are you comfortable promising me that someone will say kadish for me when I am gone?"

Principle by which my cabinets are organized:
   One pantry is for food and one for ingredients. Some things, like dried beans and like sugar, are hard to categorize, but there are only two pantries to look in. So nothing that we store is truly lost.

11:57 a.m. Nov. 10, driving to see the rabbi, nicest thing my husband has ever said:
   I love you, you know.

Rhetorical question I must never ask Elizabeth again:
   Do you have any idea what this is costing us?

11:59 a.m. Nov. 10, emotion that overwhelms me as we enter the synagogue hand in hand:
   Sadness.

What I am wearing:
   A black skirt and a black turtleneck. My earrings are made of miniature compasses that actually work; and my brooch is a teeny tiny

triptych of an Italian landscape. They all sort of go together because both the triptych and the compasses are framed in gold.

Noon to 12:12 p.m. Nov. 10, minutes late the rabbi is for our meeting:
Twelve.

Noon to 12:12 p.m. Nov. 10, thing I try to do for twelve minutes:
Not to think the rabbi is keeping us waiting because he thinks that I am a bad Jew.

Letter I will never send:
To The Authors of *The Half Jewish Book, A Celebration*:
First I would like to thank you. For celebrating me. Because I think that you're correct and it isn't done nearly enough. In my opinion. And thank you as well for making a few other points. Like that half-Jews are also half something else. That the other half isn't just a blank. That's a very important observation and one which I agree does get lost in the shuffle all too often.

But now I have a terrible confession to make: I hated your book. First of all there's no index which is a pain in the ass, but that isn't my main issue here. I only mention the index problem because after I read it, something struck me as odd and I went to look "religion" up in the index. And there wasn't one. "Religion" or "Religious Observance" or "Practices of Mourning." Anything like that. But there was no index, and I'm pretty sure, having flipped through the pages again, read the chapter headings, absolutely no discussion of how half-Jews might comfortably handle issues of loss and of mourning. What the role of ritual is. No real examination of the pain that might be inherent for some of us in having nowhere obvious to turn. Because, while I do leave room here for individual choice, there does appear to be, judging from history and all, a pretty strong and common human pull toward wanting to believe. And toward wanting to know what it is that you believe. And what you don't.

And even toward belonging to a community who share at least some of your beliefs. And who can help you, I don't know, perform rituals without thinking them through. Without having to make decisions about it all the time.

Is that a crime?

I personally find that an impossible thing to have.

Because every step toward one half is a step away from the other.

So I do agree with your basic premise, that there's a need to stop treating us all like the problem children of the Judeo-Christian era, but who's kidding whom here?

Simple, it is not.

Reason I will never send that letter:

I really haven't figured out why I hated their book so much. And it was kind of nice of them to celebrate me. And, as it turns out, I'm not particularly articulate on the subject of their book. Not yet.

Occasions for the grief that left me feeling at sea:

I lost two pregnancies, two babies I very much wanted to have.

12:25 p.m. Nov. 10, thing my husband accuses me in front of the rabbi of being that I deny:

Angry.

12:42 p.m. Nov. 10, statement I hear coming out of my own mouth:
I feel like I am betraying my father.
At a particularly inopportune time.

12:47 p.m. Nov. 10, thing the rabbi accuses me in front of my husband of being that I deny:
Angry.

How I feel at being accused of being angry:
Well, angry. Of course.

Snippet of conversation I have had with Elizabeth, time and time again:
HER: Why do I have to go to Hebrew School?
ME: Because nobody made me go.
HER: That doesn't make any sense.
ME: (*sigh*) I don't care what you do when you grow up. Honestly. I just want you to make whatever decisions you make from the inside. The inside of something.
HER: You make it sound so simple. Do you even know what we actually do?
ME: Humor me. I'm a mother. I'm allowed to make mistakes. Maybe this is another one.
HER: I don't think it's a mistake.
ME: So what's the problem?
HER: It's just boring, that's all.

What I have written so far of the speech I hoped to give at Elizabeth's bat mitzvah:
Just about thirteen years ago, when I was new to mothering, and

was very close to drowning in the joy of having you, somebody, a friend, watching how I reveled in your every moment, said this to me. She said: enjoy these days, because you know, the very first step that your child takes is taken away from you.

At the time, I thought that she was very wise, and maybe she was. And her wisdom wounded me, because all that I could feel was the completeness I knew in pressing you to my skin. So this image of you leaving me was painful for me, because it did ring true. And as it turns out, as I now see, it is true that with each day, with every new challenge you take on and meet so well, you do take steps away from being the baby I nestled against myself. You have likes and dislikes that differ from mine. You shed with every passing second another need you have for me. As you gain competence, strength, independence, tastes of your own. These qualities you have so beautifully acquired, and that you carry with you so gracefully.

But now I also know that even in her wisdom, my advisor left out the other side. The other view that I have gained, not from wisdom but through experience. The salve, the balm, the reason why every mother is not inevitably doomed to grief. For with each step that my baby girl takes away from me, a woman takes a step in my direction. A beautiful, competent, strong, brilliant, complex, compelling young woman who is my own. You are no farther from me now my love than you were when you were first born. No farther from me now than you were the moment before you were born. You are as close to me now when you stand beside me as you were pressed onto me, an infant, soft and sleeping sprawled across my chest.

The number of pieces into which my heart breaks when I learn that there is no time allotted for the mother to speak:

How many pieces are there?

12:41 p.m. Nov. 10, what my husband says as my eyes begin to fill:
   "Are you sure , Rabbi? It would be a really great way for her to feel involved."

One of many reasons I love my husband:
   Moments like that.

12:41 p.m. Nov. 10, the rabbi's response:
   "I'm afraid that isn't possible."

12:43 p.m. Nov. 10, obvious thing that suddenly occurs to me for the first time:
   This bat mitzvah isn't about me.

Reason my mother stopped lighting shabbos candles when I was eight years old:
   She realized that she was just going through the motions; just reduplicating the customs of her home; and that she didn't believe in the ritual itself.

Two things Elizabeth invariably does at take-off in a plane:
   Prays in Hebrew.
   Holds tight onto her mother's hand.

12:56 p.m. Nov. 10, the one thing I know for sure:
   I want to go home.

Letter I may actually send someday:

Dear Rabbi,

It may not have looked like it to you at the time, but meeting with you when we did turned out to be a tremendous help to me. I actually had to eat some fairly good size crow with my husband afterward. He had said seeing you might be helpful. I, well to be frank, I scoffed.

I think that what you said to me that helped the most was . . .

Reason that that sentence never ends:

I don't really understand why it helped. And to the extent that I think I do, it had nothing to do with him. And, I just don't think you can say that in a letter of that kind. A thank-you note to your rabbi.

In fact I think this is just another letter I will never send.

What I will do while my husband recites the parental blessings in Hebrew:

Stand next to him. Hold his hand. And keep my lips sealed.

Question to ponder:

If the rabbi had told me I'm a bad Jew, why would I care?

Fact that also needs to be pondered:

I would care. I would care a great deal.

Question that persists:

But why?

Odds that someday I will talk to a Christian minister about settling this sense of dislocation in myself:
  Fifty/fifty.

The most likely reason that my father will not be attending Elizabeth's bat mitzvah:
  He will be dead.

What it looks like when someone draws their dying breath:
  I can only tell you what my mother's mother looked like. I went to the door of her room, to check on her, because we knew that she wasn't going to last much longer. I loved her very much. She taught me how to cook. And when I saw her chest move up and then move down I thought to myself *well, she's ok*; and I stood there, in her doorway, relieved and safe because it hadn't happened yet. She lay buried deep in blankets, nothing much left of her, her long hair splayed out gray across a pink pillow case. And as I leaned against the door jamb, the side with the mezuzah fastened there, watching her I slowly realized that her chest had never risen after that, and that what I had just witnessed was her death.

What my daughter eats when I have scrambled eggs and bacon:
  Scrambled eggs.

Where I am left to turn when I am in pain:
  Here. There.
  And everywhere.

A funny question, repeated one more time:
    What exactly is my religion?

Answer that increasingly appeals:
    The Patina Approach:
    A short period of endurance
    For something that is so lovely
    It takes your breath away.

North Pole, South Pole, the Sea of Carcinoma

Dev Hathaway

Dev Hathaway was born April 15, 1945, in Norfolk, Virginia, and died June 18, 2005, in Shippensburg, Pennsylvania, at the age of 60. This essay was published posthumously in the Gettysburg Review.

Say everyone gets cancer, no matter who. It's our be-all and end-all, birthright and deathright, our sign, our rock. Say cancer or another, equally final.

Say it straight up, Death is our gift. That without which we'd be selfish, slothful, and probably worse. Add the poet's corollary: Beauty, as we know it, would go unborn.

Call this the high ground, the philosophic view.

The lowdown and dirty is disease is a pisser. Arbitrary, cruel, for the living and dying.

Just frighten me good, we'd gladly bargain, I'll always love my

neighbor and smell every rose. And Jesus please get me out of
jail for free.

The high, the low—they're the mortal poles.

I. May–July 2004

I don't know for sure how long I have. Twelve months, two years.
Depends on the treatment. Being low prognosis but still pretty
healthy, I made a clinical trial and got lucky in my draw. Have both
drugs, the old and the new. Two others in my boat, the Renal Carcinoma, came out with one each to keep the study in thirds. The old
works for 15–20 percent. The new might be better. In eight weeks we'll
see how our luck really runs, who stays afloat.

I know, it sounds grim. And was worse yet at first, the shock-and-
awe stage. With all the standard denials. & oh kidney cancer, swell.
Notorious for silence until metastasis rages. And radiation and chemo
won't help for long. Chances are you can't go there with bald-people
jokes.

It took a month to adjust, not to get clocked every time I forgot.

To say Fuck a Duck like five hundred times.

Make friends with pain on the one-to-ten scale.

& to contemplate the poles.

SOME GOOD HAPPENS, too. Friends and family rally around—I've
had this in spades. Cards and calls, long distance visits, covered dishes,
a DVD player the size of a book from everyone at work. You might call
this stage the Victory Tour.

Plus oncology goes from awful to normal. Dozens like you yet of all
different walks get help without pity, like regular folks.

& you do something lavish—cashing in stock and getting a screen porch built was my lark of choice—and you're glad for the chance. "Hey this cancer ain't bad," I say to a friend, settling back on my new wicker couch. You learn to make light.

BUT POLES BEING poles, the grim will swing back.

May the forces make us strong.

Roto-Rooter, Piano Tuner

What are the odds that, on the very same day, Tom, the drain cleaner, in his blackened blue work clothes, comes trundling in, his snake on its roller, and while he's filling the basement with deep dark twizzlings, dapper Mr. McMillin, in his three-piece suit, shows up with his tool case and sleek Steinway apron to do the piano.

Oh the music they make, of the awfullest kind, wonderfully discordant—thrumming and metallic twisting below, banged-on one notes, over and over, here up above. This goes for two hours. "That'll do her," says Tom, rolling on out. And with a run of the keys—all of them in tune—Mr. M gives up a resounding rendition of "When the Saints Come Marching In" and then an "On a Clear Day" encore.

They charge, give or take, $250 each for the house to run true, and I have, as a bonus, a composition for cancer.

Meditation

One way to see Being: everything yearns. Gravity, valence, biochemical combinings. Each thing reaches for a kind of fulfillment. Atoms and molecules, organs and organisms. The chain of being all the way down to pre-animate matter. Stages line up, tropisms abound, and in time all will flower and follow the sun.

Okay, okay, a pat metaphysics, complete with platitudes.

& so why would this be? The force that drives blossoms is built in throughout? Or if spirit is the answer, it has to be manifest to actually be? & needs to risk mutability. Just as God in some form hazards *coming among* in most religions. Isn't that the deal?

In res deus, the grand substantiation. Or some such imperative.

. . . Beyond my back porch the spring rush takes over throughout the garden, enlivenment splurging in green fleeting things.

Calamity Family

What is the film where like the sheriff rushes in, all out of breath, upon a scene of destruction? "Is everybody hurt? Is anyone okay?"

You get used to that, if disaster and illness befall your whole household too many times. Pancreatitis, Crohn's disease, emotional breakdowns & their whole pharmacopoeia—and I'm forgetting a few. House fire destruction, all the dead cats, an ice jam that pours through the living room ceiling. The list goes on. Calamity family.

"And now *this*," says a friend, when my biopsy's back.

But we're not them at all, I always want to say, the ones to be pitied. Five people cursed with steep IQs and a rash of hard luck, with striving hearts, fragile natures. A homeful of books and boxes and plants and yes in total disorder.

Why, we've danced our way through the eye of a needle many times over, and look at us now. *So what* about *this*? We're a step ahead of debt and grown up ironic and way *au courant*. & generous, courteous, humorous, kind. Loving, even. You think *that* can be stopped? Not on my watch.

But First, These Messages

You gotta start with good hurts to get a handle on your pain, say that gnawing in the belly, an itch that loves raking, the disconsolate erection. Old bruises you can press on over and over. Cultivate the habit, work up from there.

First my ribs hurt like hell, like a bolt was anchored front to back, and sometimes I imagined I was cranking down the lug with a giant socket—I could make it hurt more, much as I pleased. *E-uuu* it was a mother. And this *before* they said it was cancer.

And all the meds to help out. Ultracet, Tylenex, Oxycodone. First thing from surgery (for my honking big tumor) I had morphine, you bet, to let me cough out my lungs. & what a friend I had in *Jesus*. Then the catheter came out. Yowee zowee—well that wasn't so bad.

Oh yeah and the ten scale, that trick of the trade. Saying "seven/eight" beats wincing all to hell. & sing do-re-me.

Richard Pryor tells the story of his catching on fire. The wonder of it all—nigger damn near burned *down*. And *hurt?*—*holy* God, that's some pain-ful *shit*. Yet Pryor made it through, thinking upon Jim Brown, the running back and actor. Fire jump on Jim Brown, Jim Brown he say, *Whuuh*.

Body and Soul and Farewell to Willy

We were ready so long for my brother to die, he caught us off guard.

Forgot my Saturday call, missed him on Monday, Tuesday forgot, so had him on my short list Wednesday morning when the cell phone rang.

The night nurse said he wheeled out for a smoke and came back in cold. Needed help to get his scooter to his room. He "looked like death" then, and when they checked on him later, around 4–4:30, he "was already gone," dead for an hour.

Two weeks plus past my kidney surgery, I wasn't going to miss the funeral service. I knew if I didn't see his body laid out, suited and shuttered, I wouldn't get it in my head he really wasn't there. I'd keep thinking to call.

Also there's this. Almost sixty, I'd never yet been to an open casket, and felt the need, like a kid, to see for myself.

On the long trip down, nodding in and out, I imagined his box was a Mercury capsule, a bobsled, a rocket. Strap 'em tight, say goodnight, pull the lever, to forever.

Ba-da-bum, ba-da-bum, the highway seams sang.

Of course I saw soon enough it wasn't him at all, only the hide of the person he was, propped and macabre. "Godspeed, Willy," I said, laying in my rose, but knew already this was after the fact.

But then that's the jolt you reckon at the service—a life force runs out, and someone who was, isn't at all. Time is moving ahead, and he hasn't only died, he's begun to recede. And the soul, the spirit—the "peace," the "better place"—well that's comforting for us. "He gave us a gift, going when he did," somebody said. I don't know about that.

My mother, dad, sister, and I had a meal the next day, the four of us there, eating our salmon and potatoes in the quiet. My dad grew peevish at nothing—his portion—then we all soldiered on.

On the car ride back home, my sister and I went for miles between talking. In my mind I kept struggling with the who and the how—was death like a head-on, the body wiped out but the soul thrown clear? No, wasn't it instead that they both had to perish, as they'd mated for life?

I remember when Bill lost his leg to gangrene, and a ghost leg remained. That's how it feels now. From the cordless phone I'm the new amputee.

Fuck a Duck

You can say that again.

Meditation II

Now then, Best Beloved, in cancer's first bloom, that shock-and-awe phase, I see colors intensely. Primary mainly—red, blue, and especially yellow. A mug on the windowsill glows like an icon. A daffodil—wonders! Holy mortality! Jumping Jehoshaphat! And so many moments sharp and binocular, things razor clear and layered one on another. Indeed, time collapses.

One day after needles and nuclear Kool-Aid, I have an afternoon off and take a magnified drive to a hardware emporium. Clouds slide up mountains, making the illusion that the ridgelines are cresting. Highway signs loom, grow giant and flee, trailing flares of strange letters. And no cop pulls me over!

At the home supply warehouse, blue pipes and hanging lights run high over shelves that themselves need ladders. Home expert associates in snappy red vests glide up and down aisles, pushing truck-bed-sized carts. I loiter on the concourse of exterior lumber, passing as a regular, sizing and appraising board feet and grain. Think I'll have a dozen of that 6-by Southern pine, and a pallet of cedar for the back porch we're building. Settle for a scraper and a tape measure unit with a big silver clip to go on my belt.

Outside, the parking lot in a sudden burst of sun makes a grand panorama. A vendor standing under a striped yellow awning hawks gargantuan pretzels. I spring for one, and a Coke to go with, and stride to my car in all of God's glory.

Side-Effect City

I was gripping my shopping cart, glad for a walker on the long swing through produce, when I bumped into N., another soldier for cancer. He asked how it was. I made my best clown face and sighed when I said it: "Side-effect city, man, side-effect city. You know how it is, morning sick, runs, food tastes like pennies."

"I hear ya, oh I hear ya."

& so commiseration-ville, for two gnarly vets, sharing a moment, in the township of onions and garlic and potatoes.

Life on the Brink

It's not for nothing that you get to gaze upon yellow pine flooring and the many geometries of porch frame and screen, the run of soffit and sill and lath board and roofline. Oh, no, there's a price. It takes installments from the heart—this is almost too much, having all of it now, built to your specs. And which is, *because* . . .

And there's a telescoping pull—that binocular effect—from sitting room door, to porch door, to porch—where you feel going out in delectable gradients, like taking off layers, until the faint skin of screening is all that's between here and out there. And the draw of precipice that extends into prospect, the inkling of verging as you stand at the edge.

The yard drops away down the daylily slope and runs past the hemlocks and pine to the park. A grassy fairway, a visible gap, carries out half a furlong to far-off oaks. Thin stripes of sun fall across this long reach. Blink and you could teeter.

In the Navy I liked taking the midnight watch, Flight Deck 1, forward of the "island," on the catapults and spit of sloped deck beyond. A carrier at sea doesn't pitch as much as shudder, and the steady, smart gale of being under way and into a wind will hold you up stiff leaning out on that spit. When the moon is out and you're ninety feet up over oncoming seas, it's a rush to live for.

At one corner of the porch, you can stand just inches from a cherry tree's reach and see the pinnate veining in every leaf, the wild fruit ripening—oh so close.

OUR CATS NOW pretty much live on the porch. We moved their food and water out here last month. They come and go through a tear they've made at the bottom of the door. They're out all night, bringing home half a rabbit, a fledgling robin. Only now and then are they inside the house, and never for long.

I know where this is going. It's a matter of time before my soul grows wilder, my heart goes feral to out-fright the fear. The day will come—or rather the night—when I slip from the porch and take on the dark, not to come back.

Beating the Odds/Buying the Farm

The Smarty Jones story really made me choke up. I guess welcome to the club. Smarty's life-opera saga—a trainer murdered, the farm nearly sold, all but two horses. Then one bashes in his cheek first time in the gate but somehow he pulls through. That was Smarty, of course, named for the woman whose birth date he shared. The little horse who could, who didn't lose his eye & took to running like a dart.

When he won I got weepy. My chest even heaved.

Or Sylvester Croom's story, the first black head coach in SEC football. His traveling all over Mississippi, introducing himself to halls full of whites. Like some change is gonna come, just like in the song.

Or the Tony awards. Or Reagan's funeral—Patti Davis and her mom, together again—oh the great leveler! Then Ray dies himself— just like the river, I been running ever since. Oh it's been a long time, a long time comin' . . .

More shuddering breaths—*Fahrenheit 9/11*, the Wimbledon finals.

Maggey, my wife, claimed it's my feelings running close to the surface, and no wonder, she said.

"Ah hooey," I tried. And *that* nearly got me.

My good friend John from Chester County, near Someday Farm—
his stepmom for Pete sakes knew all the Chapmans—John got me a
sharp-looking Smarty Jones ball cap. Then my son looked it over. So
was it "that horse?"

"Smarty Jones," I replied.

"I don't believe in racing," he judged with a scowl.

"Oh I don't either," I gave him right back, "but as long as they're
running, Smarty's my pony."

World Enough and Time

Into June, after a week of chill and rain, the sun comes back out with
its emerald glow through overspread leaves. My daughter, Marie, and
I go in our sock feet, porch door closing, a light bang behind us. We
fall to marveling at delphiniums in bloom, plucky nasturtiums,
new daylily plants we drove over the mountain for and planted
yesterday—Penny Lane and Orchid Candy—gazing at their bud-
scapes and the others' rising in the greened bed. We catch sight of a
tiny garden spider at its miniature web, strung from a shepherd's
crook, and bow down over a Stewartia bloom, its white frill and folds
and tawny blush in alternating leaflets. We examine the foxglove's
dark, speckled throat and a no-name flower that looks like a parrot.
And everything likewise we patrol and inspect the length of the yard,
our voices low and benedictory.

Oh, yes, our sock feet get soaked in the dew, and yes the klutzy cat
Salvatore tagging through our beds maybe snaps a few stalks, and
another spider runs from its thread—true, true. But there *is no cancer,*
all our while in the garden, none whatsoever.

Outpatient Two-Step

As we say on the floor, it's an ill wind gathers no moss, a stitch in time's worth nine in the waiting room, and don't throw out the patient with the IV bag—not yet anyway. Let's wear that biohazard logo proudly there, friend. Remember, Med Wastes R Us.

Of course we're all pretty much in the slow lane here, with our canes, walkers, and caregivers' shoulders, our Simpsonesque mouth masks. How we feeling today? Can't complain can't complain. That's good that's good. Stoicism rocks.

There's a really buff wig shop down in the lobby, where nobody goes. Bald is way big. "Who Needs Hair with a Body like This." And so the woman from Remulak opines away in her chemo recliner—on anything she chooses—her dome aglow. Her deep throaty laugh says God this & God that. I mean court is in *session*.

A lotta "Ain't Dead Yet" is what's up here, Doc. And screw the word *survivor* and groups for support.

It's what you have to love about the joint. We holders of the C cards are a privileged set. Swiping 'em for entry like medical pros. The establishment's *ours*. How else to say it—we feel *whole* in here. Alive and dying—and very vice versa.

Meditation III—Ashes, Wishes, Dorothy, Sedna

In evening's dim light I'm again off the porch, leaning over daylilies, checking for buds, nodding as I verify plants on my chart due to bloom soon this June. As usual my sidekick, Salvatore Cat, slithers through the beds to assist with inspections, and as he does the first fireflies rise from the foliage, popping into view like bubbles in a tank. A quick glow and glide, then they're floating higher yet—and suddenly I'm seeing my brother's scattered ashes—or rather, his embers—like the swarm of blinking sensors in the weather movie *Twister*, the "Dorothy" experiment.

Oh how they rise, ashes in the sap of the pine where I spread them, down in the needles; rise as new candles, as fireflies and moths, chimney swifts and vultures, as meteors and planetoids—that new one named Sedna—as galaxies so far the Hubble has to find them, teeming by the millions. Matter to matter & ad infinitum.

You precede me, my Brother, in blooms where we'll rise, in our sweet glow and glide, in those faraway reaches.

Skyline Overlook

4 a.m. I have lain awake naked after making love and counted the seams in the Skyland Lodge paneling, made my eye try to follow one blade in the fan whirling slowly overhead. Readjusted my pillow. Eight hours ago my wife and I watched strangers like us, seated in their bodies, eating trout flesh on rice. Then we folded our napkins and stared out from our chairs at first lights in the valley. A few hours before, in the broad of day, we'd stood at a CCC overlook wall and peered down at a world where I lived long ago, in a haze of blue hills only eight miles away.

Down there I was homesteading—he of a couple that turned an old mill into a livable castle, with a garden and woodlot and chickens and bees. Day led to day, in maintenance and newness, mountains as boundary of picturesque life, nothing more, nothing less, and change came on gradually, year after year, until the night I blurted out I was leaving for another. Then the cavernous mill echoed with cries that a boarder we had—his name long forgotten—surely heard in the dark. And when I left in the morning, had God or a vagabond stopping by the road, or say our boarder turned seer, mentioned a man, a sixty year old with his wife of twenty years, with grown kids back home on the mountain's other side—of his gazing one day from the overlook there at his life in the past—what would I have cared? For I was so very sure of what I was doing, a new passage was at hand, and oh its guilt and thrill were everything there was.

Lingua E Tempus

It's almost touching, the faith he has in words.

—"The Cure," Andrea Barrett

Two years on and off, I've been going back and reading *The Tapir's Morning Bath*, Elizabeth Royte's book on biological studies in the Panamanian rain forest of Barro Colorado. Royte, who was there in the late 1990s, finished her account some time in 2000; it came out in '01. Yesterday, June 20, 2004, I pulled it off my shelf, blew dust off the jacket, and found my old place on page 137, in "The Rainy Season." A few pages in I recalled how enthralling it was to the senses, and numbing to the brain with all the data broken down. The very sort of book to take a chapter at a time.

Time, in fact, is part of the appeal, each time I go back, layers of years before and after writing that I'm adding to in reading. Continuity, in passage, or in discontinuity—I'm not sure how to put it. A fluid disjuncture.

Last night on the porch in growing dark, a candle burning low, barely wavering, I understood *in time* through its *out of time* flow, like a traveling bubble. Something so sublime it subsumes its duality, yet commonplace as well.

It's like the time warp one feels with a deadly disease, both out *and* in—reading Royte's book. Out as removed from, lifted, outside of, conscious of, short of. In as immersed in, flowing in, lost. And having footing in both, what a dizzying state!

Here's a passage from yesterday, carried page to page, hers to mine, an additional remove:

Sometimes the rain was soft; sometimes it came down in torrential sheets that turned gutters into geysers, culverts into cataracts. At those times we'd take plastic trays from the dining room and ride them, hydroplaning, down the steep path between the labs.

What did that take, maybe ten or twelve seconds? List the referents of *that* & hold all in mind at once.

Another way to put it, think when did this happen and through how many intervals of interrupted wording does it now come recounted?

And your bonus toss-up: how slippery a term is that little word *now*—meaning, dear reader, *when* exactly?—and am I *living* now, or dead?

Roto-Rooter II

Oh the dark clouds gather, Best Beloved, and our hero-slash-victim, flush from a spider bite visit to the doctor, hustles up the road to his root canal appointment, administered by Dr. *Devey* and his young assistant *Devin*. As the sky grows black (in less than an hour an F-3 twister will rout out a neighborhood twenty miles away) and the mouth guard is readied, plain old Dev waves for a pause and asks do they think their trio has been called together for a reason? A first lash of rain answers at the window. "Spooky," offers Devin, and helps snap in the guard. Another whip of rain blurs up the pane, then drums extra hard. "Oo you aa a ackuk kenerator?" cracks our fey patient.

"Nope," says Dr. D, lowering the drill, "you'll just have to pedal!"

The Sea of Carcinoma

It's a tough draw to play, wife of cancer. The bride of unknowing, the one who gets to fill out the caregiver's questions. Where's the item that says rank how much it sucks? Or how pamphlets overwhelm—*Tools for Navigating the Cancer Journey*. Where's the traveler's guide to this sea of carcinoma? Talk about your dead reckoning. No really let's not.

And there's fielding each kindness, the curious, the dolorous, the overmuch earnest; endless updates you're on stage to provide and give a good spin—"he's hanging in there"—when you're dangling by a thread. Oh and who is he this morning, the one you're to speak of—Bog Man, Piltdown, The Living Dead? Names like old wrestlers' he dredges from his bone scan and drags about croaking to humor the kids.

Then today your blithe husband brings you a story for a hard final proof. It's rural-style story line, coming of age, tomboy toughness, machinery and such, and, oh, by the way, the death of the farmer. Your feelings aren't fooled, and when he thanks you for the read, you wave at your eyes, but it does you no good. Now, the tears are springing like a rag being wrung, and what does he give you but stock soothing words, "It's okay, let it come." Where's the item that says how you wish you could throttle him and how this ranks right there with that fan in your face the night you gave birth? Remember that fury—girl, you let him have it *then*.

Sometimes, you want to say I can't do this anymore. Sometimes, like every day, with its West Nile tiredness and paralytic dreams, its spiraling dread. But then he's here with your coffee, just like in the old life, with a shrug and a hug and his ever-lovin' do-list. A man to your liking, whatever his game. And what's a gal to do but haul up out of bed?

How I Know Jesus

By the History Channel B-grade special with C-grade stand-ins in seaside tableaux. The voice-over line is the grabber for me, scholarly psychology on Jesus seeing Peter for the figure he would be—almost because of his failings early on—and so needling him now into the person needed later. Very provocative, very backdoor. Ragtag actors, Spartacus togas.

How would I make my own Church of Jesus? With the ratted look, say, of a dirty ghetto market, but à la Rube Goldberg, with flaps of tenting and wash lines on pulleys strung from upper windows above alleyway narrows, with Mexican lanterns, some of them lighted, some broken, swinging free, and the marketplace abuzz with scrabbling commerce, a few bronzings of sunlight angling through smoke, grilled fruit and flesh. And a crier now rushing from stall to stall, spreading the rumor: "He was here, he was here!"

& how I once wrote about "the Garden" from my bench in the yard:

. . . If things didn't change, what would we see? What would we hear? Sameness and sameness, *yeses* stretched out to sibilant sounds, extrasonic hisses that get in our ears. I'd turn to concrete, here on the bench, stopped from becoming.

All this reminds me of The Garden of Eden in Lucas, Kansas, somebody's lifework that filled his whole yard—trees and animals and everything else—cast in cement. He even had himself buried in a concrete mausoleum, complete with a window to be viewed forever, immune to change.

As an image it's how I see the Biblical Garden, a permanent environment, facsimile reality, an artful diorama encased in yeses as the curator wishes. Forever summer. Think about it, in the story of the Garden there were naming and dominion—meaningful states and holy actions, each in their way. But only one act with dynamic dimensions: human opposition. Dare we say it—*Hallelujah*.

And another thing as well: matter's too fickle to work that way, to hold to perfection. The material gives, as in "fails" and "allows"—so the Spirit's only options are enliven and evolve.

Or look at it like this: we "fell" because this is the falling place, where creation is collision, where everything possible precipitates strife, where nothing outlasts, concrete included. Where soon as there's a self, then another and another, it's a world of strife, on top of the physics. But as well it's the realm for goodness and beauty—how else can they be, without consequence and foils? Nothing can, or can only exist (forever summer). And so aren't things as they ought in the world we have? Robert Frost, he thought so. "I don't know where it's likely to go better."

And religious pitches for life ever-after, like retirement in Florida or early release for good behavior, dwelling "in the house of the Lord forever"—what's with all *that*?

Isn't *this* the house of the Lord?

Isn't *this* the Garden I'm sitting in now?

Cemetery Ten

First impression: there's a lot of people here I see didn't make it.

Were those piles of dirt with the weeds growing on them brought in or dug out?

Are plastic flowers in really poor taste or just the right thing?

A *New Yorker* cartoon with a toaster for a headstone.

A real headstone chiseler who calls in to *Car Talk*, asking for mileage with towing capacity. (Tommy's standard answer, the Subaru Outback.)

The inscription "Called Back." Way to go, Emily.

Remember the grave ghouls rising in "Thriller." Ah innocent gruesomeness. And tunes you could dance to, before Michael Jackson . . .

Let's dig up the bones five years hence like in old-world Greece. If one's flesh hasn't rotted, you bake cakes for his enemies.

The kindergarten ditty: Ashes, ashes, we all fall down.

Fuck a Duck II

Don't cry in your beer. *Simon says,* Don't cry in your beer.

& the deal is this: fear and trembling, the Victory Tour, sympathy cards, porch celebrations, other buoyant novelties "shall pass," to quote Simon.

But any day now, won't the grind wax glorious and I rise above?

"You *wish,*" injects Simon. "Soon," he says, "it's just down to the grind." Or like a scuba-diver's brush with a whopper barracuda, crisis reduces to the one that got away.

"But, but," I say, "it takes a lot to face having incurable—the *Jaws* of disease—and go on living your life."

Simon replies, "On form alone, pal, a big ix-nay on that."

"And so nothing either about low platelet counts, the nausea, not knowing . . . ?"

"*What,*" Simon says, "did I *just* finish saying?"

Hello, Camp Sunshine

Something's not right. A guy at the hand dryer's talking nonstop while he's wringing his fingers. He is not, I can see, singing along to the James Taylor song piping from the ceiling. Outside the restroom, in the service plaza proper, a short, scowling woman of uncertain years stands puzzling mightily at vestibule doors, her whither-shall-I-go likewise impervious to JT's ballad. I see others as well who fidget and frown, murmur and low. And none of them seem to hear "Shower the People You Love with Love."

Finally, I notice the dutiful attendants, a threesome herding their charges toward the doors, and all becomes clear. *Passage,* I gather, is the problem of moment, the thrall of transit. Yet slowly they make it, coddled and steered. The burble of their thrill gradually fades as Sweet Baby James takes us on home with "love love love."

... How long Maggey's been standing by my side is hard to know. Her arm is in mine as I gesture to what-all she's already seen, and she pats me in a way that says, "Yes, dear, I know" and "Now *we* have to go." She's doing the steering.

Outside, we watch them clamber to their van, robin's egg blue, *Camp Sunshine* in white bridged across the side. Then we're here at our car, where I stop a moment in the throe of a vision I pictured in the plaza, as James T showered us all—see, I *saw myself* there: as a *tree* looking down, *and* a tree that had fallen, covered with fungi, with ferns all around. Observer and observed. Alive and long gone. And the rush, like a blessing, is as much as I can stand.

I could raise my hands now and pass it on in the sway of the song, though the Sunshine campers wouldn't even notice. But that hardly matters. This is *my* gift, from them.

Funny Thing Happened

Rob and Gardner's toddler, Jimmy, all worldly from day care, decides he better call somebody Mommy. So he gives Rob the nod. And it's obvious, we say, a butt that substantial, those pushover peepers, his *je ne sais femme.* & on and on till our cheeks hurt from laughing.

Our pals, K. & M., might have diverticulitis. If they go all the way and get bags and spigots, my colon cancer buddy N. and I are challenging them to a three-legged race. Strictly for charity.

Jon Stewart, on *Larry King Live*, says Edwards is really a bad choice for veep—so idealistic, and once he learns a VP has to drop the F-bomb on congressional colleagues, it will ruin him for life.

Man Compares Self to Racehorse, Gets Prison Time. As one can imagine, here in Smarty, PA.

Chicken and egg lying in bed. Chicken's smiling, smoking. Egg sighs and says, "Guess we know now."

It happened after surgery, peeing one day, a sound like a duck call.

Looking around, I had to conclude there was no other answer—my member passed gas. *Oh great*, what *now*, and so I called up the nurse. Oh it's not that unusual, she managed to say—but be sure to let her know if the "quacking" didn't stop.

ANNE FRAHM, IN her book on fighting cancer, explains the chemical benefits of bouts of laughter, how they boost the brain's production of endorphin and give a sense of well being the body has to have to keep its battle systems going. In other words, medicine à la *Reader's Digest*. As much as that hurts.

Fast Forward and Counting

1.

Our gal Sluggerella looks over the daylilies, seventy varieties in bloom at one time. "They last just a day?"

"They'll all be goners middle of the night," I say, picking a deadhead from yesterday's Show Girl and handing it to her. "New class tomorrow & graduation day." (Did I really say that?)

"That's incredible—Jesus." Slugger's thirty-five-ish, with lots of va-voom, from boxing and beauty. "My garden's a nothing, everything is just—bleh." She does a slumping gesture, a very nice nodding flower.

"You'll make it work. Put things in pots. Hey we'll dig you some lilies."

"You're such a saint."

"Anything for an angel."

2.

The day comes when I'm scanned head to toe for signs that the drugs have put a hold on the bad boys. I'll go check on our flowers before we drive down, late-blooming lilies—Jen Melon, Cinderella, Ravishing

Rosalie. I'm of the school that says talk to the blossoms, tell them they're lovely, cupping each bloom in a V of your fingers, saying some words for the here and now before moving on. It's good for us both, I'm fond of thinking. A little like the Pope.

The news from these tests will say a good deal as to next time around, whether I'll order new flowers for June—Strawberry Lace and Fuchsia Kiss—those high on my wish list. That school I'm in says brace for the worst, take it in stride, push on from there. If anything better, you can breathe and look ahead, go tally that list. Have thought of this a lot and am pretty much ready.

Angels of Mercy

Yes the usual divas, Madonna (now Esther), my own Paula Zahn. And that Maria Sharapova! Ah womanly glory.

But oh my e-mail darlings—Debbie and Mindy and Sharon and Dara—so much passion online. We're *friends*, I admit—but when you open your wings so like Emma Thompson over *America*, and all the cleavings there are in spirit and body, like in Li-Young Lee, together, apart, and both held in mind; and how you surprise me in streams of sweet words, in yin and yang; and when I utter some folly like the moon is ablaze or beauty is a lily or life is a carwash, you are flame and blossom and those buffeting brushes, all in one; and even when I pass—especially then—it's right, it's all right, all will be fine, as I imagine you'll sigh, like a siren's song. & shhh, & shhhhhh.

Meditation IV

We sit on the porch in a light rain tonight, Maggey and Marie, the dog and cats. Our sons come and go, nodding hello. Three trains trail by off in the distance in the course of two hours, and every so often we praise ourselves on how nice the green walls in the sitting room look, the room leading out that we've just finished painting. We have a candle burning as we usually do, the Virgen de Guadalupe. And I've strung Maggey's prayer flags at the far end up high—now they're always here too. The rain picks up, turns steady for a time. Marie hears a rumble. The sill by my chair grows gradually damp, and my arm near there, with mist on the hairs. We sip our beverages, talk this and that, and are silent for stretches.

Now one of the cats stands and turns, then settles on his cushion. And all of the atoms that get to be us this time around are in tune and content.

II. May 2005

A whole 'nother year eked from the docs, and I've about run my string. Lesions have set up camp in my brain. Short-term memory's squishy. This is pretty much the deal.

But there's a keenness to things, like I clearly get to see my car crash approaching. As though all is a blessing and bad dream at once. A gift and a curse.

So I praise everything, and though don't bite for Christ, find how much room there is in my heart to sanctify roundly.

I see both of my exes and tell them I love them, and dozens of friends.

Sit outside with Maggey and hold for dear life—my wife, my wife. & my daughter and sons, whom I've seen growing up.

. . . A gift and a curse. Gift and a curse. & how to reconcile these? Like one really can.

I'll save that for last business, out on the porch.

Thirteen More Ways of Looking at a Blackbird

DORIE BARGMANN

In her non-writer's life, Dorie Bargmann, of Austin, Texas, is a private investigator—an ideal background for her compelling and in-depth "investigation" of blackbirds. "Thirteen More Ways of Looking at a Blackbird" was originally published by Prairie Schooner, *one of the first literary journals to include creative nonfiction.*

1.

In one of its past lives, the Commodore building in downtown Austin had a food court and a three-story atrium. The food court attracted grackles, which scurried in through the swinging glass doors. The atrium's roof leaked, forming a mini-swamp among the large potted plants on the fourth floor landing. The combination of greenery, dripping water, and trapped birds flying to and fro created a lovely outdoor feeling, enhanced by the building's crickets and geckos.

New management has wiped out the food court, which should discourage the wildlife. I do not know management's plans (if any) for evicting the ghost from the Commodore's upper floors.

2.

The Hyatt Regency sits just south of downtown, across the Colorado River. At dusk in November thousands of great-tailed grackles often roost here in the trees and shriek. "What are those birds?" an out-of-town man yells at me over cocktail chatter. "Grackles," I say. "Crackles?" he yells back. I am indoors at a noisy reception for urban administrators. I have just read research suggesting that dogs evolved to fill the ecological niche created by human garbage. Grackles often carry around bits of garbage, and I propose to this man that the birds be trained to clean up his city. He looks puzzled; possibly he can't hear me over the shrieking humans.

I am taking a proactive approach. Because it's just a matter of time before the grackles take over his city, as they have mine, and I want to nip potential hostility in the bud. Because I hear very little appreciation for grackles in Texas. "Garbage birds." "Rats with wings." "Greasy street chickens." They displace the songbirds, say my suburban friends. They eat grains and grapefruit, say the farmers. "Widely regarded as pests," say the naturalists. What can I offer in reply? That they eat grasshoppers? That they recycle hamburger buns? That, as scavengers go, they are remarkably good-looking?

3.

A neighborhood cat was chewing on a young grackle. We frightened off the cat and caught the bird, still alive. At first, he sat rigid with his eyes closed and beak pointed skywards. I fed him softened pet food, bread, and fruit. His swallowing reflex was good; he left light-green droppings in the cage. He was well-feathered, though a bit bald about the neck, with a buff chest, long tough legs, and a long tough beak. The only visible injury was at the base of one wing.

He chirped at me once, at 6:30 pm. *Tsik!* This sealed my affection for him, because my sister makes the exact same noise when she sneezes. I let him stand on my finger. His claws were firm, and his beak grasped my hand to adjust his stance, but he used these tools courteously, not to hurt. He lived a good twelve hours; at 10:00 p.m. I found him keeled over. He had never quite lost the expression that said, Someone's been chewing on me.

Earlier that day I had run into a lawyer who had the same puzzled, slightly cross, slightly distracted look as my grackle. We were not on intimate enough terms for me to ask who had been chewing on him.

4.

Breeding season. The winter grackle conventions break up into small groups and disperse throughout the city. The males strut their terrains and fend off challengers. They tussle and tumble beak-over-tail in the dust and chase each other up trees. Or they square off on the ground, point their beaks to the sky, and try to bend their necks back even further, in a sort of competitive grackle ballet. Finally the losers fly away, and the dominant male takes up residence on a high perch and begins a noisy come-hither call.

Male great-tails are designed for courtship and—it appears—for little else. Their black coats are uncomfortable in the Texas heat; they pant in the summer and regularly dunk themselves in water. Their long tails are a burden on windy days, when one good gust can bend the tail 90 degrees from the bird's body. Male grackles die off in larger numbers than females in winter, and it is thought that the males' greater size and poorer flying abilities make survival difficult when food is scarce.

But in courtship, the male is a star. His glossy black feathers shine blue and green and purple in different lights, and he stands on tiptoe in the tip-top of trees and sings. First a rough noise, like bad radio static; then a wavering musical note, which crescendoes; then a burst of static again; then several loud, rising whistles. When the smaller, grey-brown female happens into his territory, the male flies to the ground, puffs up his feathers, fans out his tail, and flutters his wings, looking rather like an animated Elvis wig. He runs around the female, chittering. If she ignores him, the male's feather volume dies down abruptly, and the casual observer is left to wonder about the evolutionary value of Big Hair.

5.

One evening outside the (now razed) club Liberty Lunch, we passed a tree full of raucous grackles. Inside, we were bludgeoned by music. When we came out again, around 2:00 a.m., the tree still seemed to be singing. Had the amplifiers damaged my ears? Surely these birds must sleep? Naturalist Alexander Skutch set my fears to rest. "Especially at the outset of the breeding season, the [grackles] slept lightly and repeatedly awoke during the night to shatter with shrill calls the monotonous humming of insects." Or the monotonous beat of reggae.

Austin's famous Congress Avenue bridge bats are resident from March to November, but visitors in the off-season need not feel gypped. In February, simply move three blocks west of Congress Avenue, to the South First Street bridge, and you may get to witness Shrieking Hour. On some evenings, hordes of dark birds gather on the bridge rails, on the trees along the river bank, on the roofs of stores and restaurants, on the wires, on the light poles—thousands of birds perching shoulder to shoulder, shouting for all they're worth, drowning out the noise of traffic, calling cheerful hosannas to commuters crossing the bridge from downtown, welcoming them back to South Austin.

6.

Science recently settled on *Quiscalus mexicanus* as a name for the great-tailed grackle. Thirty years ago he was *Cassidix mexicanus*. Eighty years ago an Austin zoologist listed him as *Megaquiscalus major macrourus*, and gave him all kinds of English a.k.a.'s: Jackdaw, Big Crow Blackbird, Texas Grackle, etc.

Even the genus name *Quiscalus* gives scholars a case of the frets. Does it come from the Latin *quis*, what, and *qualis*, of what kind? But why? Or from *quiscalis*, quail? Or from the Spanish *quisquilla*, quibble—a reference to the noisy, chattering birds? Or from the Latin *quisquiliae*—refuse, dregs—the diet of the garbage bird? Linnaeus, who designated the genus, was not known to invent names, but in this instance he has left other naturalists guessing.

Mexico has separate gender terms for the grackle—*clarinero* or *clarinete* for the males; *zanate* or *sanate* for the females. *Clarinero*, trumpeter, is an obvious choice. *Zanate* comes from the Aztec *tzanatl*, meaning blackbird or grackle generally. The 15th-century Aztec ruler Ahuitzotl was fond of the great-tailed grackle and had it imported from the coast to what is now Mexico City, where it became known as *teotzanatl*, divine or wondrous blackbird. Seventy years after Ahuitzotl's death, Fray Bernardino de Sahagún reported: "If anyone stoned them, they chided one another; the common folk said to one another, 'What are you doing over there? Do not shout at, do not stone the lord's bird!'"

7.

In 1989, a federal court in Illinois found Henry Van Fossan guilty of poisoning two mourning doves and two common grackles with strychnine. He was fined $450 and given three years' probation for violating the Migratory Species Protection Act.

In 1992, the federal government authorized the killing of 164,478 grackles nationwide. In Texas alone, in fiscal year 2000, 17,095 great-tailed grackles were poisoned under the auspices of the federal Wildlife Services program.

If you are going to kill a grackle, it's best to wait for the words, "Simon Says."

8.

In Managua at a bus stop I was sitting on a metal ring circling a thick pole. About a minute later, two things happened simultaneously: a great-tail issued its piercing, rising whistle, and an electric current traveling the metal ring jolted me to my feet. Many years later, when I first heard the grackle colonies in Austin, I felt an instant—you could say electric—affinity with them. I was passively familiar with the rest of their vocal repertoire—the squeaking and gargling resonated in memory. I must have heard them often in Central America, but I had not bothered, then, to connect the noises to a bird. Those were serious times, and I was a serious person, and the serious people I knew did not engage in birdwatching.

9.

In 1925, Austin zoologist George Finlay Simmons noted the existence of one colony of four hundred breeding great-tailed grackles in the Austin area. "Very noisy," he reported. "Possibly the noisiest of birds."

What would today's Highland Mall birds, or the South First Street bridge birds, make of these their humble origins? Four hundred birds would fit into just one large tree, and present-day colonies command whole groves. In our nation, great-tails were restricted to the Rio Grande valley in the early 1900s, but today they have been sighted in over half of the United States, as well as in Canada, and if they are not already there, they are coming soon to a town near you.

For those of you in unbesieged cities, here is how to recognize the great-tail. The adult male can grow up to seventeen inches long; his tail accounts for almost half that span. He is slender and black—a tuxedoed gentleman of a city bird, as compared with the pouchy, rumpled pigeons. The female is smaller, maybe two-thirds the size of the male; her grayish-brown coat and yellow eyes give her the coloration of a Weimaraner dog. Male and female great-tails are so different they initially seem separate species. But they have the same eyes, and the same sturdy beak, and the same savvy and irritable expression—like that of a parent who knows exactly what you've been up to and is contemplating discipline.

Juveniles all look like females until the young birds molt. A feather blanket once burst in my back yard; that is roughly what the ground looks like under a large grackle roost when the birds start molting. Except that the grackles' feathers are darker, and they fall with a certain regularity, often quill-down, spiking upwards through the lawn like grass blades themselves. As though someone had cast birdseed on the lawn, and the seed had begun to sprout literal birds.

10.

Why Austin needs the grackles #1: Austin calls itself the live music capital of the world, and grackles give many live, loud, and free performances. Why Austin needs the grackles #2: Great-tails are archetypal Texans—big, brash, and promiscuous. I use the word "promiscuous" advisedly, since the archetypal Texan now has a bit of a split personality—on the one hand, there's the five-times-married former Lieutenant Governor Bob Bullock, and on the other hand, there's the Bible Belt crew currently running Washington.

Why Austin (and the rest of us) need the grackles #3: Black birds are part of our psyche. In the 1990s a local theater company performed Charles Staggs' *Tower Massacre Musical*, which deals with one of the ugliest incidents in Austin's history: the gunning down of fourteen people by a sniper on the University of Texas tower in 1966. I know of the musical only through its reviews, which were favorable, and which describe, among other things, how the souls of the dead are transformed onstage into shrieking grackles. Charles Staggs, Wallace Stevens, Edgar Allen Poe, even the Beatles—black birds haunt us all.

11.

A dead grackle dropped head-first out of a tree onto the sidewalk. Another male flew down on top of him. Several females, clacking excitedly, fluttered out of the tree to surround the pair. The second male began pecking at the first, dislodging feathers. One female grabbed the corpse's tail and dragged it a few inches before the male drove her off. The females flew back to their tree; the male kept pecking at the dead bird until I came nearer, whereupon he also retreated. The dead grackle lay long and straight except for curling legs and claws. His beak was broken at the tip, and the gap between upper and lower mandibles was lined with blood. He was a sturdy, well-feathered, mature male, his back still shining blue.

I have searched the literature, but I can find no description of fatal battles between male great-tails. And the broken beak suggested violent impact, not bird wrestling. Here is my best theory: the bird hit a window or was struck by a car; it then flew, damaged, into another male's territory. The male may have attacked it, or it may have died of its injuries; in any event, after it died and fell, the females attempted to drag the corpse away, to avoid attracting predators to their nests. It is harder to understand the other male's continued aggression, unless it was simply baffled by the dead bird's behavior. The weaker male is supposed to fly away.

In 1821, John James Audubon caught a number of common grackles, as well as other birds, to send to Europe. After a few days, the grackles suddenly became violent, killing the other species as well as the weaker of their own kin. "I look upon this remarkable instance of ferocity in the Grakle with the more amazement," Audubon wrote, "as I never observed it killing any bird when in a state of freedom."

12.

Here are two stories I can neither confirm nor deny. First: a landscaper reports that grackles shadow him when he mows lawns. This, I think I believe: the birds are there to snatch the grasshoppers that flee the machinery. A power mower would frighten off most animals, but the grackles' tolerance for noise has me half-convinced they're half-deaf. In the cities, it's lawnmowers; in the countryside, tractors, no doubt; two hundred years ago, it was the plow, as Audubon also noted:

> Thus does the Grakle follow the husbandman as he turns one furrow after another, destroying a far worse enemy of the corn than itself, for every worm which it devours would else shortly cut the slender blade and thereby destroy the plant. . . . Every reflecting farmer knows this well and refrains from disturbing the Grakle at this season. . . . But man is too often forgetful of the benefit which he has received; . . . no sooner does the corn become fit for his own use, than he vows and executes vengeance on all intruders.

I am more doubtful of the second story. An acquaintance told me he once saw a parrot—presumably an escaped pet—in a local city park. While he watched, several grackles flew up to the parrot and dropped bits of food at its feet, as though they were worshiping it, bringing it offerings. Where can I find precedence for this? To date, only in 1 Kings 17:

> And the word of the Lord came to [Elijah], saying, Get thee hence, and turn thee eastward, and hide thyself by the brook Cherith, that is before Jordan. And it shall be that thou shalt drink of the brook; and I have commanded the ravens to feed thee there.

13.

I was on a green lawn at the pink state Capitol, feeding a flock of grackles half of my enormous sandwich bun. The wind was blowing. There was a whole festival of grackles at my park bench. They rushed and snatched and pushed but did not peck at one another. At last I ran out of sandwich and told them so. They blew out in the wind, broke up in patches like clouds after a rain. All but one. An old grackle, too creaky for tussling, was eyeing me. I showed him my empty hands. He drew himself up, like a scraggly, stern old prophet, and he fixed me with his yellow eyes, and he informed me that henceforth I was always to withhold a portion of bread from the rambunctious youngsters, and when they flew away, then I was to minister to him, the venerable. But I have no independent confirmation for this story, either.

What Is the Future of
Diagnostic Medicine?

MICHAEL ROSENWALD

---

*Michael Rosenwald took the concept of "immersion" in creative
nonfiction quite literally, even to the point of taking off his clothes,
all for the sake of this story, written for* Popular Science.

W hat's left of the General Tso's chicken is on the coffee table. The
sauce that eluded my mouth is congealing on my T-shirt.
American Idol just started. And Megan, my fiancée of three days, is
getting ready to swab the inside of my mouth with Q-Tips that are
nearly as long as chopsticks.

"OK, open that mouth," she says. "Wider."

She is a doctor. I do as I'm told.

"You know, these look like little Pap-smear brushes," she muses.
My mouth snaps closed.

"C'mon, open up," she says. I stall.

"I love you," I say. "Kiss me."

"Let me concentrate," she says. "What if I don't do this right?"

THE AUTHOR, READY FOR HIS CLOSE-UP. (*Popular Science Magazine* / John B. Carnett)

"Then," I reply, "I guess I'll never know if I'm gonna die."

Megan, at my behest, is after my DNA, because I am after the future of my body. This was my assignment: to take every medical test I could get my hands on to predict what will happen to my body 5, 10, 15 years from now. I set out to find the most advanced diagnostics available, early examples of technologies that would get me as close as possible to the future of medicine, when doctors will use genetic and imaging tests to predict what diseases a person is prone to developing. When illness does strike, treatments will be tailored to each patient. The researchers, doctors and drug companies working on this new gene-based paradigm are calling it personalized medicine. Their buzzphrase: "The right treatment for the right person at the right time."

In many ways, my editor handed me my dream job. I have nursed a rather robust interest in my robust body for some time, starting when I asked my parents, at the age of 12, to take me to the doctor because I felt a lump under my left nipple. They indulged me—and they did so again a few years later when, during a tour of colleges, I was so certain that I was dying from a urinary tract infection that I made them rush me to a hospital in Columbia, Missouri. The diagnoses: normal nipple, normal urine. Before I met Megan, I had no idea doctors called people like me "the worried well." This was good news; I had assumed I was just a hypochondriac.

Sitting here on our couch, though, my fiancée and I have to acknowledge the peculiar irony that something could, in fact, be wrong with me, that I might be harboring genes that will send me into the ground sooner than planned. That this might be bigger than my nipple.

"If it turns out that you're going to get some crazy disease, you can sell the engagement ring and use the money for your treatment," Megan tells me, only half joking. She tilts my head so she can grind the swabs deeper into my cheeks.

Sounding like people do when they have a dentist's fingers in their mouths, I ask, "Are you doing this right?"

"I am not an idiot," Megan says, sounding just like herself. I slip each swab into a padded envelope with extra-sticky sealing, so as not to leak bodily fluid on the FedEx man. In a couple weeks I hope to have a good idea of what will kill me, and when. I smile at Megan.

And she says, "I should have waited for the results before I agreed to marry you."

IT'S 2015, AND I want you to meet someone. Her name is Betty. She is 25 and healthy, although an uncle has had some heart problems. Her doctor suggests that she have her genome sequenced. Betty worries that if the results are bad, her insurance company will drop her, but Congress has finally outlawed such discrimination. The test results aren't good: They show three gene variants known to increase risk of heart attack fivefold. Betty and her doctor immediately begin a prevention program based on diet and exercise, of course, but also medication selected to work specifically with her genetics. Fifty years pass.

Betty notices no heart trouble, but one day her arm starts to hurt. Too much gardening, she figures, but her doctor knows better with a glance at the genetic results in her file. He diagnoses a mild heart attack and puts together a customized treatment. Betty lives into the 22nd century.

Today, though—in 2005—Betty is just a dream. She is the poster girl for personalized medicine, a creation of Francis Collins, the National Institutes of Health researcher who helped map the human genome. Collins, along with Craig Venter and his company, Celera, identified the 25,000 genes that serve as the construction manual for the human body. Although geneticists had already been able to home in on diseases caused by a single mutated gene—disorders such as cystic fibrosis, sickle-cell anemia, Huntington's disease and Tay-Sachs—laying out the entire sequence of our DNA allowed them to begin exploring diseases with more complex roots.

Mapping the human genome gave scientists a view of the entire canvas of our genes, including the small aberrations called single-nucleotide polymorphisms, or SNPs ("snips"), that occur in everyone's DNA. Some of these deviations are harmless, but others, when they interact, create instructions that produce some of our most serious disorders: cancer, heart disease, diabetes, Parkinson's, schizophrenia, and on and on.

Now there are dozens of companies painstakingly comparing DNA samples from people who are sick with those from people who aren't, looking for SNPs associated with those disorders. If they pinpoint aberrations exclusive to the disease sample, they can create reagents—and thus tests—that identify the SNPs from blood or DNA swabs.

Celera's scientists, for example, have discovered SNPs in the past two years that indicate at least twice the normal risk of heart attack—putting people who carry the aberrations at the same risk as diabetics, smokers and those with high cholesterol. Such is the cruel science behind seemingly healthy people dropping dead of a heart attack at age 47. The promise of personalized medicine is to be able to find those people who would otherwise have no reason to worry, monitor them closely, and get them started on a preventive regimen.

I would love to take Celera's test, but it won't be ready for at least a year. And although there are about 800 genetic tests available right now, most of them screen for diseases that rarely show up in humans. The 13 tests I took—from DNA Direct, Genelex and Kimball Genetics—are for common conditions that turn up in every walk of life, and they're all for single-gene mutations. Celera and other companies are focusing on the multiple-gene problems, but that will take years, so researchers are also looking at the grunts that do your individual genome's dirty work. I am speaking now of proteins.

Built with instructions from genes, proteins go on to build your entire body. When the instructions are bad, the proteins do bad things—disrupting normal biological functions and causing disease. The emerging field of proteomics is about identifying these proteins, and it's an important secondary tactic in the push for personalized medicine, because any given gene may or may not become active, but the presence of a certain protein can tell you unequivocally whether you'll get a certain disease. Already many doctors test for high levels of C-reactive protein, a biomarker for inflammation that plays an early role in heart disease.

Other proponents of personalized medicine, including Geoffrey S. Ginsburg, director of Duke University's Center for Genomic Medicine, say that getting the science right is just one hurdle to making gene-based predictive tests part of the standard physical. Federal health agencies exercise little to no oversight of testing protocol or accuracy, or even of how a patient's DNA should be safeguarded. None of the companies I bought tests from were suggested to me by a doctor; I did my own research, checking the reputations of their labs and that they're run by bona fide geneticists. But for all I know, one of the labs with my DNA could be planting it at a murder scene right now.

Then there's the insurance issue: Few companies pay for genetic testing. And while the U.S. Senate has passed laws forbidding discrimination based on a patient's genetic test results, the House has yet to follow suit. I just hope my insurance company doesn't read this.

I'M LYING ON the couch watching TV, thinking about popping an Ambien. I take the little white pill a few nights a week to help me sleep (worried wells are often up at 3 a.m., worrying about one thing or another). Suddenly, though, I'm desperate to stay awake. Charlie Rose is on, and tonight's guest is surgeon Mehmet Oz, director of the Cardiovascular Institute at Columbia University Medical Center. Rose wants to know about the controversy surrounding full-body CT scans, a procedure central to the aims of personalized medicine—a procedure I'm scheduled to have next week. Hundreds of doctors' offices now advertise the scans as virtual physicals, offering you peace of mind knowing that your organs have been examined for structural abnormalities. Others warn that the scans also expose people to high levels of radiation.

Indeed, one of Oz's colleagues at Columbia, radiation biologist David Brenner, has shown that having a full-body CT scan in middle age carries a 1 in 1,200 risk that you'll eventually die from radiation-induced cancer.

Oz is alarmingly nonchalant in his caution. "Well, you're scanning the whole body. How do you keep protected?"

Rose looks flummoxed. I sit up. "But the bigger issue is that you uncover problems that aren't problems . . . and that starts a cascade of evaluations, which in themselves carry risks. You'll cause cancers, probably as many as you're going to find."

In the week leading up to my scan, I had other mail-in diagnostics to deal with. Aside from using our genes to see what diseases might be in store for us, researchers want to use them to customize treatments. Because drugs act differently in every patient based on his or her genetic makeup, biotech companies are developing tests to identify which drugs will function best in which patients.

Biotech giant Genentech has developed Herceptin, a breast-cancer treatment targeted at the 25 percent of patients who have too many copies of a gene called HER2. Tumor cells that have too many copies of the HER2 gene overproduce a protein that promotes increased cell division and faster growth. Doctors look for the HER2 gene malfunction using two FDA-approved tests, and if they find it, they prescribe Herceptin.

Genelex, a small biotech company in Seattle, and Roche Diagnostics, a global pharmaceutical company, are competing to sell tests that predict whether someone will have a bad or potentially fatal reaction to widely prescribed medicines, such as antidepressants, narcotic pain medications, and beta blockers. About half the U.S. population has gene mutations that either hasten or slow the absorption of these drugs into the body, mutations that can create adverse reactions.

Genelex sent me a test tube in a small white box, which looked like it might contain a watch. I had a phlebotomist at Megan's medical practice draw my blood, and I sent the tube off in the mail. The lab would use the blood to determine how my body processes hundreds of drugs. I hoped, in the meantime, that I wouldn't need Prozac or Oxycontin.

Jaunts into the future of medicine can take one to the strangest places. I wind up in the Allegheny Mountains of West Virginia, at the stately Greenbrier Resort, which for decades has managed to maintain pristine ratings from the varied likes of AAA and *Andrew Harper's Hideaway Report* despite a design aesthetic built around searingly green carpet. The main building is an 803-room mansion that looks a lot like the White House, which is fitting—for 30 years, until 1995, it hid a secret bunker that Congress could use if the Capital came under attack.

Even though the resort exists in a state known for its high poverty rate and its starring role in the movie *Deliverance*, some of this country's richest people make it their summer retreat. It has three award-winning golf courses, croquet pitches, a mineral-springs spa, and a skeet-shooting range. On the day I arrive, the morning edition of *The Greenbrier Today* announces a falconry class: "Learn the history of the sport of kings, and interact with our trained hawks and falcons."

I have no time for fun and games, though. I've come for a workup at Greenbrier's world-renowned health clinic, which caters to executives whose corporations have a vested interest in preventing them from suddenly keeling over. Greenbrier has, for instance, a Philips Brilliance CT 16. It is one of the fastest CT devices in the world, capable of scanning the entire body in 30 seconds as well as snapping images of the heart between beats, a method that can detect the presence of tiny bits of plaque that will eventually cause blockages.

But Greenbrier's brand of personalized medicine predates CT scans. The clinic's founding principle, in fact, is to catch problems before symptoms arise, which—in addition to using good technology—requires close attention (read: time) from a doctor. That works in a place where patients can sidestep the limitations of managed care by paying for a $950 full-body scan with a credit card rather than a referral. But it raises questions nobody in personalized medicine has been eager to address: How will people afford medical care under the new paradigm? Will insurers shift payouts from treatments to preventive measures? Or will only the Greenbrier regulars of the world have access to the best that medical science has to offer?

―――――

It's 8 A.M., and my workup starts with an hourlong chat with one of the clinic's 10 doctors, a gentle Southerner named Jeffrey Graves. He prods me for my medical history before poking at me in a puke-green examination room. This is where anything resembling a typical physical stops. Graves puts me through a battery of tests that will have me bouncing around the clinic for the better (or worse) part of 10 hours. What's remarkable about this place, I discover, is that it amasses diagnostic equipment from a vast array of medical specialties under one roof. It's a hypochondriac's wonderland.

And so I find myself doing things I've never done: I sit encased in a sound reduction chamber as a technician checks for early hearing loss (none!); I get an EKG, a test that people don't typically get unless they have chest pains (my heart rhythms are normal); I blow into the plastic tube of a spirometer that checks my lung capacity, an indicator of asthma and lung disease (my wind bags are mildly restricted); and I lie on a hard table, staring at "Got Milk?" stickers on the ceiling, while a low-beam X-ray arm scans my bone density (far lower than average).

Thankfully, I'm only 30: In the 20 years until even the most ardent supporters of personalized medicine would suggest I need a colonoscopy, I'm counting on science to find a better approach. (A Canadian medical-device company is developing a test to identify a sugar in rectal mucus that's associated with colon cancer.)

I have my blood taken three times, to provide enough for tests on my liver and my heart and my lipids. In addition to breaking down my reading into HDL ("good") and LDL ("bad") cholesterol, Graves plans to send a blood sample off to Berkeley HeartLab, which a few years ago became one of the country's first private labs to offer further analysis. Standard cholesterol tests count just the number of cholesterol particles present; they don't identify their chemical makeup. But Berkeley examines the LDL for the nastiest, most dense particles, which more easily penetrate the artery wall. The presence of these particles increases heart-disease risk threefold.

Between tests, I sip on a quart of toxic-tasting contrast agent to light up my bowels on a computer screen during my full-body CT scan (which, I found out, will dose me with radiation equivalent to taking 100 mammograms back to back).

I ask Graves about the controversy over CT scans, and he says he can see both sides of the debate. He tells me about a healthy patient who had a history of normal stress tests and EKGs—not an obvious candidate for any kind of scan. But when the machine scanned his heart, snapping pictures as it contracted, Graves could see that the patient's arteries were dangerously calcified. The man could have dropped dead, but instead he got an angioplasty. I am convinced.

A nurse gets me situated on the gantry, which slides my body through the scanner, and inserts an IV with even more contrast agent. I lie perfectly still. I close my eyes. As the table moves back and forth, allowing the camera to take aim at each of my organs, I think, "Once and for all, I'm really going to know if I'm a dead man."

It's the waiting that kills you. I'm slouched in my doctor's office to get news of my genes. Kimball Genetics, a small lab in Colorado that I ordered several tests from, had sent the results to my primary-care physician, as is its practice. I wait for at least an hour, contemplating a bleak future. What if I do carry the Tay-Sachs mutation? I mean, I'm Jewish. Jews carry Tay-Sachs. If Megan carries it and we had a child, that child would have a 25 percent chance of developing the disease and dying a horrible death—first going blind, then deaf, and then losing the ability to swallow.

What if I carry an ovarian- and breast-cancer mutation that, in men, makes it 12 percent more likely that I'll get prostate cancer? If I had a daughter, there would be a 50 percent chance she'd get the mutation, putting her at a 54 percent risk for developing ovarian cancer.

My god, I think, why did I do this? Do I really want to know this stuff? I put down my magazine; the sweat on my hands has made the pages damp. The nurse calls me back, and I wait a little longer. My doctor comes in. I ask her for refills of my blood-pressure medicine and Ambien. As she settles onto her stool, she starts flipping through my genetic test results.

"Well, you don't carry the Tay-Sachs gene," she says. "That's good."

"OK," I say, holding my breath.

"You're clear on narcolepsy." I'm not surprised at this one.

She goes on: No periodontal disease. Negative for HLA-B27, a gene associated with inflammatory disorders. Negative for Apo E, a culprit in coronary disease. Suddenly I'm thinking that maybe I got ripped off.

"So are these tests a bunch of crap, or what?"

"No," she says. "This is good stuff. This is for real."

She flips another page and says, "Oh, now this is interesting." Apparently I carry one of the two genetic mutations required to develop hemochromatosis, an iron-overload disorder that destroys the liver. But it's unlikely that I'll develop the disease without the other gene. Still, my doctor asks me to come back in a few weeks for blood work to see whether I'm retaining too much iron. (It turns out I'm not.)

Several days later I get an e-mail telling me that a genetic test I ordered from DNA Direct is complete and that I can log on to the company's Web site anytime to view my results. I am negative for thrombophilia, a blood-clotting disorder. I'm relieved. But then I think, "When is the other shoe going to drop?"

The next day my cystic-fibrosis results are ready. I log on. Negative. Yes! I mean, excellent! Through DNA Direct, I had also taken the genetic test for the mutation suggestive of prostate cancer. DNA Direct does not believe patients should learn on the Internet whether they have cancer—and at this point in my odyssey, I fully agree—so a genetic counselor calls with the results.

"Give me the bullet," I say.

"Your tests were negative," she says.

Life is beautiful. I told all this to Dr. Graves as we sat down to go over the results from my physical. He was pleased. I asked whether Greenbrier would one day offer these tests. He said he sure hoped so. As of now, there wasn't much interest from patients, but more important for Graves, the available tests still can't look for the kinds of widespread diseases that primary-care doctors regularly come across. He thinks those tests are at least 5 or 10 years down the road, an opinion shared by those seeking to advance personalized medicine.

And then he got to my tests. My CT scans showed an irregular left kidney. Might be a good idea to follow up with a urologist, Graves advised, and instantly I thought of what Mehmet Oz said about discovering things that looked like problems but were not. There was absolutely nothing clogging my arteries. No tumors had formed in my body. (Of course, these scans looked for existing tumors, not for the cells that could cause them to form.) Then Graves said something I will never forget.

"You're in good shape," he told me. "There's just too much of you." I am 80 pounds overweight. My cholesterol is borderline high. My glucose levels are flirting with diabetes. I am a prime candidate for a heart attack or stroke. At that moment, sitting there across from Dr. Graves, I had to face the reality that, until the more powerful tests come online, I am back to where I was before starting down this road: fat. I had been conveniently ignoring the fact that I could have predicted what will be wrong with me just by looking in the mirror. Mutated genes aren't all that can damage a body. A body can be damaged by eating French fries twice a day, by eating chicken wings twice a week, by eating cookies for breakfast, by eating a lot of General Tso's chicken.

I asked Graves what to do.

"Lose 10 pounds," he said.

"Just 10?"

"After you lose 10," he said, "then lose 10 more." And so on. It was all very simple. For now.

Like a Complete Unknown

MIMINEWYORK.BLOGSPOT.COM

W hen I first saw her, the eyes weren't so much lobotomised as scared rabbit. Rippling folds of baby pink flesh nestled beneath buds of breasts—dangling like a suckling cow too young to be reproducing but forced into it by the cattle market. She's scared, this bitch; scared beneath the thick, black lines painted round blue depths of inane youth. When she dances, it's with a fixated grin boring into your face to distract from the body she doesn't want to show; the body her parents probably think is still covered up with cheap H&M even as she sends back the big fucking dollars to pay for their post-communist rent, their American beers. "How do you dance, plis?" she asked me, and I just shrugged, nodded to the vodka clasped in my hand, the glass misted from the heat of my palm, ice crackling and fizzing, emitting little puffs of gas into the arid, chilly air. She took the drink and she grimaced, the little rolls of flesh rippling up from her baby stomach up through her baby breasts, into a face whose cheekbones sank beneath pre-pubescent pudge.

"Listen sweetheart," I said, and I leaned in urgent, like I gave a fuck, grabbed her hand, stared into those pretty blue eyes, felt my hand tighten against a round, pink forearm, saw my skin ghoulish, white and taut against this fucking honey-blossom oozing the nectar of nineteen and new in Nueva

York. "Get out. Get your fucking money, get back to Russia. This place isn't for you. Drink what you need to do the fucking job, keep your wits about you, don't suck cock and you'll be fine."

She looked scared, now I think about it, but her brain was still working because the pupils contracted as she shrank away, disappeared to a corner, thought about the cash, got back to her pathetic faux-grinding in mid-air. That same fucking grin, the blonde hair, dark roots delineating the stark white flesh of her scalp bobbing up and down in the white light, the disco flashes from the sad glitter ball, there since '83. Familiar. She was always there, in her corner when the lights tracked across the club. Another crappy stripper. Kind of gawky, kind of cute.

I didn't give it another thought, just turned up for work, saw her around. Didn't notice that shy, sly smile slowly flailing like a weak sapling beneath the cancerous weeds of something sicker.

When I went back it was all different. Different because you get away and you become the person you were before, the person slowly asphyxiating beneath the thick, caked layers of shitty panstick. You become daughter, sister, friend, whatever. You become what you aren't when you're in that fucking place, caught between the rapid beats of bad house music like a heart patient on amphetamines, the jarring, listless gyration of the dance. The two never meld, surprisingly. You'd think if you spent 40 hours a week in this place you'd get some fucking rhythm. Just a discord. A discord like the sour taste from too many cigarettes counterpointed against no food for a week, the dark stench of alcohol roaring out of your mouth like a sewage drain, drenched in Orbit sugar-free. So I got back and probably I noticed more. Saw things. Felt things more, released for six weeks from the ritual of dousing my liver to make my head go away. She was the first one I saw, but now the pretty blue eyes were lobotomised with the scalpel of money, hard fucking cash, and she led the old dude with the bad breath up the fucking stairs to Never-Never Land, 'cause I've never been there and I don't intend to go, the private private rooms, more private than the others, where your dick up her peachy-ass costs 300 bucks, and ramming the back of her throat will go for a Ben Franklin, and straight-up pussy probably about 250. And you wonder what it was like for her—the first time. Whether it was as bad as her stage show, as transparent as the scared rabbit eyes, which were a glass mirror right into her fucked up little Russian head, allowing the sense to leak out like a soft-boiled egg cracked swiftly open. It seeped out as easily as that dress peeled off, that spangly, glittery g-string curled up in the corner of the room like a dead spider, that dignity was shed.

Before the night was over I went quietly upstairs, past the girls drunk and waving cigarettes around in the locker room, talking about their asshole boyfriends from the Bronx fucking bitches while they earn the rent. I dressed, scrubbed the crap off my face. I left the shoes for the girl I shared my locker with, but I took my name off the door and threw it in the trash. I didn't say goodbye to anyone. It's not a big deal, retiring. We all do it, when we're too old, when the fucking stink has gotten too much, when the new ones barely bleeding and out of their fucking training bras undercut you 'cause scared eyes looking up from the end of your cock are so much more satisfying than the middle finger pointing between your screwed up little piggy gaze, in a pathetic gesture that says more about you than them. But I wondered as I walked home through the East Village, the night pouring onto me with damp, false caresses, warm, stinking sweat—I wondered if it was all worth it. If staying someplace, trying for what I wanted—or not even wanted, something I had to do, have to do because it's all I know—I wondered if trading in ignorance for this unbearable sadness, this knowing, this dull, deep ache—is ever going to mean anything besides poverty, a Bob Dylan song, spending my last twenty bucks on a six-pack and some cigarettes, sitting down and doing what I know best. Ratcheting it up from my dark, boiled heart as the a/c whirrs and Manhattan starts to slowly wind down in preparation for the reprise, which continues regardless.

My Mother's Touch

ALEXIS WIGGINS

"I am just beginning to understand the nature and power of the truth in creative nonfiction—how it's clear and hard and beautiful as a cat's-eye marble. How it asks me to be naked and confident, honest and inventive, a writer—in control—and a subject—powerless—all at the same time. I have never felt my writing truer, more powerful or purposeful," says Alexis Wiggins.

This essay first appeared in Brevity, *an online journal of concise nonfiction.*

When my mother tries to touch me, I flinch. I don't like her to touch me at all, ever, and I don't remember a time when we cuddled or hugged or she took me "uppy," although it happened. My grandmother has proof: the old black and whites of me in my mother's arms, in a cracked, brown leather album that says, "OUR FAMILY," in faded gold letters on the front.

I dread our every embrace. I feel her bones, smell her breath—sharp, like the smell of New England Novembers—hear the excitement in her voice at welcoming me home, and I can't wait to pull away. What kind of daughter am I?

My mother and I have the same hands. They are exactly the same: veiny, bony and large-palmed. I wonder if my daughter will have my hands, my mother's hands passed down twice.

Her hands:

Once, when I was 17, she refused to take me to the doctor when I had an earache. I couldn't drive, and she said it wasn't her responsibility to take me. I went to sleep and woke with a circle of brick-red blood, the size of a silver dollar, on my pillow. She felt terrible and took me to Dr. Marsh right away. She scrubbed the stain out of the pillowcase later, in the sink, under the faucet, by hand.

Once, when I was 8, I was in the front seat of the car and must have said something smart, because she hit me hard with a backhand across the face. It was harder than a slap, because I could feel her knuckles and her rings, which scratched my cheek and nose. Later, she felt sorry about the rings.

Once, when I was at boarding school, she spent many hours writing me cards in her enviable, flawless penmanship, her right hand moving steadily across the page. Each line was perfectly straight, and all the *f*'s and *q*'s slanted the same, beautiful way, like morning light through a window pane. The florid words always added up to the same thing: I was manipulative; I was trying to sabotage her in her job; I was blaming her for my father's leaving us; I was the cause of her illness and near death the year before; I needed to grow up and face these facts. She always sent the same cards, reprints of Impressionist paintings. I had a box full of them, but I preferred not to read the cards more than once. I hid them under my dorm bed, content to let Monet's gardens flower in the dark.

So I can never tell her how much I don't want her to touch me with those hands. I just let her embrace me, like the frozen juice around a Popsicle stick, and wait, desperately, for her to let me go.

66 Signs That the Former Student Who Invited You to Dinner Is Trying to Seduce You

LORI SODERLIND

This piece, from PMS poemmemoirstory, *is structured as a list, a neat trick that lets the writer view an entire evening through a single analytical lens.*

1. She is an older student, and you have heard somewhere that she is married but you have never seen her husband and she has never worn a ring.

2. When she invited you to dinner, she didn't ask if you planned to bring a friend.

3. You did ask her if there was something you could bring, wine or a cheesecake for instance. She said, "just yourself."

4. As you think of this now, dressing to go to your former student's apartment, you struggle seemingly without reason to decide what pair of shoes is most appropriate. Chunky boots? Skateboard punk sneakers with broken laces? Your "Jesus sandals" with the leather straps that show your, well, your sort of cute toes? You choose professorial loafers and hope that they don't look too grave.

5. You wonder why you are wondering about this.

6. When you arrive at her apartment, the Billie Holiday disc is already playing. The apartment is well appointed, though small, and immaculately kept. The ceilings and doors and windows are all very high and the room is airy; the family photographs are all professional portraits. The carpet is plush. You sense that you are impressed.

7. The very short tour she gives of her apartment begins in the bedroom. In fact it involves looking at the unusual door to the bathroom, which is off the bedroom, and this leaves you standing in the bedroom right next to the bed. And you notice the bed, that it is neatly made without a wrinkle in the covers, very clean and not slept in. You notice the bed is the primary feature of the bedroom, that it faces out through open French doors, across the living room to the very tall windows, so that if you were lying in it you would have a fifth floor view of the lights of this small city. And it occurs to you that you could walk naked without a care in the bedroom with the French doors open and the view of the city staring back at you because the city is such a quiet and empty place at night that there would be no one out there to see you. You could be jumping on that bed naked and no one would see. You know that no one would see because you know the city is empty because in three years living there and teaching college classes there you have met so few people that you really care for, and you have been a little lonely as a result.

8. You realize you are staring at the bed, and that she is no longer talking about the bathroom.

9. You comment out loud about the view of the city through the tall windows across the living room and you quickly head for them and stare out. When you notice she is no longer standing near you, you go off toward the kitchen, where she has begun preparing a meal.

10. She slides a wine bottle down the counter and casually hands you the corkpuller as if opening the bottle has been your role in the

kitchen with her for seven years or more of happy marriage. She asks, as she places the corkpuller in your hand, "Would you?"

11. You do.

12. The wine is cheap and from her native country. She laments that there are so few wines from her native country available in yours. You remember that when the whole class (you invited them all, not just her) came to your house for dinner you served them soda. In plastic cups. You fill the glasses with the cheap foreign wine.

13. You ask her about the exam she had in a music theory class that caused her to cut the last day of your own class so that she could study. You deliberately use the word "cut" and tap your professorial loafer as you say this, briefly restoring your sense of control. You remember that you are a mere adjunct professor and that she is a returning student very close to your age and she is not saying any of the self-conscious things you would be saying if you were cooking in front of someone else.

14. You remember that you are never really in control, not even in the classroom.

15. You notice her legs and wonder if she wore shorts for a reason, since it is not very hot outside, and then you notice her shoes. They are not loafers. They are sandals. They show the tips of her little, painted toes.

16. Her toes wiggle and you look somewhere else immediately.

17. She reveals that her husband lives in Chicago, which you know to be about a thousand miles away.

18. You feel somehow embarrassed that you forgot about the husband. You consider that maybe they just don't believe in wearing rings; now that she mentions him you remember the husband from a class discussion. And with that memory the whole scene changes. You discreetly rub your eyes with the thumb and index finger of one hand and try to restore a sense of reality to the situation. Reality is really nicely dull. You hope you have not been sending her inappropriate sig-

nals; perhaps she sensed your tension from the moment you came in and stared at her bed, you creep. You are relieved and a little embarrassed to realize you misunderstood what you were not sure you understood in the first place, let's just forget it.

19. You glance at the unslept-in bed that is partly visible from the kitchen, like a leg glimpsed through a half-open door, and you rub your eyes again. You were her teacher, forgodsake!

20. She says as she stirs at the stove that her marriage is rather unconventional.

21. She begins telling an interesting story about how the faculty of the women's studies department, in which she is a major, is self-conscious about the reputation that all women's studies majors are lesbians and that the chair is thrilled whenever married women come into the program; they like to trot them out at functions.

22. You wonder if she even knows you are a lesbian, much less someone she could be setting up for some kind of tawdry lust-filled thing you keep realizing you are trying not to think about. You think, "of course she doesn't know!" You never mentioned it, after all. You feel great walls of sexual ambiguity growing right up around you and you sit at the kitchen table and cross your legs and swing your loafer. You feel almost smug. You are so mysterious.

23. She is still stirring and not looking up and she says, what a riot that women's studies chair is, presuming a woman is heterosexual just because she's married.

24. You swing your loafer faster.

25. ". . . because even my husband knows that I am a lesbian," she is saying, as she stirs.

26. You nod your head thoughtfully and your loafer drops and as she turns to look at you her expression sort of suggests, "could anyone doubt it?" She waits for you to look equally dumbfounded. She waits for you to shake your head at how crazy it is to think any woman anywhere could possibly not be a lesbian. She waits for you to agree with

her that every woman everywhere should know there's nothing like being with another woman baby, yeah baby, like you and me baby right here. Right now. Let's go.

27. You ask her if she watched the recent political convention on TV. You suck down a mouthful of wine.

28. She returns to her cooking.

29. The plates are on the small table in the kitchen where you have been sitting while she cooks. She has remembered that you are a vegetarian and has made a creamy meatless meal. It is fine. The sun goes down and she lights a large candle in molded glass.

30. You keep trying to talk about politics. The conversation keeps drifting back to female sexuality.

31. You repeatedly surprise yourself by being so candid with a former student about female sexuality. You wonder if she has noticed that you are no longer sounding like a professional educator, but more like a life guard at an all-lesbian beach party. You keep trying to suppress unexpected references to casual sex.

32. She tells you a story about a gay man she knows who spent six months in Italy and had sex twice a week with a stranger he met in a bar who spoke no English and her friend speaks no Italian but somehow, she isn't sure how they arranged it, they just knew that twice a week they would meet and go home with each other and fuck.

33. She asks if you think women can just do it like that. You know, just fuck. Without strings.

34. It is clue number 33 that really gets you thinking.

35. "The Italians just elected a whole new parliament, didn't they?" you say.

36. Yes. Well. She says she doesn't really think sex can be that anonymous for women. It's always necessary for women to talk, at least eventually. Do you agree?

37. In your heart, you know that you do not agree; you know that there are women who make a hobby of seduction and probably put

lipstick hashmarks on their bathroom mirrors to tally up every trick they can get in and out of their bed without speaking even once. But you do not say this. You begin to explain instead that you actually feel strongly that casual sex is not a feminist value despite the poster campaign of the early '90s that showed all those young sleek beautiful pairs of lesbians climbing over each other in assorted steamy positions, and indeed, despite one or two lapses in your own case history that you don't care to get into, the point is that you personally are not very promiscuous, you tell her, and you cross your legs.

38. She says, "define promiscuous."

39. You look thoughtful for a moment as you try to get clear in your head whether you are having a great debate with an intelligent woman or you are being seduced.

40. When you inevitably ask her to show you one of the many interesting essays she has referred to over the past two and a half hours of talk about female sexuality, feminist values and Italian politics, she rises and hurries into her living room. She seems to be spending a long time looking for a book in her shelves. When it becomes apparent that she is not coming back into the kitchen, you rise and go to the living room to rescue yourself from the fidgety wait. She finds the book, and instead of returning to the nice square table across which you had been talking, she flops herself on the couch, shedding the open-toe shoes, tucking her legs up beneath her body.

41. You stare at the couch for a moment, with her on one end, and an empty place at the other end, and the curtain across the stage of your life rises to reveal a cast of characters and a gallery of scenes of infamous past couch moments.

42. You take five steps and sit down in a chair next to the couch. It is positioned so that you are essentially reading safely over her shoulder, looking at the book she has drawn from the shelves. This seems natural. You become distinctly aware that you are taking special pains to look natural. It is getting harder to do.

43. As you read from the book together your tension mounts. But now it is a tension directly related to your growing sense that it will be very difficult to get out of this room.

44. You realize that you have, in fact, decided that you want to leave the room, and once you know this you also know that you must do it at the soonest possible opportunity.

45. There is no longer anything casual in the conversation. You are clipped, monosyllabic, done. Each word fumbles for the clasp on this moment, seeking release. Your lips are pursed, like there is something in your mouth you are trying to hide. What is in your mouth is your life. You fear for your life. You slap your thighs emphatically, once and with finality. "Well." You smile at her. "My dog will be angry if I don't get home soon."

46. You know that there is something unfortunate about your choice of exit lines but you console yourself by remembering that it's true.

47. You stand. You begin preparations for takeoff. You are saying a number of things about the good meal and the nice evening and the fine wine from her native country; after two sentences you have no idea really what the fuck you are saying but you keep making the noise while you wait for her to join in the parting rituals and show you to the door.

48. She stands there in front of you, saying nothing.

49. As you continue to speak you scan the room and see that you are boxed in by the chair, the couch and the standing former student. You must pass one of these in order to leave.

50. You continue finding ways to say thank you and you put your hands in your pockets to search, distinctly and perhaps even dramatically, for your keys. You jingle the keys in your pocket as if it will distract her long enough to step around her. You step around her, very carefully avoiding any chance of looking into her pouting, expectant

face. You turn sharp right at the French doors that lead into the very-prominent-bed room, where the bed seems to be straining to run after you but can't force itself to move, and you pick up speed with the straining bed and the pouting former student close behind, and you head down the homestretch to the hall.

51. When you reach the door, you work the lock yourself, and you say, "thank you for a very nice evening," as you step through the door and then and only then, you turn around.

52. She smiles faintly and says, "Yes, well, nice talking to you."

53. During the thirty-minute drive home from your former student's apartment, you find yourself visualizing her naked, slightly overweight body, and how it would feel to see her smiling and looking up from a pillow completely thrilled to be naked with you at last and how she would be soft to lie down on and press hard against and you shake your head fast.

54. You imagine it again.

55. It is after midnight when you get home. The dog looks up and is completely thrilled to see you, as he is every single time you come home, and you begin scratching his ears with frantic affection and he is dancing like a 60-pound Chihuahua on his hind legs with his leash in his mouth and you are about to live happily ever after.

56. The phone rings.

57. You walk over to the phone on the third ring, pick it up and say hello cheerily, and motion to the dog to sit still and stop jumping up and down with the leash in his mouth. He sits and drops the leash and listens.

58. "Oh," you say, "hello," as if there was even a remote chance you could be surprised, as if you might have even possibly expected it to be someone else.

59. She tells you that she had been thinking and decided that it's best to be honest, rather than to keep this to herself and always won-

der what you might have said, had she told you; that is to say (and here she seems nervous for the first time) she wants to tell you that she has developed these feelings . . .

60. You think, "I can handle this. I can handle this." You are aware of the possibility of three to five years in a sordid relationship with a married woman who is a former student all because you couldn't handle The Phone Call.

61. And she proceeds to say sweet and most sincerely flattering words to you, and you really take it in because her choice of words is so original, and kind. You wish that as her writing teacher you had been responsible for this proficiency with the English language but you know that the outpouring has come directly from her own heart and you can take no credit.

62. So you are not lying when you tell her that you admire her for saying what she has said, because it was bold and brave and it was said so nicely. But it is equally true that there is no possibility for romance here, and that is what you say.

63. You realize of course that there has already been romance.

64. You talk for a few minutes about why it would be impossible, and she accepts the answer with grace, and you thank her one more time for dinner before you say goodnight, and listen to her accented voice as it echoes yours, "good night," and you hang up the phone.

65. Do all teachers fantasize that their students will fall in love with them? Is this what it is like? As you lay in bed putting off sleep for a few minutes of reflection, you wonder how it could be, if you're the teacher, that you had actually been so dumb as to think she was "just" inviting you to dinner.

66. And then you remember that you have always loved teaching precisely because, to do it, there is so much you have to learn.

Wild Flavor

KARL TARO GREENFELD

"One of the reasons I became a writer is because of a desire to enter-tain," says Karl Taro Greenfeld. "Yet so much journalism and non-fiction is written to educate or inform, and the notion of entertainment is reduced to clever turns of phrase or similes. That's not really entertainment, that's verbiage." This story, from the Paris Review, *communicates a great deal of information about economic development in China, and its ramifications, through the story of one man.*

Fang Lin woke to the usual din: the bleat of a truck reversing; the steady, metallic tattoo of a jackhammer; the whining buzz of a steel saw; the driving in of nails; the slapping down of bricks; the irregular thumping—like sneakers in a dryer—of a cement mixer. Up and down the coast, from Shenzhen to Fuzhou to Shanghai to Tian-jin, this was what you heard. They were building—a skyscraper, a shopping mall, a factory, a new highway, an overpass, a subway, a train

station—here, there, everywhere. Fang Lin had just arrived in Shenzhen and already he was accustomed to the ubiquitous cacophony, as
regular and familiar as the breath in his nostrils.

Fang Lin was the son of rice farmers from Nanpo Village in Jiangxi
Province. He'd come of age during the era of reforms. The Cultural
Revolution and the Great Helmsman were no more relevant to his life
than Genghis Khan. Even the great events of his childhood were
shrouded in the obfuscating gauze of prehistory. To Fang Lin, Tianan-
men was just a square in Beijing and Mao was the guy on the money.
And it was money that mattered now. Mao—or was it Deng?—had
said it himself: "To get rich is glorious." Fang Lin's parents recalled the
hardships of China's great upheavals in the 1950s and '60s and were
grateful to be allowed, in exchange for payoffs to local officials, to
own and farm their ancestral plot; to slaughter their own chickens,
ducks, and pigs; and to trade their own rice harvest. After decades of
sacrifice and poverty, they'd bought a color television and were saving
for a mobile phone. They could eat as much pork as they wanted and
watch pirated Hong Kong action pictures on their video-CD player—
and they were thrilled. But Fang Lin and his contemporaries were not
content to gaze at other people's better lives on TV. They wanted to
have those lives.

When a cultivator gives up farming for some other kind of work, it
is called *li tu*—"to leave the land"—which suggests a kind of exile. For
Fang Lin, the decision was easy. As the second son in his family, he
didn't stand to inherit any land. It would all go to his older brother
and his brother's wife, a village girl with bad skin who seemed to
go through a box of Choco Pies every day. Fang Lin warned that
she would become fat, but there had been no fat people before the
reforms—the whole country had subsisted on a starvation diet—
and in his parents' peasant eyes even obesity appeared a virtue. But
although there was food in the village, there was no money. The
money was in the south, along the coasts, in the boomtowns that

appeared on television. China was becoming rich around the edges while it stayed poor in the middle. So people in the hinterlands were hitting the road, hopping a bus, truck, or train to the coast and seeking employment in a factory or a construction crew, a restaurant or a brothel. The newspapers called the migration the Hundred Million Man March. Someone from Nanpo seemed to set out every day, especially after the harvest in early winter.

FANG LIN BORROWED five hundred yuan (about sixty dollars) from his brother, packed his extra shirt in a vinyl duffel bag, and walked out of town to the road that ran along the river. He thumbed a ride with a truck, buying the driver a bowl of noodles at a gas station. Then he caught a local bus south to Nanchang, where he paid a hundred yuan for the upper berth on a sleeper bus to Shenzhen. He lay in his bunk and watched the TV mounted in the roof above the driver, but soon the bus was so thick with cigarette smoke that Fang Lin could barely make out the newscaster.

He rode for thirty-six hours. In the night the villages gradually gave way to county seats and the rough farmland yielded to workshops and factories. By morning, Fang Lin was in Guangzhou, rolling south along the Guanshen Highway past multiacre industrial compounds with corrugated-metal-roofed workshops that were bigger than his whole village. Entire mountains appeared to have been hollowed out for gravel and cement. There were stretches where the landscape was practically lunar: just a few stones and, hunched amid swirling dust, a handful of shacks made of scavenged wood and cloth. Occasionally, a family farm would appear to be holding out between the encroaching factories and construction sites, its crop—usually tropical fruit—obscured by a thick coating of dust.

Fang Lin saw all this and he thought it was beautiful. Amazing. Progress. Soon there would be no more farms at all. Just factories as far as the eye could see. How many people worked on a farm—one, maybe two? But in a factory, he could not begin to count.

At the central bus station in Shenzhen, he found a pay phone beside a cigarette stand and called a number he had for two other Nanpo boys who had come south, Du Chan and Huang Po. In his thick Jiangxi accent he asked the woman who answered if he could leave word for his friends. She told him he could leave a message, but it would only be delivered if the recipients were willing to pay a yuan for it.

"Why would anyone pay if they don't know who it's from?" Fang Lin asked.

"How would we make any money from this otherwise?" she shot back. "If it's important, he'll pay for the message."

Fang Lin told her who he was and that he would be arriving shortly. He doubted anyone would ever pick up the message. He bought a pack of cigarettes and a bottle of sweet lemon tea. He showed a slip of paper with his friends' address on it to the cigarette seller, who told Fang Lin to follow the signs south toward the border with Hong Kong. He set off on foot, stopping every few minutes to show his slip of paper to another pedestrian. Few understood his accent, but they could read the paper and point him in the right direction.

He was disappointed by the buildings here. He had imagined they would be taller, grander. But these were no higher than those in Nanchang, the provincial capital of Jiangxi. And the roads were no wider here. And the people seemed no better dressed. But there was more of everything: more tall buildings, more wide streets, more pedestrians. There were more shops, selling more clothes, more televisions, more VCDs, and more fake-fur coats. There were more rich people and more bums. More cripples and more whores. And there were more migrants. Half the people he asked for directions couldn't help him because they were new to Shenzhen themselves.

By the time Fang Lin found his way to where his fellow villagers were supposed to be bivouacked he was thirsty and hungry and the neighborhood was swathed in darkness, the narrow alleys and dirt lanes obscured by smoke and steam. In a corner storefront, a woman sat behind a counter flanked by five booths in which five different men were shouting into phones. Fang Lin showed her his slip of paper. She read the names, nodded, and told him the charge would be one yuan. He paid and she handed him the phone message he had left for his friends earlier that day. At least that meant he was in the right place.

Fang Lin kept asking around and was told by another migrant from Jiangxi that Du Chan and Huang Po had gone north to find work in a factory that made the machines that make sewing machines. He didn't know anyone else in Shenzhen, but from the voices around him he could tell that many other men from western Jiangxi had preceded him and he took comfort in the familiar. From a stall set up on a narrow alley, he ordered a plate of chicken intestines, scallions, and red peppers—a Jiangxi dish—and a bottle of beer, which he shared with two other fellows he had just met. In turn, they offered to share their room with him. They charged him ten yuan and told him to bring some one yuan coins along to feed the meter box that provided the room with electricity by the hour.

That night in his sleeping pallet on the floor, Fang Lin turned away from his roommates and thrust his red plastic wallet into the crotch of his pants. When he woke, his roommates had already left. They had rummaged through his duffel bag and taken his cigarettes. His wallet was safe between his legs.

SHENZHEN WAS ONCE not so different from Nanpo—a rice-farming village with a few thousand residents. Then in 1979 it was designated China's first special economic zone. When Fang Lin arrived, twenty years later, metropolitan Shenzhen sprawled over seven hundred square miles and was inhabited by seven million people. The central government's plans for the city had all been rendered obsolete before they could be implemented, as wave after wave of migrants swamped the planners' ambitions. Millions of the city's new residents had arrived without the proper permits to live in a special economic zone; they survived in a legal limbo, tolerated as long as they could be exploited by local officials, manufacturers, and land-lords. The city had no choice but to embrace the chaos, as thousands of new buildings were put up and thousands of miles of new road were laid down every year. Shenzhen became the richest city per capita in China and its population, with an average age of twenty-five, among the youngest in the world.

At ground level, in the shopping malls and restaurants, the first impression of Shenzhen's boom was the sheer volume of goods and services that were on sale. Chinese advertising was still pretty much all about bargains—there was very little aspirational marketing—so in Shenzhen the plastic surgeons promised cheaper eyes, lips, and breasts, rather than better, and for every Dunhill or Louis Vuitton boutique, there were a thousand no-name shops operating out of retail space let by the day or week. Although Shenzhen sits atop Hong Kong, it had become, in many ways, Hong Kong's underbelly.

Emporia the size of football fields were given over to cheap plas-tic toys, cut-rate kitchenware, stuffed animal zoos, and narrow aluminum-pan alleys, making Shenzhen seem like a ninety-nine-cent store ballooned into a city-state. There were enough crappy vinyl purses to have outfitted the entire Brezhnev-era Soviet Union and, it seemed, enough nail clippers for every toe in town and a hairbrush for every strand of hair. Everything was on sale, all the time. Suggest a price, any price, the vendors would meet it or beat it. Everywhere you looked, Hong Kong families were returning from the surrounding fac-tories with all manner of household goods loaded onto wagons—new storm windows, heaters, blenders, car radios, tires. Money in Shen-zhen was made on volume. The attitude was: sell as much as you can today because more of everything is arriving tomorrow from factories up and down the Pearl River Delta.

In China in the last years of the twentieth century and the early years of the twenty-first, the greatest mass urbanization in history coincided with, and perhaps catalyzed, one of the most vertiginous economic booms. It was a time of incessant multiplication, of more piled upon more, and nowhere was the superabundance greater than in the Pearl River Delta. As China's economy grew by nearly ten percent a year through the late nineties, entire swaths of Pearl River marsh and paddy lands were drained to make room for factories and container ports. Consider that there were more than a hundred and twenty car companies in China, more than two million trucking companies, and hundreds of vacuum cleaner and television manufacturers; that, according to one estimate, China manufactured enough televisions to replace the entire global supply every two years; that fifty percent of the world's phones were made there and at least thirty percent of the world's microwave ovens. Look around your home: that frying pan, blender, coffeemaker, hair dryer, sewing machine, shower curtain, doormat, flowerpot, pencil sharpener, ballpoint pen, broom, mop, and bucket—all were made in the Middle Kingdom, probably in the Pearl River Delta, where more is always good and cheaper is always best.

THE TYCOONS OF more—the factory owners, the landlords, the real-estate brokers, the pimps, the party officials, the scalpel cowboys doing four dozen eye-jobs a day—defined the tastes of the boom by the way they spent their money. They spent it on mah-jongg and Audi automobiles and karaoke girls and cognac in ceramic bottles cast in the shape of Napoleon on his rearing steed. They spent it at a brothel in Dongguan, reputed to be the world's largest, which had a choice of more than a thousand women on display behind a glass viewing wall.

And they spent it on wild flavor—the cuisine so emblematic of China's new conspicuous consumption that Chinese spoke of the boom years as the Era of Wild Flavor.

Southern Chinese have always eaten their way through the far reaches of the animal kingdom more adventurously than others, but during the Era of Wild Flavor the sheer variety and volume of creatures they consumed came to include virtually any obtainable species of land, sea, or air. Wild flavor was supposed to give you face, to bring you luck, to make you *fan rong*. *Fan rong*, which means "prosperous," had become the preferred term in the Pearl River Delta to denote anything that was cool. And *fan rong* could get extreme: there were rumors that for the right price one could order a soup made from human babies, which imbued the diner with fantastic virility. The rumors told you that nothing was out of bounds. Restaurants opened daily offering an ever-wider range of snakes and lizards, camels and dogs, monkeys and otters. Hunters as far away as Indonesia, Thailand, and Canada became the front end of a supply chain that met the demand of Chinese traders hungry for the empowering wild flavor of tiger penises from Sumatra and black bear gallbladders from Manitoba.

The director of Wild Animal Protection at the Guangzhou Forestry Bureau, Lian Junhao, told me that in 2003 Guangzhou alone had two thousand wild flavor restaurants. The Forestry Bureau has regulatory authority over these restaurants, but the number seemed too round to believe. When I pressed him, he admitted, "Nobody really knows how many there are." I spent an hour in his office and in that time he issued four licenses for new wild flavor restaurants. Before I left, he mentioned that the Forestry Bureau had imposed a ban on selling snakes in Guangzhou, but an hour later I was standing in front of a writhing bag of cobras at a wild flavor stall at Xinyuan market. I counted twenty-five burlap sacks of snakes at this stall alone and there were at least twenty more stalls specializing in snakes in the market.

Ten years ago, when I first visited these markets, there had been about thirty stalls in all, selling a wide variety of wild animals. During that trip I ordered snake, turtle, and boar, all of which went from the seller to the carving board to the pot right before my eyes. The meat was served at a communal table beneath a corrugated-fiberglass roof. The boar was disappointingly flavorless, but the rest—washed down with green beer—was excellent. The atmosphere of the market was genial. Kids chased each other between the animal cages and women sat around on stools, chatting as they washed vegetables. Walking between the stalls, you could look up and see stars.

Now this style of dining, which was once a quaint local custom, had become industrialized. In one cage at Xinyuan I counted fifty-two cats packed so tightly that their guts were spilling out between the wire bars. There were fifty such cages in that stall. There were fifty-two stalls along that row of vendors. There were six rows of vendors in that market. And there were seven markets on that street.

A sharp, musky smell overwhelmed me—the excrement of a thousand different animal species mingling with their panicked breath. I saw at least a dozen types of dogs, including Labradors and Saint Bernards, and there had to be at least as many different breeds of house cat. There were raccoons, dogs, badgers, civets, squirrels, deer, boars, rats, guinea pigs, pangolins, muskrats, ferrets, wild sheep, mountain goats, bobcats, monkeys, horses, ponies, and a camel out in the parking lot. And these were just the mammals. The choice of birds and reptiles was every bit as diverse. Predator was sometimes stacked atop prey. Damaged animals—those that had lost a paw, say—were kept alive with intravenous drips. And because wild animals were more valuable than farm-raised creatures, I was told that some traders would slice off the hind paw of a civet or badger to make it appear to potential buyers that the animal had been trapped in the wild.

I had brought a list of banned animals from the Wild Animal Protection Office. I asked for the rare bird species, the monkeys, the tigers.

"No problem," I was told by a smiling trader with buckteeth who said he was from Guangxi.

"What about the authorities?" I asked.

"No problem." He pointed to a fellow in a gray and blue uniform sitting on a white plastic chair, flicking his cigarette ashes by a bag of banned snakes.

"OK, how about mountain lion?"

"No problem."

"Black bear?"

"No problem."

I decided to push my luck.

"How about panda?"

He shook his head. "You must be sick."

ON HIS FIRST morning in Shenzhen, Fang Lin explored his new neighborhood. Ka-Ta, or the Click, was a perfect grid of sixty-four white-and-pink-tiled, eight-story buildings. The Click had got its name from the electricity meters that ticked away outside most apartments. Due to the peculiarities of Chinese zoning laws, the neighborhood was technically a distinct village and remained under the jurisdiction of the farming cooperative that had owned the land when the special economic zone was formed. Elsewhere in Shenzhen, city planners, politicians, and architects controlled construction practically by fiat, but the farmers in charge here had contracted independently with a real-estate developer to put up these housing blocks for the zone's rapidly expanding middle class. But the developers had left so little space between buildings that the Click was forever shrouded in darkness and there was little chance of attracting such dream tenants. The narrow, unpaved alleys were bathed in fluorescent light day and night—except at high noon on sunny days when the sudden appearance of yellowish natural light was almost confusing.

During the damp summer months, the Click's pathways turned to streambeds and even in winter they remained soggy. The neighborhood's original plan had provided for commercial space in each ground-floor corner unit, but enterprising tenants had rented other ground-floor apartments then punched their way through the brick walls facing the alleys to create prime, street-front retail space. In the absence of urban zoning laws, there was little anyone could do to restrain such sledgehammer capitalism. Many of the apartments had been subdivided into smaller one-room units, some without water or even windows. Electricity was pirated through jury-rigged lines, and once a month ChinaGas workers arrived in groups of ten to snip away illegal cables, which quickly grew back like vines. The interiors of the buildings had been similarly modified with power lines and broadband cables nailed to the walls in tangled masses that occasionally emitted bright showers of sparks. There were buckets of sand deposited at every landing in case of fire, but these were so full of cigarette butts that one wondered how they would contain a blaze.

Illicit commerce thrived in the alleys of the Click. There were several small piecework factories of three sewing machines each; the workers slept under their machines at night. There were four shoe repairmen and a man who converted old tires into sandals. There were a half-dozen key duplicators and no fewer than a dozen doctors in one-room practices—fifty-square-foot storefronts that usually featured a bench covered with newspapers, a cabinet full of pills, maybe a diploma on the wall, and a stool on which the M.D. sat smoking cigarettes. The doctors all specialized in treating venereal diseases and a frightening few also practiced cut-rate plastic surgery. But it was easy to bypass the doctors and head straight for any of the half-dozen pharmacies that did a thriving business in aphrodisiacs and antibiotics. There were barber poles swirling red, white, and blue—a beacon that very often marks a brothel—and hookers in skintight Lycra pants and tube tops would grab your arm as you walked past. There were the pay-by-the-call phone centers, the pay-by-the-hour hotels, and the pay-by-the-tablet ecstasy dealers. You could buy anything in the Click in the smallest possible increment: one cigarette, one nail, one phone call, one injection, one sheet of paper, one envelope, one stamp, one match, one stick of gum, one bullet, one brick, one bath, one shave, one battery, even one feel.

The disorderly, bursting, subterranean energy of the Click made it a perfect microcosm of Shenzhen. Everyone was winging it. Many residents didn't even know their addresses. Their telephone, if they had one, was a mobile. If a message were truly important it would be text-messaged to them via their phones. They'd be moving in a week or two or three, so what would be the point of giving out an address? And since the floor plans and roadways were as impermanent as sand castles, it was impossible for the police to keep tabs. But the city, in some sense, thrived on this chaos. There were certainly risks—I was robbed in Shenzhen twice—but for the quick-witted and flexible, there were great rewards. You may not know where you are going, but neither did anyone else.

One afternoon in Shenzhen, I decided to look at a few apartments, reckoning that it might be cheaper to rent a place than stay in hotels. I walked into a realtor's office where the broker said he had several apartments that might interest me, one of them in the Click. He borrowed a set of car keys from another broker and we set off in a rented Hyundai. After a few minutes' drive, I noticed that we kept passing the same giant video display terminal on which a plastic surgeon was promising a "cheaper, bigger, more womanly bust."

"Where are we going?" I asked the broker.

He explained that he wanted to show me a small apartment in Laohu.

"But why are we going in circles?"

He shrugged.

I asked my real estate broker when he had arrived in Shenzhen. "Two days ago," he said.

MAO ONCE SAID that environmental woes affected only capitalist countries. In that regard, China's transformation to a market economy was complete. In the Pearl River Delta the normal color of the sky was a smudged brown; in Shenzhen on most days it looked like it was about to rain. You noticed the pollution first as an itchiness in the eyes, then a sore throat, and finally a hacking cough that stayed with you throughout your visit—or, if you stayed long enough, landed you in the hospital, where doctors had observed a steady increase in respiratory diseases. Similarly crime, which was also dismissed as an ailment of the decadent West, had surged in China. In Shenzhen in 2003 a police officer claimed that kidnappings were up seventy-five percent and murders were up thirty-five percent. Some of these murders were the work of serial killers, who have proliferated amid the migratory flux of China's boom. In a three-week period last year, arrests were made in three unrelated serial murder cases. In Shenzhen the victims were eleven young women, in Henan they were seventeen boys, and in Hebei a man was arrested on suspicion of having killed sixty-five people in four provinces. In the damp, dark back-alleys of a migrant-workers ghetto like the Click, a killer could lurk without being discovered for a long time. During the Era of Wild Flavor, the biggest such killer turned out to be a virus—severe acute respiratory syndrome or, as it came to be known, SARS.

WE—HUMANS—HAVE always died in cities at greater rates and from more varied causes than we ever did as nomads or villagers. Mass urbanizations have always been accompanied by epidemics of emerging or reemerging diseases. Smallpox ravaged the great Roman cities; plague overwhelmed the cultural capitals of the Renaissance; the commercial centers of England's Industrial Revolution were bazaars for the swapping of cholera and tuberculosis bacilli; and Africa's urbanization may have been a key catalyst for the AIDS epidemic. Each of the four major modes of disease transmission—water, air, animal carriers, or human contact—is facilitated by urban life. And, in the early twenty-first century, China's health-care system was in a virtual state of collapse at the precise moment that its cities were being inundated and overwhelmed by new bodies.

In the Maoist past, rural Chinese could count on a few basic medical services, usually provided by the armies of so-called barefoot doctors who tromped through the countryside providing rudimentary care, setting broken bones, giving prenatal exams, and vaccinating children. This service, which was essentially free, helped bring about the virtual eradication of smallpox and sexually transmitted diseases in China and partially accounted for the near doubling of the country's life expectancy between 1949 and 1990. But with the sweeping economic reforms of the past decade, health care in China was privatized as rapidly as the country industrialized. Today, fewer than thirty percent of Chinese have health insurance and for the uninsured in China, just like their counterparts in America, this system has meant the end of preventive care. Tuberculosis and hepatitis B have been allowed to spread largely unchecked; AIDS had afflicted a million Chinese before the government declared it a national health crisis; asthma, exacerbated by air pollution, afflicted as many as one in four children in the Pearl River Delta. In the cities, doctors saw outbreaks of diseases they hadn't encountered in a generation: schistosomiasis, measles, meningitis, dengue fever, malaria, and encephalitis.

Measles needs a population of at least seven thousand susceptible individuals in order to maintain a chain of infection. Shenzhen's migrant neighborhoods could provide many more receptive immune systems than that. Unvaccinated migrants were arriving every day, ensuring a perpetual supply of meat for a new epidemic. In such communities, where roommates often don't even know each other's names, it would be extremely difficult to trace a disease outbreak back to its origins or determine who should be vaccinated or quarantined.

Everyone in the Click seemed to have a hacking cough. For those who suffered, the primary objective was to stay out of the hospital where a bed for the night could cost half a month's wages even before any intravenous drips or special tests might be added to the bill. So the alleyways of the Click were lined with the offices of doctors who would have you open up, say ahhh, and sell you a box of pills. And if you were really sick, you handed over a few more yuan and the barefoot doctor, who now had shoes, would jab a needle full of antibiotics into your ass. (Who knows how many potential measles outbreaks have been thwarted in this manner?) So many residents subsisted in a perpetual state of low-level illness that Fang Lin thought nothing of it when he came down with a cold during his first months in town.

FANG LIN HAD settled in a building that housed mostly Jiangxi natives and he quickly discovered that jobs and trades tended to be divvied up according to one's province of origin. People from Henan, for example, were into waste hauling and recycling, while most shoe repairmen and key duplicators came from Anhui. The construction trades were dominated by Fujianese and Guangdongese, Uighurs opened restaurants or set up begging networks, and men from Zhejiang generally became garment workers. And for those from Jiangxi it was easiest to find work in restaurants as dishwashers or busboys or "cut-men," who were hired to chop ingredients. New restaurants opened every day throughout Shenzhen and within forty-eight hours of his arrival Fang Lin had found a job working at one managed by three brothers from Sichuan.

He had cut his hair so short his scalp showed through. This allowed him to economize on showers, which cost a yuan each. With his wide forehead, bulging brown eyes, sturdy nose, and thick lips, the crew cut made him appear almost menacing—until his stutter and diffidence betrayed him. A few weeks after his arrival in Shenzhen he called his parents. His mother was excited. She reported that his grandparents had made a down payment on a burial site—a south-facing plot close to the village with very good feng shui, an auspicious starting point for the afterlife. Fang Lin heard his mother's pride and knew what was coming next—the cost, eight thousand yuan. The plot was bought on an installment plan, his mother explained, so Fang Lin need not worry that his grandparents' souls would go wandering for lack of worldly funds. After his grandparents' down payment of five hundred yuan, the family had to make monthly payments for the next four years of two hundred and twenty-two yuan. Even the number was good luck, his mother pointed out. "That's good news," he said before hanging up. But he understood. He was the only member of the family who earned cash instead of, say, rice or coupons for rice. He would bear the burden.

WALKING HOME ALONG Dongmen Road, Fang Lin saw that a nightclub, which had featured Russian girls when he came to town, was being torn down. Already a new building was going up in its place. The sign on the construction sight promised "International Commerce." Fang Lin walked past a Häagen Dazs shop and turned down a narrow alley on his way back to the Click. There was a wild flavor restaurant at this corner called Heartiness and Happiness. It, too, was expanding. The spirit of more was irresistible in Shenzhen. Fang Lin had his own dreams: to smoke Panda cigarettes and slap down mahjongg tiles while he talked on a flip-phone with a camera function. He wanted to sing karaoke with Korean girls in slit dresses and drink ten-year-old grain liquor. And, like so many in the Delta, he dreamed of feasting on wild flavor. He read through the Heartiness and Happiness menu and wondered what camel hump tasted like. He'd had pangolin, but what about marmoset? Or badger? And what was a turtle-fish? When the menu offered monkey brains, did that really mean the brains of a monkey? Or was that a euphemism, the way they wrote phoenix instead of chicken?

"Do you want a job?" a woman asked. Fang Lin saw that she wore gold earrings and a pearl necklace. When he didn't respond the woman asked, in the flat tones of a Jiangxi accent, where he was from. When he told her, she clapped her hands together sharply, a sudden gesture that caused Fang Lin to jump back a step. "I already have two boys from there," she said.

Fang Lin asked, "What's the job?"

"Assistant driver," she said.

"How much?"

"Seven hundred a month."

Fang Lin nodded.

"Come back and meet the boys."

She led Fang Lin through the restaurant, the kitchen, and a darkened, fetid menagerie of caged animals to a narrow dirt lot. A diesel truck stood next to a pen in which two peacocks and a boar were tied to pegs driven into the earth. Sitting there on concrete steps, drinking dense tea from plastic mugs, were his old friends, Du Chan and Huang Po.

To have found his fellow villagers and a new job on the same afternoon made Fang Lin think that perhaps—despite the cost of his grandparents' burial plot—his luck was changing. Over cigarettes, Du Chan and Huang Po described the job to Fang Lin: how they rode with the drivers, collected the animals from local markets and farms, unloaded them at the restaurant, and then slaughtered them as the chefs called out the orders.

They showed Fang Lin the animal pens, the peacocks, and the boars—very *fan rong* they all agreed. Then they took him around the other side of the truck where there was a giant bird with feathers two feet long.

"What's that?" Fang Lin asked.

The animal was coated in dust and snorted like a giant pig.

"Ostrich," Du Chen explained.

Every night the restaurant went through about a dozen pangolins, twenty badgers, two dozen civets (in winter, when they were in season), three dozen snakes, and a half-dozen lizards. You had to move fast with the badgers and the civets or they would take a bite out of you. In the winter, the lizards and snakes were usually too sluggish to be a problem. But just in case, the men wore thick rubber gloves.

IF THERE WAS a soundtrack to the Era of Wild Flavor, it was high-energy techno music. The relentlessly upbeat dance tracks poured from every karaoke bar, fitness club, barbershop boom box, and taxicab radio. Grannies playing mah-jongg in the back of noodle shops and old men smoking Cocopalm cigarettes in front of their knockoff handbag stalls had it cranked up to ten. No one seemed to know the names of any of the tawdry, yet infectious, songs. In fact, the CDs they played in Shenzhen were often pirated mixes. In other words, someone had ripped off someone who had sampled someone else and packed the compilation in a jewel box labeled: *Feel Good Music! Dance Forever! Wild Flavor Mix!* If this music were an edible substance it would be cotton candy injected with steroids. In Shenzhen's narrow streets and muddy alleys, while you were stepping over a legless man or skirting a woman picking rice from a trash can, there was something disconcerting about this much enforced feel-goodness.

Fang Lin barely heard the music even though it pounded through the cab of the Heartiness and Happiness truck as he and the driver, smoking Honghe cigarettes, made their rounds of the wild animal markets. The sound had become as familiar to him as the sound of jackhammering or drilling. Back in the restaurant's chopping room he would sometimes work his knife in time with the beat, though he never noticed when one song ended and another began.

It was hardly a surprise that the work left him insensate. The restaurant went through as many as two hundred animals a night. The high volume creatures—wild rats, cats, and dogs—were stacked near the kitchen. Snakes and other animals that might take a bite out of you were under the two fluorescent lights in the middle of the room, while more docile creatures, which could be extracted from their cages with less risk, were in the corners, further from the light. In the summer, the temperature in the kitchen would climb to a hundred and ten degrees. The only good thing about the heat was that it made most of the animals sluggish.

When an order was called out from the kitchen, Fang Lin picked through the wooden-and-mesh cages until he found the beast he needed. There was a specific technique for retrieving each animal. For a snake, one pinned the head until the tail could be located and used to swing the animal, smashing its skull against the brick floor. A lizard had to be thumped in the head with the fat part of a knife blade. Cats were easy: reach in with the thick rubber gloves, pull them out, and chop the head off; it usually took one clean blow with the cleaver. The female civets were easily extracted and decapitated. But the males could put up a fight. So one cut-man would pin the animal to the back of the cage while another would bind its legs with duct tape. Fang Lin would treat it like any other animal—pull it from its cage, skin it, bleed it, and separate the organs into those that were prized for their various invigorating properties and those deemed inedible or inauspicious. At last, it was ready for the hot pot. The chefs would further slice the animals according to their own recipes. Some dishes, like civet and snake, tended to be heavily seasoned, while rat, for example, was usually skinned, basted in sweetened soy sauce, grilled, and then chopped up like an order of barbecued pork. Occasionally an animal would get loose before the coup de grace was administered and the three cut-men would have to chase it through the chop room and the kitchen and—in one particularly frightening incident involving a wild boar—into the dining room of the restaurant itself.

By the end of the evening the floor of the chop room would be slick with blood and entrails and feces and animal urine. Fang Lin became used to all the noises—the construction, the music, and even the shrieks and screams of dying animals. But he never got used to the smell. He kept a cigarette lit constantly, clenched between his lips so that the trails of smoke were always pouring into his nostrils and obscuring some of the stench.

Between dishes, the chefs would stand beside their woks, smoking and slugging from screw-top jars of grain liquor. A couple of chefs sometimes expressed disgust at what Guangdong people were willing to eat. One night, when several of the chefs and cut-men were sitting around on the back steps passing a jar of grain liquor, a chef named Chou Pei looked at Fang Lin and said, "You've got blood on your face."

Fang Lin rubbed his cheek.

"Other side," Chou Pei said.

Fang Lin wiped the other cheek and his hand came away coated in blood. That entire side of his face, in fact, was covered with some animal's gore. He shrugged and wiped it off with his T-shirt.

"It's still there," said Chou Pei.

"What?" Fang Lin asked.

"The blood."

Fang Lin shrugged and wiped it again, this time smearing some of it into his eyes. It wasn't the first time one of the cut-men had got animal blood in his eyes or nose or down his throat. But what did it matter? People were paying a fortune for the stuff.

———

FANG LIN BEGAN to feel feverish at the end of the summer—or, as he put it, around the time the big Yao Ming advertisements for mobile phones started to appear on billboards around the city. After a day and a half, when the fever didn't break, he consulted a local physician, a man with one eye and a rusty stethoscope. Fang Lin described his symptoms: in addition to the fever, he had nasty diarrhea and his muscles ached when he woke in the morning. The doctor nodded and without saying a word removed a box of tablets from a glass case.

"How much?" Fang Lin asked.

"Five yuan each."

Fang Lin bought four tablets, swallowed two right there, and went to work. Riding around in the truck that day, he felt better but still feverish. At one point, as he was tossing caged animals into the truck, he felt so weak that he had to sit down. The driver offered him a cigarette.

"Here," he said. "That'll make you feel better."

Fang Lin made it through the day and night, when he told his colleagues in the chop room that he didn't feel well, and they offered to cover for him. But there was no way that just two of them could do the job without slowing down the kitchen, so Fang Lin kept on chopping, although he often had to pause to catch his breath. He took frequent cigarette breaks.

The next evening, when he sat down on the back steps for a cigarette break he couldn't get up. The fever had climbed—he guessed his temperature had reached a hundred and three—and no matter how deeply he breathed, Fang Lin felt perpetually winded. His body ached no matter what position he stood or sat in; it felt as if his muscles were being pulled from his bones. When Du Chan found him and asked what was wrong, Fang Lin told him that he didn't know.

Chou Pei came out and handed Fang Lin a bottle of grain liquor. Fang Lin took a tiny sip and immediately vomited a stringy pool of yellow bile.

"You need to go," Du Chan told him.

Fang Lin nodded, but couldn't get up.

Du Chan and Chou Pei helped him to his feet and loaded him onto the back of a motorcycle taxi. Somehow, Fang Lin managed to hold on for the five-minute ride home. Even in his addled state he knew he needed medical help. He presented himself to another storefront doctor, who told him to stand still, then to stand on one leg. The doctor asked him where he ached and what he'd eaten in the last few days. He also asked where Fang Lin was born, whether his mother was taller than his father, and what direction his bed faced. As Fang Lin answered, the doctor ran his hands over Fang Lin's blood-stained shirt, gently squeezing his chest and arms. Finally, the doctor pronounced Fang Lin's chi to be unbalanced and advised him to face south more often. He also sold the patient vancomycin and proparacetamol tablets for fifty yuan and told him to drink a certain type of fungal tea that he sold by the can.

Fang Lin made it back to his north-facing room but he never went back to work. The medication did nothing to assuage his fever. On the contrary, for a time his temperature seemed to be rising. Twice he was unable to rouse himself from his sleeping pallet to reach the toilet in the hall, each time soiling his pants. He hadn't eaten in three days, he gasped for every breath, and he grew progressively more disoriented. In a state of near-hypoxia, he lost all track of time in the constant darkness of the Click. He was vaguely aware that his roommates were sometimes sleeping alongside him and their steady, deep breathing reminded him of how frantic and shallow his own breaths had become. Standing up was out of the question: even the slightest movement—rolling over or attempting to sit up—winded him completely. When he begged his roommates to open the window, they could not bring themselves to remind him that the room was windowless. Fang Lin managed to sip from the cans of herbal tea, but when his roommates brought him a Styrofoam bowl of soup with pork dumplings, he left it on the floor.

Du Chan brought bottles of beer from the restaurant and plastic jugs of bright-blue sports drink. Fang Lin could bend his head forward just enough to pour a little of the liquid down his throat before falling back in pain.

One of his roommates suggested he go to a hospital.

"No hospital," Fang Lin muttered. "No money."

Who ever died from a bad cough?

WHAT TERRIFIED Fang Lin most when he was conscious was the sense that he was running out of air. No matter how freely he breathed, he felt that he was inhaling not oxygen but some other odorless, tasteless gas.

He now had to remain perfectly still. To move was to suffocate. Stay still. And breathe. Breathe as deeply as possible.

He fell into fitful, angry patches of sleep during which he would systematically recreate and recount his days since leaving Jiangxi. Bits of conversation he'd had were steadily repeated and turned over in this dark semiconsciousness. It was as if he was trying to make sense of something someone had said, but the meaning eluded him and he woke dissatisfied—unsure whether he had slept at all.

He could still hear the city outside, the steady clanging and banging racket of construction, the constant clomping of other residents' feet coming and going, the sounds of doors opening and slamming. He had never felt as alone as he did then, hearing the working girls returning from their nights and, a few hours later, the day laborers and construction crews rousing themselves and setting off. Sometimes all these sounds would converge into one dull tone, leaving him frustrated at his lack of comprehension.

Around the sixth day of his illness, Fang Lin lost all track of his environment. From then on there were only dark dreams and the sensation that his life was being squeezed from him. The muscle aches came in steady, rolling waves that peaked in cramps around his spine, his neck, and his upper legs, a dreadful tightening that would coincide with a constriction of his ability to draw in enough oxygen.

Fang Lin could not have known that even as he lay fighting for breath—and for life itself—just a few miles northwest, in Foshan, an entire family had been afflicted by the same mysterious ailment and was already in intensive care. He could not have known that elsewhere in Guangzhou, patients with complaints like his were presenting themselves at emergency wards, and that within days the health-care workers with whom they came in contact would also become gravely ill. He could not have known that these symptoms often presaged death, because no fatalities had yet been reported from the disease that would later be identified as SARS. But as he struggled to hold still and to stay awake—fearful that if he fell asleep he might forget to breathe—it occurred to him that perhaps that's what dying is: your body forgetting how to breathe.

He began to drift off, always remembering, even in his unconscious state, that he must stay still. Any movement, even a wiggling of the toes, even blinking, used precious oxygen. That was air he didn't have. So he lay perfectly still and in the moments between severe cramps and muscle aches, when his bowels were settled, he would fade into dark snatches of unconsciousness—a cruel sleep that never let him forget his suffering. He felt very far from home and very alone. Fang Lin had never really thought about what happens when you die. His parents and grandparents had always been adamant that one must die and be buried as close to one's home and family as possible—and now, finally, he understood. Then he thought of something else: even if he were to make it home, who would pay for his funeral?

Notes on the Space We Take

BONNIE J. ROUGH

"When I was moving to a house that felt a bit too big yet, I wondered, 'Well, how does a hermit crab know when it is time to move?'" says Bonnie J. Rough. "I dug in and wrote the essay just as it appealed to me. There was no need to couch it in an imagined story, no need to set it for the stage, no need to count meter or seek rhyme, and no imperative to strive for the avant-garde." The resulting essay, from Ninth Letter, *is full of surprises, small and large.*

The womb is the smallest space in which a human being may live.
      Most human babies, when they are born, weigh from seven to eight pounds—about the same as a gallon of milk.

When I was born, I weighed seven pounds, eight ounces. When my mother was born, she weighed four pounds. She lost two pounds before she began growing again. When my mother's mother was born, it didn't cross anyone's mind to weigh her.

Little babies—under five and a half pounds—are said to be much more difficult to care for than big babies.

When I stand as tall as I can, I am five feet, eight and three-quarters inches high. I most often weigh 142 pounds. Buster Keaton weighed that much, and so did a world-record-setting paddlefish caught in Montana in 1973. My weight is also the weight of a newborn giraffe, which stands six and a half feet tall the first time it takes to its feet, casting a much bigger shadow than I do.

Hermit crabs grow out of their shells—not into them.

Our little blue tent has 37 square feet of floor space—a little over 5 feet by 7 feet. It is a two-man tent. But we are one man and one woman. Still, it fits us snugly, with enough arch to stretch up an arm, and a taut wall for our toes to brush in sleep.

Hermit crabs drag their shells around a spring of fresh water on the bank of grass behind the palm trees, near our little blue tent. They hiss through the low tropical forest, among fallen fruits. They hiss onto the beach, shells scraping, making tracks crossing tracks crossing tracks.

The hermit crab, which is not a true crab, has a somewhat stiff exoskeleton but lacks a protective carapace. This leaves exposed his tender belly. To protect himself, the crab looks for snail shells, abandoned or soon-to-be abandoned. When he finds one he can back snugly into, he turns his small right-hand claw backward to grip the spiral inside his shell, hoisting the whole thing onto his back. He puts it down when he is resting or eating, and heaves it up again when he takes a walk. The hermit's left-hand claw is enormous. He uses it to gather food and fend off attackers. The hermit crab also uses his large claw as a front door, slamming it across the entrance to his shell when he wants to be alone.

Hermit crabs prefer a high volume-to-weight ratio when selecting a shell to live in. A light, roomy shell is ideal. A hermit crab will look for a new shell when his old one becomes dirty, broken, or otherwise unsuitable—or he will change shells for no apparent reason at all. When a hermit crab molts—sometimes more than once a year—he sheds his old skin. He peels it off and slides it over his head like a full-body disguise. The crab then experiences a few days of terrifying nakedness, when his new skin is soft and supple. Finally, the new skin hardens. Only during his few days of soft-skinned vulnerability may a hermit crab grow. When he emerges from his molting hole in the sand—if other crabs haven't already found him and eaten him alive—he searches out a bigger shell for his newly bigger self.

Scientists and activists note a dire situation on the world's beaches: a shortage of snail shells for hermit crabs to move into. One way for a hard-up crab to find a new shell is to select one from someone else's back. "Shellfighting" ensues—one crab twisting the other out of his shell, and the evicted crab scrambling for cover. Scientists have observed that when a shiny, roomy new shell is placed on the beach, a crowd of hermit crabs will converge upon it. But instead of mayhem, a ritual of great civility follows. The crabs arrange themselves in order of size. The largest crab exits his shell and climbs into the shiny new one. The crab just below him in size takes his old shell, and so on down the line, until every crab, down to the teensiest, has a comfortable new home. It is clear to everyone involved that the teensiest crab is pleased with his take, and would be miserable in the largest shell—perhaps even unable to lift it. In his case, the ideal home sits right up against the belly with a smooth plate of calcium carbonate, and has a doorway no larger than his own left hand.

Under duress of a snail shell shortage, hermit crabs have in recent years been sighted carrying plastic pill bottles and airplane liquor bottles on their backs. Elizabeth Demaray, a New Jersey artist, proposes a rescue operation: the distribution across American beaches of custom-molded plastic homes for hermit crabs. Since pollution and consumer excess are blamed for the decline of shoreline health and the resultant tumble in snail populations, the artist suggests that corporations be made to pay for the plastic hermit-crab homes (which have an irresistibly high volume-to-weight ratio). In honor of their support, these corporations would have their logos printed on the plastic.

More than one million Americans call a recreational vehicle their primary residence.

There are no reliable statistics for the number of Americans who live in cars and trucks. But people who live in cars and trucks by choice say they like the convenience of a cozy, warm place to read and then sleep, even if it's hard to host a party. People who live in cars and trucks by necessity are less often interviewed.

Cars, trailers, tents, yurts, gers, tipis, wikiups, wigwams, and benders are houses you can pack up and take with you. But sometimes, houses move from place to place only in the mind. For some Inuit people, the work of building an igloo was a daily task, like building a fire. A new evening, a new landscape, a new house. These were houses not meant to be lived in more than once, and certainly not by more than one family.

Some people find ways to bed down away from the land entirely. Some live in boats on water, some sleep in airplane cabins, and some astronauts subsist in weightless space.

For kids, NASA uses an apple metaphor.

"Pretend your apple is the planet Earth. It is round and beautiful. It is full of good things. See how its skin hugs and protects it? Cut your apple into four equal parts. Three of those parts are water on Earth. You may eat these three parts. The fourth that is left is dry land. Cut that dry land part in half. One part is land that is too hot or too cold.

Eat this part. Cut a little more than one half. Eat the smaller part. It is too rocky or too rainy. Food can't grow on this part. Peel the skin from this part. Eat the inside. Look at the little part that is left. This shows us all that we have to grow food for the world. Some of this little bit has houses, schools and malls on [it]."

Earth provides about 58 million square miles of land. 23 million square miles of that land is considered habitable by human beings—as long as food can be brought from elsewhere.

The average American home has 2,200 square feet of livable space—a little more than a singles tennis court. The average American family consists of 3.86 persons. The average home space an American inhabits is 570 square feet—the size of the two rectangles into which tennis players must serve.

Before we married, my husband and I lived in a house of 550 square feet. When we married, we moved into a house of 1,175 square feet. When we finished graduate school, we moved to the city, into a house of 1,800 square feet.

Unlike hermit crabs, my husband and I have given ourselves room to grow in our new house. If we don't fill it with the work of our brains and hands, we will create children to share our space with us, thereby decreasing the relatively high space-to-human ratio in our home.

Biltmore Estate, in Asheville, North Carolina, is America's largest home. It has 250 rooms, including 34 bedrooms and 43 bathrooms. It has almost as many fireplaces as bedrooms and bathrooms combined. Tycoon George Washington Vanderbilt finished building the Biltmore in 1865, when it had four acres of floor space—enough for three football fields.

In terms of Earth's geologic history, space was not a gift to life, but vice versa.

Fed up with oversimplified guidelines for what size tank will fit aquarium fish, scientists G. J. Reclos, A. Iliopoulos, and M. K. Oliver offered new formulas in the June 2003 issue of *Freshwater and Marine Aquarium.* "The best known [rule] is the 'one liter of water per cm of body length' (or 'one gallon of water per inch of fish') rule, which, in our opinion, is useless. . . . The statement that shows the impracticability of this rule is 'Twenty neon tetras each measuring 1.5 cm may fit a 20 liter tank but one 30 cm fish will not.'" In place of this shoddy guideline, the authors provide the following (along with easy formulas for tank height and width), where L = tank length and FL = maximum expected fish length:

Peaceful fish, peaceful tankmates: $L = FL \times 4$
Aggressive fish, good swimmers: $L = FL \times 5 \times 1.2$
Aggressive fish, poor swimmers, ambush predators: $L = FL \times 5$
Aggressive fish, cruise predators: $L = FL \times 5 \times 1.5$
Mild temperament, cruise predators: $L = FL \times 5 \times 1.3$
Pair of aggressive fish, cruise predators: $L = FL \times 5 \times 1.5 \times 1.2$

There is a range of literature on the proper way to design zoo enclosures. Some guidelines say that most mammals need an enclosure that allows them to explore changing landscapes, work for food, search for mates, get away from the viewing public, and simply investigate its territory. On the other hand, at least one scientist states that in designing zoo enclosures, keepers need only bear in mind that "Animals will usually only move to find food, escape danger or find mates."

I have seen six smooth belugas negotiating space in a single aquarium pool, raving polar bears pacing zoo pens, and caged birds wedging their beaks between bars.

Belugas are the only all-white whales, colored to blend with the edges of Arctic ice fields, where they dwell all year. Gray whales migrate much farther—up to 12,500 miles every year—but at home near the ice, belugas dive a thousand feet deep.

Polar bears move in enormous, private northern arcs. They wander thousands of miles every year on paths programmed inside their brains. At least one bear has been tracked pacing the ice 3,000 miles from Alaska to Greenland—then back.

The Arctic tern migrates between the north and south poles, a journey of 10,000 miles twice a year, perhaps experiencing more sunlight in its lifetime than any other species on Earth.

Clipping a bird's wings, obviously, does nothing to diminish its impulse to fly.

The urge to migrate is deeply rooted in human ancestry.

I was born in Washington State, and grew up 70 miles from my maternity ward. When I was three, my parents and I moved from a one-story house to a two-story house a mile away. When I graduated from high school, I moved across the state. When I graduated from college, I moved across the country. By this time, I had discovered flight. I traveled to a new continent every year, and wore out many pairs of shoes.

For over 99 percent of human history, we moved as nomads: with the seasons, in small groups, to the places most likely to provide edible plants and game.

Travel writer Bruce Chatwin loved the idea of human migration. In 1970, he wrote the following in "It's a Nomad, *Nomad* World":

> Some American brain specialists took encephalograph readings of travellers. They found that changes of scenery and awareness of the passage of seasons through the year stimulated the rhythms of the brain, contributing to a sense of well-being and an active purpose in life. Monotonous surroundings . . . produced fatigue, nervous disorders, apathy, self-disgust and violent reactions. Hardly surprising, then, that a generation

cushioned from the cold by central heating, from the heat by air-conditioning, carted in aseptic transports from one identical house or hotel to another, should feel the need for journeys of the mind or body, for pep pills or tranquillisers, or for the cathartic journeys of sex, music, and dance.

Chatwin also said it simply. "The best thing is to walk."

My neighbor is a retired mail carrier. He takes a three-hour walk every morning, returning in time for lunch. Then he takes a three-hour walk every afternoon. He walks in all weather, under all manner of clothing. Puzzled by his daily miles, I asked if he misses delivering mail. No, he said. He misses movement.

People who seem small end up in small spaces.

The best way to shelter a child is against the body. But humans who do not enjoy wearing infants against their bodies, and who do not want their infants to get away, often store their babies in small enclosures, such as baskets, plastic carriers, cradles, bassinets, playpens, and cribs.

Some people set up house in cardboard boxes. Sometimes they are children in trim backyards, and sometimes they are grown-ups on public property.

My grandmother has just moved from her two-story home overlooking the Puget Sound into a room at Merrill Gardens at Mill Creek. She had to pass a test to qualify for lower monthly rent. She had to prove she wouldn't require too much assistance.

I keep telling my grandmother that her new home is going to be like college, or nursing school, all over again. Friendly faces in dorm rooms up and down the hallways. She seems only partly convinced, perhaps because dropping out means something different now.

Tiny people, huge people, hairy people, albino people, legless people, and two-headed people could all be viewed for the price of a coin
in the U.S. between 1840 and 1940, when freak shows were wildly
popular. Lots of times the freaks were displayed in cages or other small
enclosures, but it seems they were released after the show.

Judges in many U.S. states have declared that a prison cell should
allow no less than 60 square feet of space per prisoner, but this edict
is rarely followed in U.S. prisons, which are endemically overcrowded.
The American prison at Guantánamo Bay features prison cells of
approximately 48 square feet—about six inches larger on all sides
than our blue tent. Humans have been—or are—stored in much
closer quarters: hulls of ships, forbidding camps, airless train cars
lurching in the night.

It would take 3.4 billion Biltmore Estates to swallow Earth's livable
space. It would take 294 billion average American homes, or 13 tril-
lion Guantánamo cells. Earth's population ticks upward every second.
At the time of this writing, the planet supported about 6.55 billion
human lives.

Perhaps, then, it should be no surprise that humans commonly discuss the colonization of Mars, the moon, and other planets in the
Solar System.

Claustrophobia is the human fear of small or enclosed spaces.

Rose Hill Cemetery in Whittier, California, is the largest cemetery
in the United States. It is the size of 106 football fields. Only a handful
of people with claims to fame are buried here—a few professional ath-
letes, a few musicians—and there is space available for newcomers.

Less than half the size of Rose Hill Cemetery, Arlington National
Cemetery is the second-largest burial place in the United States. Former presidents, astronauts, and Supreme Court judges are buried

there. Arlington has some space available, but to be buried there, one must have been a U.S. president, a prisoner of war or other unusual veteran, or their spouse or child.

When there is no more room for the dead, or when we try to hide the dead, humans bury bodies one atop another. When there is no more room for cemeteries, humans build homes and markets and parking lots upon them. In Alexandria, Egypt, for example, archaeologists were recently able to dig down into 2,000-year-old Necropolis, a city of hundreds of tombs, only when a building was torn down to make room for a highway. After a whirlwind excavation, workers sealed the tombs over again.

Despite the inevitable tight fit, thousands of people every year purchase small plots of land for their bodies, or little lockers for their cremated remains.

Some traditions allow corpses to feel the freedom of space. They place their dead in trees, or slip them into rivers, lakes, and oceans.

My grandmother has asked us to check the "discard" box on the funeral parlor's form when she dies. She will not have a coffin or an urn.

In the summer of 1926, escape artist Harry Houdini bought a bronze coffin and first performed a new trick. Stepping inside, Houdini bade his assistants close the lid and lower him into a pool of water. Ninety minutes later, the assistants pulled up the coffin. The magician emerged, smiling. But Houdini was able to perform this trick only a few times. A stomach illness killed him that fall, and he was buried in the bronze coffin.

A standard coffin is 80 inches long and 23 inches wide. The largest regularly produced coffin available to U.S. funeral homes is 88 inches long and 36 inches wide. It is capable of respectfully accommodating a 500- to 600-pound corpse.

The tiniest coffin available is made for premature infant deaths. It is ten inches long, and five inches wide.

Tell Me Again Who Are You?

HEATHER SELLERS

"I write creative nonfiction because what I can try to accomplish in this form, and nowhere else, except perhaps in prayer or meditation, is a kind of physical holding of the ineffable: interior experience in a matrix of fact," says Heather Sellers. This story, about her struggle to discover the roots of her difficulty recognizing people, first appeared in Alaska Quarterly Review.

1. Harvard University

For the test, my first Harvard test, I am lying flat on my back.
I'm at the university of my dreams.

Finally.

I'm taking the test. I'm one of the people who loves taking the test. I'm one of the girls who thought: I should go to Harvard. But I never knew how. Or where it was.

For the test, my body and brain are wedged in this white plastic

MRI tube in a dark room in a dusty lab by a navy yard. My arms are pinned at my sides, and my face is in a white plastic cage with metal wires, stuffed with packing material, sponges in this case, lodged all around my face.

I could be shipped to the Alps.

Mark me fragile.

The test is called Same Different. Same Different is created by a neuroscientist, tiny slim Galit Yovel. She keeps popping in to check on me.

Faces, morphed by a computer to 10, 20 and 30% difference, denuded of hair and ears, flash before my eyes on a tiny computer screen duct-taped in the top of the MRI tube.

In my sock feet, black yoga pants, and a paper-thin white T-shirt, perfectly still, on my back, I click Left Same. I click Right Different.

A bug, trapped in a giant's drinking straw.

If I can't tell what faces are the same and which are different, I am diagnosed, I am prosopagnosic. Face blind. Able to see faces, but unable to *read* them.

I HOPE TO fail this test. I am trying my hardest. Because I want an accurate score. But if I fail, I have a diagnosis, a passport, a Greek term: *prosopagnosic*. A way to explain, a reason to say tell me again, do I know you?

Because so far, I have been winging it.

When I was a child, my mother was one people called peculiar; people said you are like your mother and don't be like your mother. Everything wrong seemed like it came from her. I was a nervous person. (Because of her.)

When I was dating, and could not tell the men at the bar apart, which one was the one I came in with, I got lucky. I got lucky a lot.

When you are twenty, and adorable *I had a great ass no one appeared to be using faces* it's called flirting.

But then I got married. Fast, at nearly forty years of age, and I couldn't recognize this man, at the grocery store, wrong man, at the races, 5Ks we ran together, only not together. Dave is fast, and kind, and he said, "I don't think you can tell people apart." We were watching a movie. I was asking, "Have we seen any of these people before?" And he said, "It's like with Gayle Kuipers. When you didn't know her." And I said, folding into his good arms, "Oh my god. It's a thing, isn't it."

And then I did what we do now: Web research. I did what my mother used to do: I wrote the government a letter. The Department of Rare Neurological Disorders. (You can have a thing where your family members seem to be imposters, people pretending to be the real members. Who hasn't had some version of that? Who isn't intrigued—wanting to have that *just for a day*.)

The government sent a packet of information.

Like in the old days!

This was not the first time I contacted my country for mental health information.

One of the Web sites they directed me to: www.faceblind.org. At Harvard.

DIAGNOSIS: A COUPON, a passport, an apology, and an invitation, maybe a cure. At least maybe it's a kind of fraternizing with the concept, the cure.

But in the tube, I can't breathe. My chest feels wrapped with bands. I want out of the tube very badly, even worse than I want to be officially Face Blind, Officially Explained to at least my husband and myself.

To get calm, I try to imagine Harvard's brick buildings around me, the beautiful church I saw when I walked across the diamond shapes of grass. *It's going to be worth it! Soon you are going to know! The mystery will be solved, the marriage healed!*

But when I try to imagine the rest of the world outside the dark room, the bright tight white tube, I feel like I have to get out of the tube.

I feel like if I don't get out now I will die.

Sometimes I feel that way about being in the world.

I AM NOT actually in a tube at Harvard University, but I will not figure that out for several weeks. When an $80 check comes from MIT. And I write Galit, and the e-mail goes to MIT.

MIT!

My whole life I wanted to go to Harvard and study, be a lawyer or an architect or famous. When I was in junior high, I was turning primitive. I was in the white-kid classes, the Academic Track, but I was not able to read books, only eat them. I craved paper, I had to always have some paper in my mouth. I began skipping classes and failing them, spending my days at the Orlando downtown library, dreaming I was a scholar, and Harvardian, as I researched pica. The craving for unnatural substances. You could crave shit, stones, leaves, string. I read about everything that could go wrong with a person and I felt better.

I just had one thing.

I diagnosed my classmates. Those girls in orange University of Florida sweatshirts, the boys who rooted for Duke. When asked, I said (or, more often, wrote—there were weeks I couldn't speak) "Harvard or MIT."

"You are not," Andrew Snedeker said one day, sneering. And I said, "I know."

And that afternoon I read about the component parts of the sperm.

And sexual addiction and homosexuality and pedophilia. I didn't think, yet, about my mother when I was reading up on psychological disorders and dreaming about my college career.

From each page of the DSM I read, I had to tear off the corner, tops only, and eat it.

SOMETIMES, YOU'RE face blind. Sometimes, you really just can't see.

THERE IS NO diagnosis code for the inability to recognize other humans.

The science literature says prosopagnosia is extremely rare, usually caused by a stroke or injury to the head.

You pronounce it like this: pro. Like you are for something. Soap. Nice and clean. You are for cleanliness.

Agnosia, there's a lot of those, that's the easy part. It's any kind of not-knowing. Not knowing, well, it's even more common than knowing.

Think: agnostic.

DR. ARIAGNO OF Michigan Medical and Dr. Donders, Spectrum Health, both told me to my face: this would be extremely unusual, if you had this. It's just very rare. They both said they had never seen it before.

DONDERS GIVES ME the Benton Face Test and Famous Faces. I pass with a C+ on the first, photos of women and men from the sixties in funny haircuts and sideburns, stiff clothes. The images are forty years old. We had no television in my mother's house, no newspapers, no radio. No framed things. No photos on the walls.

Those are all conduits for the voices.

"I wouldn't know these people anyway," I told the doctor.

He said the test takes that into account.

I had the urge to peel a corner of that page, the thick card-paper that held the faces of maybe Johnny Carson, maybe Shakespeare, maybe Martin Luther King.

In the tube at not-Harvard-but-MIT, I click Same. Different. Galit's faces are just faces—real human faces from contemporary times, with their hair and ears brushed away. The faces pop and zip across the computer screen; these are the fastest faces I have ever seen.

Lodged in my left hand is a plastic ball, like a baby ear irrigator. That's my emergency squeeze. That's my Get Me the Fuck Out.

It also means, if I am asked a question over the loudspeaker, Yes.

If I freak out, I can't scream. They will not hear me. Over the amazing pulsing roar.

In order to explain this to other people, I have to understand it myself. To understand myself, I need to look inside.

I'm on a listserv with 117 other face-blind people. Some of the face blind are experts at diagnoses, and list like advanced degrees, letters after their names, ADHD, B/P, IBS, CAP.

Is this a good use of our time, to diagnose?

This obsession, this listing of disorders, this pronoun "my." My ADHD, my hearing loss, my topographic agnosia.

Is it a sickness masquerading as self-care?

These diagnoses, they're like popular kids, you feel you have to like them, have to want to be like them.

There is no cure. There is no treatment. If I am prosopagnosic, nothing will change. If I am designated officially face blind by the Prince and Princess of Weirdest Neurological Glitchdom Ever, I still won't know you. If you put your hair up, if you wear a hat.

If you ride by on a bike in a helmet and say "Hey, Heather!" I will call out, "Who is it?"

And you will say.

And then I will know.

It's hard to know how much of a problem this is.

Sometimes when a stranger calls my name, I look away.

"HAS THE VALIUM kicked in?" Brad says over the microphone. Tall cute Brad, a postdoc collaborator of Galit's. Brad, who looks like an actor. Not a particular actor, just tall and strong and vibrant and cool.

The kind of person who would be famous.

"Sure," I say.

I'll say anything to get inside my brain, to snag a view. And I want to be the best little prosopagnosiac they have met. I want to be invited back.

I am at freaking Harvard, and I want to do well.

Truth be told the Valium hasn't kicked in, it hasn't even nudged the door, or impressed upon the anxiety in any way whatsoever. There is no cushion other than the foam around my head. My friend Ann says about painkillers, they don't *kill the pain* at all, nothing really takes away the pain. She says, "They just make it so you aren't so terrified it won't be more than you can stand."

———

THIS MORNING, BRAD picked me up in the lobby of the Park Plaza Hotel in Boston, and we took a cab to Harvard. It was like a date. Brad was wearing the same T-shirt as the day before, a ragged pale yellow intentionally ancient shirt with a cartoon monkey on it. A monkey I have seen somewhere before. A cool-person monkey.

I asked him how he got interested in prosopagnosia. He said a friend of the family, his mom's friend, had it and he got interested. He talked about his family, asked me about mine. Did anyone else have it?

It wasn't the kind of family, I tell Brad, where you would notice something like that. I want to tell him: my parents are criminally insane. I feel like Brad, with his little monkey T-shirt, his newly beat Converse, his pinky ring, Brad can handle anything.

Instead, I told him how I couldn't recognize my husband's children at school pickup, at the theatre, how I hugged the wrong man in the grocery store, thinking it was Dave. How my colleagues remained unidentifiable after a decade, how I kept introducing myself to neighbors at the park, and how they'd point out they lived next door. "Hi, I'm Heather, I live just over there." Pointing to myself, and then my house. The weird stares.

How if the man who lives next door is standing in the next door driveway, I have no clue who he is.

"So, do you think I have it?" I asked him as the cab curled over The Big Dig. I want to know how I am sounding. I don't want to be a faker, an exaggerator.

"We'll soon find out," he said. He smiled nicely.

A NAME, A diagnosis—it's like an answer complete with love and attention presets.

What could be more seductive than that?

The search for a name, a diagnosis. Someone with hands to lay on your shoulders, a someone smart who says, "Yes. You. You are it. You are the perfect example. You are my life's work."

IN THE TERRIBLE nightmare tube, the noise is the deafening sound of a fighter jet.

I am not allowed to move my head. No smiling, I am crying. Where is the Valium, my buffer, the silk blanket of drug? Am I feeling it and I just don't know? I have never taken Valium before. Maybe my brain is Valium-blind.

BRAD AND GALIT are behind a radiation barrier; looking inside my brain for light. I want to marry Brad and Galit. I want to be always experimented upon.

I have to look up, and up is a tiny mirror, the size of the ones in a lipstick case. The size of rolling papers.

My head is anchored with sponges, vibrating as the giant roars. Tears are slipping out of my eyes, itching my cheeks, my neck, I'm getting sponges wet.

I don't know where the light is coming from, but the tube is bright from within. My brain is tilted back—I'm feeling very brainy (though I am not actually at Harvard, I'm at MIT, though I won't figure that out for two more days)—and I'm looking into a mirror at the top of my brain's cage, which reflects a computer screen taped onto the back end of the straw, where the giant's mouth would be. The glass screen has a jagged crack across it. The tape hasn't always held up.

The rooms are messy, the floors dusty, and the researchers Brad and Galit talk over a microphone, over the fighter jets and I can't actually understand a single word they say, their voices are muffled hollers.

WAB BLAH BLAH MA, HIFF OO U PLEASE SQUEEZE THE BALL?

I squeeze. There's a loud set of clicks, like angry roosters have landed in a mass on top of my tube.

The rumbling and screaming start again.

I thought the Valium would drop me off a cliff.

BRAD SAYS WHEN their supervisor did Same Different in the tube, he fell asleep. Ken, their supervisor, spoke with me this morning. He is soft, and beautiful and brilliant and calm. He has prosopagnosia, Brad says. Not as bad as yours. Not nearly. He was really impressed when you said you didn't recognize your colleagues, yeah, that was great, Brad said to me as we walked out, past the animal guards.

This made me feel like I *belonged at Harvard as I suspected I always did*. This was good weird news, the best kind.

SO FAR I have been watching an episode of *The Simpsons*. My brain is perhaps being tuned to the tune of Bart and Lisa.

Then, it's all white, with the giant scar scratch and then, fast, the faces start flashing on the broken screen.

You will want to know what this looks like. It's like a casino or bar game. It's like those pop-up menus that torture your computer.

It's a bald woman.

Flitting around with her close personal friends.

A beautiful bald woman. Like a model, everything seems large and perfect about her.

ONE TIME, DAVE (I wish so badly he was in the room, holding my foot, which sticks out of the tube, corpse-like) said, Can you describe your face?

I smiled. What an excellent question, I have never thought about that before. And I smiled again, because now I was drawing a blank.

My face?

I tried to see it.

I couldn't see it.

I know it's heart-shaped and small and cute, I said. But that is because I have been told this. We were looking at photos of me that my friend Pat had taken at the Saugatuck Dunes.

I can see it, but I can't imagine it, I said.

Dave said, What about your mother's face?

It's like she's standing there, right there, and I can put my hand through her, like those ghosts in the dining room at the Haunted House in Disney. I can almost see it. There is a face there. It's not a ghost without a face.

How would you describe the face? he said softly.

I took a sip of my wine. I leaned into him. We were sitting at my kitchen counter.

I can't describe, I said. I can see it, but then there's this weird series of gaps. Like when you are running on railroad tracks. There's her face, there's her, here I am, I see her. She has a face, but I don't know that face. It's a placeholder. It's an energy that stands in for her. For her herness.

He said, How about your dad? Your brother?

Same.

DIFFERENT.

The bald woman appears on the cracked computer screen in my little lipstick mirror in the tube. She floats—dashes really, this disembodied head, across the screen. Her face is always the same size. About one sixth of the size of the screen. She alternates her slide to the left, slide to the right. You never know where she will pop up. It's fast, it's hard to keep up. I'm never sure when I press Different. They all look the same. I can't tell if it's four women, serving in a rotation, or many, many women with subtle superfine differences.

I'm guessing.

Like I have been all along.

It feels like an arcade game, where you have to shoot the duck.

I should have told Galit, did I tell Brad? I drive on the wrong side of the road. England didn't scare me like it did other members of my high school class. All this backwards.

I don't want to do anything to wreck up the data, but this mirror, this gal is moving so fast—I don't know.

I keep waiting for a new girl, a different face. Someone with ears, something I can hang on to.

Same.

Same.

Same.

Same?

I need a question mark button.

Here's a face, different! The eyebrows look more intense, like they are underlined.

Otherwise, she looks the same to me.

PEOPLE I CAN recognize: the weirdly outlined.

The very tall, the very short, the freaks. The bent or broken, the mentally ill, the extremely ugly. People with long hair or astounding hair. Superbly frizzy, intently braided, spectacularly combed-over (thank you, Donald!). Anything big, wrong, or emphatic affecting the outline = good. Useful. Some people come with handles. Some you can't tell from all the other knives in the drawer.

————

I AM NOT able to recognize myself in mirrors, photographs, or home movies.

BEAUTIFUL PEOPLE are the sum of the perfect average; they are very difficult to tell apart. In magazines, it seems like the same model. I can't tell Cindy, Julia, Christy.

Galit says: What's amazing is that the brain can tell faces apart at all. They mostly look the same. We are interested in how the brain does that.

BRAD AND GALIT are running the tests from a bank of laptops they take everywhere, plugged in now to a hardware console with a sign atop that reads "Monkey MRI." When I asked, they said, no, no, no. There aren't monkeys in this part of the building. They are upstairs.

But I did check for short dark hairs on the bedsheet as Galit was strapping me in.

It *feels* like a monkey was here.

Same.

Different.

A dozen tests.

The first one, Famous Faces. I click on his laptop space bar, and a famous face comes up. He says, Is this familiar? I said, Yes. This test isn't timed, he said. Take as much time as you need.

"Jim Carrey?" I say. I'm feeling like I am off to a good start on this test.

"That's me," he says. "I just put that in there for fun."

I can feel my face fall. Mean trick.

I sip my water.

Stare at the screen.

"Do you look like Jim Carrey?" I say. I want to be wrong and I want to be right. That tension is at the center of the diagnosis quest.

He says he does look like Jim Carrey, people say. I give myself full credit for that one.

THE ONLY OTHER famous face I get is Robert Downey Junior. These are just *faces.* Cropped of ears, much hair. Later, I retro-identify Nicholas Cage and Julia Roberts. She was the first one. Those lips, those teeth. I think I can really see teeth. They aren't affected by the not-seeing. They can shine through.

I miss: Elvis, Brad Pitt (he looks like everyone), Mel Gibson, Jennifer Aniston, the whole crew.

AFTER THE FAMOUS faces, Brad asks me a bunch of names.

Do I know who Brad Pitt is? I do. Do I know Reagan? Do I know Winston Churchill?

I do. I do. I do, of course.

Do I know Tony Blair?

I know who he is. I don't know that I have ever seen a photo. I don't have television. I rent DVDs because they come with the *answers,* who's starring.

I see the magazines in the grocery store, I know who is pregnant. I keep up with the famous people, who they are marrying, what they hit up against, were nominated for, got addicted to.

But evidently I don't know them, not that personally. Not well enough to say hi.

Brad tells me I am the second worst person to fail this test. The only man who did worse than me was hit on the head by a car accident.

He is amazing with birds, but he can't find a face at all.

He can't even figure out what a face *is.*

2. I Do Not Recognize Myself in Photographs

The summer I graduated high school, I told my neighbor Evelyn, when she asked where I was going to college, a fat lie. "Harvard," I said.

She said, "I am not surprised."

Two months later, at age seventeen, I am on a bus headed north out of Orlando. I am going to college. Not Harvard. Florida State University. To me it sounds grand, like Oxford, like the Taj Mahal.

I am not exactly sure where Florida State University is, how far until Tallahassee.

PART OF ME is happy to be tucked safe in this metal tube on wheels; I like the leaping dog, who looks more like a fast grouchy panther, on the Greyhound sign. I like him better than the Trailways sign, which is red, white and blue. Kind of tacky, kind of trying too hard.

Part of me is terrified.

I AM ONE day late for college. I am missing orientation.

I am going to college because there is so much I want to find out. I just want to know and know and know and know.

I have three thousand dollars cash in a hidden compartment in my brown leather purse. My purse has a large cursive *H* embroidered on it in black. I have a notebook where I write everything down.

Writing it all down makes me feel like I am getting what.

At this exact moment, I just want to be going *faster*.

Harvard: I don't know how you would get there—I don't even know what state Harvard is in, exactly. It's a huge feat, one of my biggest so far, that I figured *this* out.

I sit back in my hard grey seat. I try to catch eyes with the driver in his big flat mirror.

I am trying to get him to ask me, Where are you going, little lady?

So I can say College.

So I can tell a true story.

If he would just look my way.

MY MOTHER SAYS full-time work would teach me what I needed to know. She says she believes in hard work.

My mother doesn't have a paying job.

I have worked four jobs since I was eleven years old: mowing, babysitting, swimming lessons instructor, day camp counselor; then I replaced mowing with Chi-Chis and babysitting with Disney.

She says I am not prepared for college, I will wash out. You need to work, she says. She comes by my dad's house, bangs on the door, then runs down the sidewalk, leaps back in her truck. And he yells, Go talk to your mother.

THE NIGHT BEFORE I go, my father weeps. Says don't leave him. Go to Valencia, go to junior college, take his car. But every time I went out there, to find out more about Valencia, a college named after an orange, way east of his house, I got lost.

I ended up at the beach, in Christmas, out of gas, in trouble, all of them at once. I can't go to junior college. People going to Harvard do not go to junior colleges.

AT MY GUIDANCE counselor appointment, one was required before you graduated, Mrs. Jenkins said, "I heard your boyfriend hits you."

I said no. I was crying.

She looked at me long and hard. I stared at the floor.

I had no idea what to do or say or hope for, how to plan.

She said you can go to any one of these schools. She handed me a gold form. She said, Check a box. I can write a letter. You will have to come up with $450 deposit. Tomorrow.

I said I wanted to go to Harvard.

She said those decisions had been made, long ago.

These were our choices, she said. She tapped a long skinny shapely black plastic pen on the form. "Pick one." She leaned over her snow globes collection.

I CLOSED MY eyes and cried and I picked.

THAT NIGHT, WHEN my father passed out on the sofa, Ruby long gone home, I wrote the check, and rode my bike down to the post office and under a really hot almost purple Florida moon, I stuck the thick envelope of forms addressed to *Florida State University* in the chubby blue mailbox on Orange Avenue. I kissed the envelope before I sailed it in there.

I listened: soft landing.

3. Recognition Errors

There's also a sign on the lobby door that says "Do not Feed the Scientists." I concentrate on this. I wait for the Valium. I feel like I have to get out of the tube. What's the point of this?

BLAGH MAH MAG, HAF WEE PAH PLEASE SQUEEZE THE BALL?

I squeeze.

———

I FEEL LIKE I have floated so far out of the normal Heather world. I wonder if they can see that I thought *Monkey MRI*.

It's animal rights awareness week, and that's why the extra security guards all around this building, Brad said.

THE ENDLESS BUZZING the jets and the crows, it continues, and I click my buttons, forever, Same Same Same Same trying to stay very still. If the face of this morph woman looks different, I click Different.

Sometimes I click the wrong button. The faces are coming really really fast, like a subway train speeding past.

It's a blur of faces. They pop up on different places on the screen, so that it's nothing like a subway station platform where you are standing, really, at all, but more like you are jumping on a trampoline as the train flies.

I click Same Different for an hour.

Then I say, I have to get out. I have to get out.

THE LAST NIGHT I saw her, I told my mother don't pull any stunts, don't follow me, please don't embarrass me by coming up there.

My mother said I was compounding all my mistakes. She said she wouldn't let me leave. She would call the police.

I said to her: I have one goal in life.

"What's that?" she'd said harshly.

"Not be like you."

We were in my father's driveway. She looked stronger, calmer after I said this thing. I'd been waiting, wanting to say it for years. I never thought I would be brave enough.

"Thanks," she said. "You really know how to hurt a person."

She drove away in her little truck, chugging, like she and the truck were both choked up.

I thought: this is the last time I will ever see her.

I was full of premonitions then.

THEY ARE VERY, very young, younger than me. Galit is going to teach neuroscience at the University of Tel Aviv in the fall. Brad is going to be a faculty member at the University of London in psychobiology.

Like a nightmare, I lose all sense of time and purpose. Do they know what they are doing?

What is the point of this? People are dying!

When Galit comes in, the noise stops. It feels like everything wrong with me is healed.

She slides me out. I grin. I sit up, stretch. I can't believe myself, my own bravery. I am terribly claustrophobic.

"Can we do some more or do you have to stop?" she says.

"Stop," I say. I wipe tears off my face.

"You did great," she says. "Was it okay?"

"It was hard," I say. "It was a long time."

"An hour," she says. "But it looks like we got good data." She says she will call me tonight at my hotel to tell me what they find.

If I can't see faces, she will know for sure.

I say thank you.

She says I did so well. She says thank you. For someone with claustrophobia to be willing to help them. She is just very grateful.

You did great, she says again when we are getting in her car with Brad, and I feel like a million bucks.

She says, weaving over aspects of the Big Dig, You clicked Same a lot.

I did the best I could, I say.

I sink into the backseat.

I am at Harvard, a person probably making a C−.

———

THAT EVENING I walk around the city. I stand on the Boston Common. I hear women speaking French, men Dutch, and maybe Chinese. Everyone looks smart and there are a lot of ducks and babies. I walk around, feeling smart and helpful.

I have wanted to be at Harvard my whole life. Ever since I heard about it, from my father, who said, he should have gone to Harvard. To study law. Not going was the biggest mistake he made besides leaving us kids with my mother.

In my hotel, I have dinner at a famous oyster bar. I have six kinds of raw oysters. I compare each one. Same, Different. The metal taste is good, it tastes like how being in the MRI machine felt.

While I slide my oysters into my body, I read the Bhagavad Gita, which I keep calling the Bhagavad Vita. I order a second glass of chardonnay.

I listen to the conversation next to me, two men, drinking water, eating chowder, talking about running, how many miles a week they go. They are forty, they say, like me. I want to add to the conversation—I am forty, I run—but I'm very very happy with my oyster shells, my book, my wine, my perfect mood. I have accomplished this huge thing today I lay in a tiny terrible scary tube. All by myself. For one hour. I donated my body to science. I don't want to do anything to mar my good mood. So I stay quiet. They leave.

The most difficult school. I would never get in, my dad always said. What I needed, he said, was the school of hard knocks. And he'd bang me on the head, and laugh, a laugh that sounded like he was forcing something bad out, something in him that refused to leave.

In my hotel that night, I take a bath and wait for Galit's call. I have gobs—too much—Estée Lauder Intuition bath bubbles coating my skin like a bad idea. I soak and sweat. I get out, not feeling cleaner, just coated. I flash back to how she and Brad flicked open their laptops, how their very own laptops ran the MRI. How I'll want to tell my husband, Dave, what kind of laptop, Apple? That's part of the story he'll like. If it's Apple, if I know what kind.

I wait for the phone to ring, for the red button to light up. I'm wanting this terrible news: your brain doesn't work like a normal brain. I need this sentence, as a passport, so when I travel in the country of normal people, neurotypicals, I can say, it's proven. See?

I'm not like you, but trying really hard.

So I won't feel insane, just helpful, when I say to both of us, Can you tell me again.

Who are you?

4. Affinity for Likeness

On the bus, above my head on the rack, like a cheerful white cloud, I have my own white suitcase, filled with my dad's old college clothes, because it's up north, Tallahassee, it gets cold there. A mustard alpaca sweater, three of his neckties from Chicago, a red plaid vest, grey wool shorts from the fifties. Wrapped in the clothes are my books, my novel notebooks, my journals, my book of wisdom quotes.

On a pale green index card: my father's address, my mother's phone number.

I get nervous and I can't remember for the life of me.

I get nervous and I can't remember a fucking thing.

ON THE BUS, I do not want to be seen. No girl, I believe, does. I want to make up a whole new life. Don't look at me now while I am trying to do that.

ON THE BUS card I'm flicking around, all you can see is O and O, with a hole in the middle of the word.

I am dying to talk to the driver. I keep testing out different words in my mouth. He is looking in his big mirror as much as he is looking at the road. I lean forward. I wonder if my face is filling up his view.

Then, we stop.

We aren't even out of Orlando, really.

I am already late to college by a day and now I am in Okahumpka, Florida, sitting in a bus.

The driver calls out "Okahumpka!"

He yanks open the doors, steps out of the bus. He lifts up the bus sides.

Okahumpka. Really, Okahumpka is still Orlando. Okahumpka touches Orlando like the pancreas touches the liver.

My mother is fully capable of driving to Okahumpka. She's driven here before, I was with her. She might have called my father. He might agree: Heather has to be stopped. There's a window in his drinking, about 8 p.m. at night, a window where she can get in, and they can sometimes agree on what to do about me. Then it closes. Then it was never there.

I review my card.

There are so many stops: Ocala, RS Ocala Pilot Station, Leesburg, Belleview, Gainesville, Alachua, Lake City, Live Oak, Madison, Monticello.

I had no idea we would be stopping at all these towns. I feel queasy knowing it now. I thought you just got on a bus and it took you where you were going.

Two black women get on the bus. They are wearing the most beautiful hats.

Three more women get on. They are in church dresses and they have boxes of food. There are no children. They do not stop talking. The driver says, "All aboard."

I close my eyes. Please let my mother not be running towards this bus.

Already, I am learning so much.

5. Losing Your Data

The phone rings and I jump off the Boston bed like electricity.

"Hello?" I say. Heather, I'm thinking, what do you really hope for here? Are you worried they found a brain tumor. Are you remembering: there is no treatment, no cure?

"I have terrible news, I'm so sorry," Galit says.

"Ah!" my whole body says. I stand up in my hotel room, which is two old rooms made into one gorgeous nice new room. Terrible news. Terrible news. I'm shaking.

"We lost all the data," she says. "I was worried when they said they were working on the machine this weekend. But we tested, we thought we were okay. The data, it's all junk."

I say. "So we do not know? If my face area lights up?"

"We have nothing," she says. "Can you come in again?"

"No," I say. "I took the Valium. I don't have another. There isn't anything I can do." At Harvard, I want to say to Galit, how is it possible the computers and machines don't work? Whose fault is this, I want to say. Do you know how hard that was, all those faces? Lying so still?

"I am sure we can get a Valium. I will call Brad. He will know someone. I hate to ask. But we have nothing. No data. I'm sick about it. And, there is another thing. My husband specializes in claustrophobia. He's a therapist, cognitive behavioral. He has helped a lot of people."

"I don't know," I say. I'm shaking all over. My hands are sweating. I wanted to know tonight. I tell her I am leaving Sunday evening.

"I have to think," I said.

"He could come over now," she says. "He thinks he can address the issue in one session. But there is not pressure on you."

"We're going to fix my brain, my claustrophobia, this is like a complete workover," I joke. "I'll go back to Holland a whole new person." I'm smiling, nodding, using my free hand to say *cheerful! Sorry!* When mostly, it just seems like things are breaking.

I can't do it again, lie there, with tears pouring out of me, for an hour, in a profoundly confused situation, a true nightmare, bald women who all look alike but some are different and I want to get the answers right. I always want to get an A.

I call Dave. What should I do?

"How was the big meeting?" he says. His voice is pushy cheerful, like a thing catching up to itself.

"We talked about that last night." I try to breathe. I'm rubbing my thigh with my free hand. I am looking up at the ceiling of my palatial Park Plaza room. "This is the face thing."

"The face thing!" he says, busted. The cell phone crackles.

I want to say, Have you been drinking a lot? When did you start today?

Dave says he doesn't think the man should come to my room and experiment.

He thinks I should just come home.

I tell him about Brad calling, not finding the Valium, then calling back, saying "We remembered, Serena!" And how I thought that was so perfect, a woman named Serena, she has the Valium, this woman named *evening, night, late, love song.* A postdoc friend of theirs. I wondered what her area of study is and Brad said: attention.

The brain on attention. This is what that looks like.

Dave says, "Do they like the book?"

And I say, This isn't those people. This isn't that. The meeting with Bedford St. Martins was two days ago. We already talked about it!

This is the face people. I don't sound happy. I wish I had called someone else.

This is my husband.

Who is, how on earth have I not seen this before, like my father.

This is my father not remembering our conversations from the
night before, the night before that. He isn't seeing me at all. He's not
even looking my way. He is drinking, he wants to be blind.

"We're breaking up," I say.

I pretend the static is a lot worse than it is. And I disconnect.

I TAKE A bus to college. It is nothing like running away from home.
Even though my father said, "Baby, don't go. Stay here with your ole
Daddy," and that broke my heart. Even though my mother said: "I will
not let you get away with this. This is unconscionable."

I'M ON THE bus, and Bird's breath is bad. Real bad. Like a can-
taloupe in a hot room. He is short, and sits turned towards me on his
seat. He got on in Ocala, and has had his arm around my seat.

I can feel the heat off his red-tan flaky skin, and the whole metallic
energy of Bird who is about as much like a bird as a bucket.

Bird smells like rubber and something melted and sun, too much
sun. Maybe beer, too, something sour. My father never smells like this.

Bird tells me his life story. It's not a pretty picture.

I close my eyes.

The driver is never going to talk to me now. He's thinking I'm going
down a bad path.

I do not know how to get rid of this Bird.

"So you've never had a boyfriend? Not a single one?" Bird says. He
has a cracker accent, and talks like he has a mouth full of loose teeth.

"I told you," I say. My throat is tight, all the way down to my stomach. It hurts to talk. There is so much I haven't said.

"So you don't like to have fun? Or you don't know about fun?" Bird says.

Be more nunlike, I command myself. Drive him away with your goodness.

Bird tells me his third wife left him because she thought he was an alcoholic. He says he likes to have a good time and there is no crime in that. Is there a crime in that? Do you think there is a crime in that?

He says he is a free man, a free bird.

He leans in closer. His palm is resting on my shoulder. I push down further into myself. Why is this happening to me?

His breath gusts across my face. "You like to have fun, right? Would you like to get down with the Bird? I'm a party Bird!" he says, louder. "Very rare species in these parts." He laughs really hard. I can hear that in him there is some kind of goop.

I lean forward, look at the floor. It's rubber-ribbed, black. Maybe I could throw up.

In Palatka, I do not get off the bus even though I have to go to the bathroom so bad. It's a long, long stop. The Bird disappears. We get a new driver. The new driver is black. First thing he does when he gets on the bus, he thanks me for sitting up by him.

"You can be my eyes and ears," he says. He has a minister's voice. "Okay? You going to see your kin? You got kin up this way somewheres? Where I'm taking you tonight, Young Lady?"

"I'm going to Tallahassee, sir," I say. "That is my final stop. Do you know our arrival time?"

We are just backing out of the stall. It's nearly dark, a heavy North Florida evening.

There is a loud knock at the door of the bus. The driver opens it. I want to shout, No, don't. I fear my mother.

Bird.

He climbs back on. He shows the driver his ticket. "I've added one additional stop—I'm going up one more stop, because I think my life is going to change. I think I'm about to become a very lucky man. That Palatka bus, it runs in the morning?"

"Ten a.m.," the driver says. He says it like you would say, "Welcome to the Promised Land."

I close my eyes, squish down into the corner as much as I can. Bird is tapping my arm, then it turns to stroking. I slap his hand.

"What?" I say.

"I brought you some gum." He acts like we have known each other our whole lives.

The driver doesn't look at me.

Bird hands me the piece of gum. It is not wrapped. Lord knows where he got it from.

"This is your stop," I say. "This is where you are supposed to be." I point out the window. I feel like a teacher. I'm surprised how strong I am.

Bird suddenly looks furious, redder. "You, get off," I say.

Someone from the back of the bus yells, Let's get going.

THE NIGHT IS hot, and the sky is spooky, the night clouds are different here than in Orlando. I walk past the Waffle House, which is anchored into a hill under the Travelodge. I am in Tallahassee, Florida, at midnight. It's August. I am going to start college in the morning, or something like college. I have finally made it.

I'm in the middle of a busy five-lane street, in the turn lane, between cars, under the streetlights. I'm trying to cross. The light is green. I'm liable to be run down by the people hollering at me. My white suitcase is banging my shins every step.

I cross the street, horns honk. I'm grinning. I'm doing fine. I smile and wag my head around, as in, I'd wave if I could, but I have this suitcase, I'm moving in.

City smart, I am thinking. Street smart.

I have bus legs—stiff, long-feeling, weak—but I try to walk strong, swag my hips, show I know my stuff. I walk in this way across campus, probably two miles. I'm staying at the Ponce de Leon Motel tonight. I walk in the lobby. The food cooking is Indian.

I smile.

"Name?"

"Heather," I say.

The man in the scarves stares at me.

"Sellers!" I say. "Sellers!" This is the right answer.

I am doing well. I'm going to be so fine. Tomorrow, I will go to late registration. I will get a terrible schedule that will make me popular and well-known: ceramics, massage, water ballet, pocket billiards, writing.

I do not want these classes.

Boys tell me it is a schedule they have in their dreams.

I will buy books for real classes, I'll go to the library every day. Six boys have asked me out. Sara says no one has asked her out. She says, "How do you meet these people?"

I tell her the truth: I have no idea.

6. A Knock at Room 1273, Park Plaza Hotel, Nearly Midnight

"Are you ready to kill the monster?" Iftal leans forward, smiling, rubbing his hands. If people are scared of bridges, but every morning hundreds of people drive across bridges, then we too can do this thing.

I have taken notes on his talking. I believe what he says, about fear. It all sounds great. Why am I going to a psychotherapist, to talk, when there is this efficient workable way?

"We kill him!" Iftal says, grinning, like a kid. He stands up.

"Right now?" I say. I've been sitting on this hard formal rose sofa in the lobby of the Park Plaza Hotel with Iftal Yovel, Galit's husband, for an hour. His degree is from Northwestern. Even I am calling it CBT now, cognitive behavioral therapy. He said it doesn't matter about the head injuries, the trauma, that's all okay. That isn't really part of what we do.

Iftal says, There is no fear, only fear *of* fear. There is no such thing as claustrophobia.

"People think they have a thing," he says. "It's not a real thing. The tube can't hurt you. The small spaces, you won't die. You feel you will die. But you are just afraid of that feeling—which is a very uncomfortable feeling, granted. But you won't die."

It doesn't matter, beaten, abandoned, tortured. When we were babies, 10,000 years ago, we were afraid if we were in a small space, in a crevice. Our heart rate went up. Our fear responses increased our chance of survival.

The mind is dumb. The body dumber. We are wired to freak out about high places, narrow places, small places, but this information is 10,000 years old, older. Iftal says small places can't kill us. The mind-body just thinks this. We are smarter. We can create a gap.

He says, "Let's go do it."

"Right now?" I say. I was thinking I would just get the book he suggested. I do not stand up. This was just a talk. Wasn't it?

"Yes. Yes. The MRI is tomorrow, yes, you are leaving? I think we can do it in one hour."

"This wasn't our hour?" I make my hands flap around, to designate *the space of the talking.* I took notes. I wrote down the books he said to read. I will never read them.

He is nodding, waiting, smiling, rocking on his toes.

Maybe he doesn't understand everything I say. I haven't understood all of his words, our accents are different. I just go with it, like I do with people, faces, after a while it becomes clear who they are, what is said, or it doesn't, and it doesn't matter.

He said he tells his clients that if other people are doing—driving over the bridges of Boston, scary, yes—in masses, we must use this—and there he hit his forehead with his palm—to override *this*—hitting the back of his head quickly with the same hand.

We get in the elevator.

"How are you in elevators?" he says.

I push 32. I'm thinking of Aristotle, and how the mind is in the heart. Maybe brain can't trump heart. Maybe the heart is too weak to face down 100,000 years. Maybe the baby wins every time.

"Fine," I say. The elevator whooshes up.

Where is Galit, the Princess of the Kingdom of Brain? Home with the twins. Where's Brad? Who am I in Boston, this Heather meeting with a CBT researcher in the middle of the night in a hotel?

I do not recognize myself.

FORTUNATELY, I AM used to that.

"YOU WILL NOT need the Valium. I do not want you to take it. You have a great chance to finish off the monster tomorrow. I am so excited for you to not take it." As we go in my hotel room, "We have to kill the monster," Iftal says. "We kill him, and you are free! You have a chance. Any chance you have to kill him a little more, always take it. The Valium, it just makes it worse."

I do not tell him: I will not do the tube without the Valium. At least a few safety crumbs.

"WHAT IS scary to you in here, this room?" Iftal says.

"You."

———

I GET IN the closet.

"What will freak you out now?" he says through the closed door. I can feel his body leaning against the door.

I can't believe I am sitting in the dark in a closet on the thirty-second floor. I can see in my mind's eye the ironing board, and out in the city, the lit-up bridges, flanging out of Boston like electric cords.

He jangles the doorknob. "Do you see the monster?" he says. "Is he near?"

Yes, I say. I'm smiling.

"Are you laughing at him? That is good! That is good! See!"

This is the weirdest thing I have ever done in my entire life. I want to call my friends. I want Dave to see.

Iftal bangs on the door, hard. Then it is quiet.

The monster grows.

WE DO it again.

Again and again and again.

He screams. Kicks the door. I sit there, and stare at the monster, and he's right. It grows smaller.

Nothing can scare me. It's just weird.

"I am cured," I say. "You must go home to Galit."

Iftal looks like he has killed the monster himself. "You are cured," he says. "No Valium needed." He throws his hands over his head. He shakes my hand.

I'll be using half Valium, half CBT. Just to be on the safe side.

"Thank you," I say.

"My wife was so upset. She was so upset. I had to help." He bows, slightly, takes his coat, and I walk him to the door.

I lock the door, change into my sleeping shirt, brush my teeth, and put up my hair. I set the alarm, and call again to confirm my wake-up call.

I get under the covers, and breathe.

I wake up at 6:59, one minute before the alarm.

IT'S OUR FIRST *college* Saturday night. Sara Simko and I sat with a lonely looking boy at lunch, and we invited him to watch the movie with us. We three are on Sara's burgundy sleeping bag in the attic of Landes Hall. Sara wears an FSU necklace, an FSU watch, and all her folders are burgundy with gold *Florida State University*! She has scoliosis. She sits with a prim stiffness. Her brown hair is lacquered back into thick wings. Fans are blasting us with hot air. Around us, kids are sprawled on the floor, eating popcorn, draped on sheets, sofas, each other.

The movie is hard to follow. This is my real life. My first real life.

I'm in a red skirt I sewed out of a vintage pillowcase. I have on lipstick, my hair is brushed and silky, and I'm pretty. I sit on my hands because they sweat so much, but other than that, I can't think of anything that is wrong. I look at the other kids in the room.

IN THE MOVIE, two people are making love.

I saw Linda, my father's wife, estranged, Linda the woman who beat the shit out of me, again today at the Spaghetti Station. Maybe it's not her. I see her a lot. A lot of women look like her. I see her every day, at least once. I see her when I open the door to the public bathrooms. And I wonder if she is following me or if I am turning into my mother.

"WHO IS THAT, have we seen her before?" I say to Sara. She shoves the popcorn bowl—a plastic Tupperware thing from her set, she has a popper, too—towards Todd.

Sara is wincing.

The lovemaking woman is now in the living room, in Africa, and the lover man is riding off on a horse.

"Have we seen either of them before?" I mean, before the love scene.

"Shh, Heather. Yes, sweetie. That's Meryl Streep. Meryl Streep. Same person. Whole movie, she's the star."

Sara whispers that she will tell me if it's ever not Meryl Streep.

All the men wear hats.

Next Saturday, I have a boyfriend.

We have so much in common. He says his parents are crazy; I say, Mine too! He's Catholic; me too. He is from New York. I am from Orlando. He is majoring in International Relations. I love to travel. He has written a poem. I tell him, I have written a novel, and I am working on a new one.

He says, "No way."

Michael Mahon takes me to the Spaghetti Station. When I come back from the bathroom, he has moved to a new booth. Because I am newly cool, I do not ask him why. Because I am sexy and fun, I sit right next to him this time, I lean over, and kiss him.

He laughs, and says whoa.

I see we have different food than our food. Different plates.

I look around. Michael Mahon, or someone who looks a lot like him, is setting down money. On our table. At my old booth.

Is walking out the door.

I run out—it's Tennessee Street, the street I came in on, it seems like years ago I rode that bus!—but I don't see him anywhere. The sidewalks are crawling with college students. In their uniform khakis and pastel polos and Miami Vice hair. Smelling of Stetson. I run through the herd.

Sunday, I do not leave my dorm room. I study for my Psychology test. And go to my experiment. Where I have to hold my hand in ice cold water until I can't stand it anymore.

I last five seconds.

"Is that good?" I say. "How does it compare?"

The researcher says she can't tell me anything about the experiment because that would ruin it. Her hair hangs in greasy strings and she calls the next person. Michael.

There's a million Michaels, it's not him.

In the hall, I wait in line for my proof form.

"They use us like rats, it's sick."

"It's totally illegal."

I have to do four more experiments. Everyone has to do five.

Sara called me all day, she says, standing in my doorway. "Worried sick!" She fiddles with her FSU necklace, and I invite her in for water.

I was at my experiment.

Did you do the cold one?

I tell her yes.

Did you and Michael break up?

I tell her no. Maybe. I do not know.

And truly, I do not. He reminded me of Bruce Springsteen, I say.

But he was very non-Christian, Sara says.

I don't say anything.

We sit on my bed. She rubs my back.

"Oh, sweetie," she says. "We have to teach you to flirt better. And I want to just try eye shadow. Just let me try. We can wash it off. Right away. No one has to see!"

I'M CHANGED back into my regular clothes at Harvard. For the tiniest moment, I was naked at Harvard.

"What's the results?" I say.

"You pressed Same a lot," Galit says. "I'll know more after I run the numbers."

"Will I get to know—" I say. I'm not sure what to say. I am expecting her to hand me a report, handouts, graphs, charts. I am thinking she is going to sit down with me and go over all this at a table, and we will have Cokes. It will take hours. But when we are done, I will understand everything about how the brain works, what mine is doing, it will be as clear as a Discovery Channel special, friendly as a Nova. Useful as antidepressants, clever as pie.

Galit says I can write her with any questions, and the article will be out she hopes in a month, and she will e-mail me the citation.

And she drives me to the museum.

The whole way through Boston backstreets, I try to think of questions. I'm feeling so let down. I'm feeling like what was the point again? That I have forgotten what it is I came here to do. That I am missing the prize.

When I get out of her car, I thank her again for the ride. And I tell her to thank her husband, it was way too nice of him to come and help me.

"It's the least I could do. And you were much less anxious, yes?"

"You can tell him, cured in one hour. I am a complete convert to CBT. Tell him it worked great. You don't have to tell him I took a tiny quarter of the Valium." I smile, and Galit laughs.

"You were very calm. Very different from yesterday."

I walk across the park to the Isabella Stewart Gardner museum and while I am walking, I call Dave. I say, I did it. I did great. I definitely have it, for whatever that is worth! My brain doesn't work. But, I made it through, I used the cognitive behavior skills, and a little Valium.

He says, "Are you still in Boston?"

There's a scratchy silence.

I wonder if he remembers I had to decide to do the MRI again. When we talk on the phone at night, by morning he's lost the data.

Every time.

Why am I the one who keeps forgetting?

"Can you believe I had a man in my room at midnight shaking my closet door, can you even believe I was awake at midnight? I think it is the weirdest thing I have ever done," I say. I am not crying. I'm not sure if I am building a bridge for him or presenting a test.

"That's right," he says, long and slow, big aha. In a tone that sounds incredibly dense and simultaneously wise and caring. "I remember something about that."

I press the red circle with the dot. Pretending it was a bad connection.

WHAT I LOVE about the museum is nothing is labeled. There are no name tags, no names to the faces, it's how art and stuff exists in your own house. So it is easy to pretend the Isabella Stewart Gardner museum is *my* house. There are a few paper labels, stuck to the walls or furniture, and signs saying don't sit here, don't place any object here. But they say things like "Oil on canvas, purchased in 1922 from Venice." And in this way they are more interesting to me than titles, the names of artists. Face after face, portrait by portrait, I move through the rooms. My legs are tired, my face is smiling, my bag is heavy, with my yoga-MRI suit, my journal, the remains of lunch. I sit in the courtyard. Nasturtium vines grow three stories high. I love courtyards, tile, fountains, light. I imagine this room in winter. I pretend this room is mine. And as I sit there, pretending to be Isabella Stewart Gardner, pretending I am her, I think about my constant need to find out *what do I have and who am I?* Am I trying too hard to see inside my brain? What is it I wanted Galit to tell me, exactly? Because I am a professor, do I believe vocabulary words and definitions are the same thing as knowledge, answers?

———

I BREATHE IN the mossy dank courtyard smell. I look up into the rest of the house, the doors open on all the floors to this central chamber, this giant square tube of light that makes the center of the house.

Some women from England pass by, and I pretend I invited them for dinner.

A string quartet finishes, and the first floor fills with noisy people.

A man tells his wife everything that is written in the free brochure, nothing in the house can be moved, she acquired these things on shopping trips to Europe, after her husband died, as though he himself has always known this information. As though the brochure didn't exist.

"You see, nothing here can be moved. That's what she dictated in her will. So that vase, the vase in the courtyard, that's tipped over? They can't even pick it back up. The paintings that were stolen? When we go upstairs, you will see just the empty frames. Because they can't do anything with them. That would be making a change. Everything has to stay exactly where it is. Forever."

The woman nods.

I stand up from the damp cement steps, and step out of the courtyard, feels like a rainforest.

I think: this is alluring, this idea that nothing is moving, nothing is changed. People want there to be one house where everything stays exactly the same. Not to mention controlling chaos from the grave, that's pretty appealing, too.

What did I want Galit to tell me?

Did I want to change the course of neurobiological research? Did I want the world to stop?

My claustrophobia is cured, perhaps, and I know, for sure, I have it and I can tell my doubtful friends I am Harvard-certified prosopagnosic, it's almost as cool as having a degree from there, having been *studied*.

I think I wanted the whole Galit article devoted to me.

Is this what we all want? Our own experience enshrined in an article or *in a museum so people can visit and know oh, this is what it is like to be you?*

I wander through the rooms, see the empty frames where the stolen paintings were, the funny wrought-iron Venetian bed, all the old letters, the dusty chairs, and tiny paintings set on tables, at right angles by windows, back-to-back because she liked to sit and stare into the faces of these subjects, and she liked them lit that way.

By the time I am too hungry to look at any more of Isabella's crazy rich wonderful weird collection, I know that there isn't anything for Galit to tell me.

My brain's responses are a sentence—maybe not even a sentence, maybe just a diamond or a circle—I would rather be a diamond, I guess—on a graph in her article.

The research isn't about me.

None of it is about me.

It's not even about prosopagnosia.

Prosopagnosia is only interesting because of what it tells about how the normal brain functions.

I think we all want someone to say: you are the single most fascinating of all the humans. We want to focus on you.

THAT'S WHAT LOVE is. *We want to devote volumes to your case.*

FLYING HOME FROM Harvard, I try to conjure fear so I can practice my monster technique, but I am not afraid of flying.

I'm afraid of Dave not asking me about the trip, or asking questions that aren't important to me. I'm afraid of not caring enough about what happened to him while I was gone.

I'm in the very back row, pressed into the window. I search around in my brain for the 100,000-year-old baby, but nothing, no discomfort. I feel like my brain has been dusted, cleaned out with one of those static electricity wipes.

Like the MRI blasted away a few layers of neurosis. Like we shined a flashlight in the crannies, and wiped.

I sip my seltzer, and close my eyes. I can't tilt my seat back, so I sit up and doze, strapped into the hard little airplane chair.

I'm a girl steering a brain, flying through space, like a neuron, with a destination, and a heart, and I am still wondering. What do I know now?

GALIT SAID WHAT she is studying is this: there are two processes, face detection and face identification. They are definitely dissociated. Do they co-occur or do they follow each other in time?

Her theory is that face blind people process faces like normal people process objects. DPs don't have the mechanism for making fine discrimination among faces.

She'll send me the paper when it's finished.

I want to ask her, will I be referred to by my initials, HS? That's how I've seen it in the articles I have been reading. I always wonder who they are.

WHEN I GET home, I circle my house, trolling up and down the blocks, not wanting to go home. Driving past people. Do I know you? Do I know you?

Driving right through. What can be known.

about the contributors

Dorie Bargmann's work has appeared in *Manoa* and *Prairie Schooner*, and her forthcoming piece in *Spurs of Inspiration* received an award at the Mayborn Literary Nonfiction Writers Conference of the Southwest in 2006. She works as a legal investigator in Austin, Texas.

Eula Biss is the author of *The Balloonists*. She teaches nonfiction writing at Northwestern University and she is co-editor of Essay Press. Her essays have recently appeared in *Gulf Coast*, *Hotel Amerika*, *Columbia*, *Ninth Letter*, *American Poet*, the *North American Review*, the *Massachusetts Review*, and *Harper's*.

Robin Black's work has appeared in numerous publications, including the *Alaska Quarterly Review*, *Colorado Review*, and *The Southern Review*. A MacDowell Colony Fellow, she has twice received special mention in the Pushcart Prize Volume and won first prize for a short story in the 2005 Pirate's Alley Faulkner/Wisdom Writing Competition.

Marie Carter is the editor of *Word Jig: New Fiction from Scotland* (Hanging Loose Press, 2003), and has had work published in *The Brooklyn Rail*, *Hanging Loose*, *Bloom*, *Spectacle* (a circus magazine), and turntablebluelight .com, among others. She completed a residency at the MacDowell Colony in

September 2006. In 2000 she moved from Edinburgh to Brooklyn, where she currently resides.

Oliver Davies, who lives in Middlesbrough, Cleveland, UK, has an encyclopedic knowledge of bad jokes and a Pekingese puppy called Lulu. He also loves food, plays guitar loudly, and cannot function in the morning until he has downed a cup of strong tea. His blog documents his applications to 100 jobs for which he is absolutely unqualified.

Louise DeSalvo is professor of English and the Jenny Hunter Endowed Scholar for Literature and Creative Writing at Hunter College. She has published four memoirs, among them *Vertigo*, winner of the Gay Talese Award, and, most recently, *Crazy in the Kitchen*, and is at work on another memoir.

R. F. Foe (miminewyork) grew up in Wales and received her BA (Hons) first class in English Literature from Cambridge University. From Cambridge she traveled the world, eking out a living from writing, teaching, sailing, cooking, and begging. In 2004 she ended up in New York penniless and without a visa, and has been there ever since. Foe's first book, *Lapdogs*, is due out in summer 2007. She is currently working on a novel in India.

Jeff Gordinier is the editor-at-large at *Details* and a regular contributor to PoetryFoundation.org. A graduate of the creative writing program at Princeton University, he has written for a variety of magazines and newspapers, including *Esquire*, *GQ*, *Fortune*, *The Los Angeles Times*, and *Entertainment Weekly*. In 2006 he won the ASCAP Deems Taylor Award for two stories about classical music. He is in the process of finishing a book for Viking.

Karl Taro Greenfeld has written three books about Asia, including *Speed Tribes* and last year's *China Syndrome: The True Story of the 21st Century's First Great Epidemic*, and was for a few years the editor of *Time* Asia. He has been a writer and editor for *Time* and *Sports Illustrated* and his work appears regularly in *Details* and *Conde Nast Traveler*; his writing has been previously anthologized in the *Best American Sportswriting* and the *Best American Nonrequired Reading* series. Currently working on a memoir about his autistic brother, Karl lives in New York City with his wife and two daughters.

Kelly Gruver (hotcoffeegirl) lives in Cleveland, works wherever someone will hire her, and used to be a Republican. She has spent time with both George Bush Sr. and Snoop Dogg, and still wonders which meeting was more significant. When properly caffeinated, she earns a living as a Web geek. When not jockeying a cubicle, she paints terrible paintings, terrorizes her small dog, and occasionally writes something of worth. She commands a legion of bloggers with her snarky, biting wit.

Lee Gutkind's most recent book, *Almost Human: Making Robots Think*, details his experiences at the Robotics Institute at Carnegie Mellon University. Gutkind's immersion into the motorcycle subculture (*Bike Fever*), the organ transplant milieu (*Many Sleepless Nights*), and other previously unmined worlds has led to nine books and many award-winning literary achievements. He is a professor of English at the University of Pittsburgh and founder and editor of the precedent-setting literary journal *Creative Nonfiction*.

Dev Hathaway (1945–2005) was professor of English at Shippensburg University since 1993 and served for three years as the chair of the English Department. He was also the author of numerous essays and short stories, including the collections *The Widow's Boy* and *Skylarking on Honeysuckle Road*.

Melissa Lafsky is a lawyer-turned-writer whose blog about law firm life, opinionistas.com, gained notoriety for its relentless skewering of the corporate legal world. Since leaving her firm's cushy six-figure embrace to write full-time, she has written for numerous magazines and journals and served as a contributing editor at *The Huffington Post*. She lives in Brooklyn with her boyfriend and cat, both of whom play prominent (if not always desired) roles in her blog.

Olivia Chia-lin Lee once worked as a high-class call girl in San Francisco and now is a taro-farmer in Hawaii. In July 2006, she started Taro Patch Small Press in the storage shed of her auntie's antique shop to self-publish three of her novels.

Debra Marquart is an associate professor and the coordinator of the MFA program in Creative Writing & Environment at Iowa State University. Her books include two poetry collections—*Everything's a Verb* and *From Sweetness*—and a short story collection, *The Hunger Bone: Rock & Roll Stories*. Her memoir, *The Horizontal World: Growing Up Wild in the Middle of Nowhere*, was published by Counterpoint Books in 2006.

Daniel Nester is the author of *God Save My Queen* and *God Save My Queen II*, both lyric essay collections about his obsession with the rock band Queen, and *The History of My World Tonight*. His work has appeared in *Mr. Beller's Neighborhood*, *Poets & Writers*, *Time Out New York*, *The Best American Poetry 2003*, and *Bookslut*. He publishes and edits the online journal *Unpleasant Event Schedule* and is assistant web editor for sestinas for *McSweeney's*. He is assistant professor of English at The College of Saint Rose.

John O'Connor was born and raised in Kalamazoo, Michigan, and attended the creative writing program at Columbia University, where he wrote his thesis on competitive eating. His writing has appeared in *The Believer*, *Quarterly West*, and *Gastronomica*, among other publications.

Sunshine O'Donnell is an award-winning poet and educator who teaches creative writing, visual art and quantum physics to underserved children in schools, institutions, and residential facilities throughout Pennsylvania. She was a professional journalist and copywriter for ten years before founding The Coffeehouse Project literacy program in 1997. O'Donnell is program director and lead instructor for Philadelphia-based Grow from Your Roots, a nonprofit organization providing experiential education in writing, art, and science to poverty-stricken communities.

Michael Rosenwald is a staff writer for *The Washington Post*. He is also a former finalist for a National Magazine Award in feature writing; his work has appeared in numerous magazines and journals, including *The New Yorker*, *Esquire*, *Men's Vogue*, *Popular Science*, *ESPN Magazine*, and *Creative Nonfiction*.

Bonnie J. Rough's essays have won the Iowa Review Award and the Annie Dillard Award for Creative Nonfiction. Other recent nonfiction has appeared in *Modern Love: 50 True and Extraordinary Tales of Desire, Deceit, and Devotion* (Three Rivers Press), *Alaska Quarterly Review*, and *Isotope*. Rough lives in Minneapolis, where she teaches at The Loft Literary Center.

J. D. Schraffenberger's work appears in *Paterson Literary Review*, *Seattle Review*, *Louisville Review*, *Poet Lore*, *Dogwood*, *Appalachian Heritage*, *Journal of Kentucky Studies*, and elsewhere. He is the editor of *Harpur Palate* and founding editor of *Elsewhere: A Journal for the Literature of Place*. He is currently finishing a book-length creative nonfiction project called *The Ground*

Beneath You, which confronts issues of globalization and environmental degradation in Jenkins, a former coal-camp town in southeastern Kentucky where his family is from.

Heather Sellers is the author of a short story collection, *Georgia Under Water*, a Barnes & Noble Discover Great New Writers selection, as well as a children's book, three books on writing, and three volumes of poetry. Currently, she is completing a memoir about prosopagnosia, entitled *Face First*. She lives in Holland, Michigan, where she is a professor of English at Hope College.

Rebecca Skloot is an award-winning freelance writer and contributing editor at *Popular Science* magazine. Her work appears in *The New York Times Magazine*, *O: The Oprah Magazine*, and *Best Food Writing 2005*, among others. Her first book, *The Immortal Life of Henrietta Lacks*, is forthcoming from Crown.

Carol Smith is an enterprise reporter for *The Seattle Post-Intelligencer*, where she has covered a variety of beats, including science, medicine, and the working poor. Her work has been recognized nationally and regionally by the American Association of Sunday and Features Editors, the Society of Professional Journalists, Best of the West, and the Washington Press Association. She has also been recognized for her investigative work, and was a co-finalist for Harvard University's Goldsmith Prize in Investigative Journalism. She was a finalist for this year's PEN Literary Awards. In addition, her work has appeared in a variety of national magazines, including *Forbes*, *Redbook*, and *Glamour*.

Lori Soderlind is author of *Chasing Montana*, a memoir. She earned her MFA from Columbia University and teaches journalism at Norwalk Community College in Connecticut. Her writing has appeared in newspapers, magazines and journals from *The New York Times* and *The Boston Globe to Montana Magazine*, *Women's World*, and the *American Journal of Nursing*.

"Waiter" is the nom de plume of a thirty-something New York–area waiter. A former Catholic seminarian and mental health care worker, he chronicles his dining room exploits on the Web site www.waiterrant.net. Waiter Rant was nominated for Best American Weblog at the 2006 Bloggie Awards. The Waiter has also signed a book deal with Ecco/Harper Collins. His book, tentatively titled *Waiter Rant: A Behind the Scenes Look at the Front Lines of Dining Out*, is due out in the summer of 2008.

Alexis Wiggins recently received her MFA from the University of New Orleans. She has spent the past three years in Spain and Hong Kong writing a novel. Her work has appeared in *Creative Nonfiction, Fresh Yarn*, and *Ruminator*, among others. In 2004, she was nominated for a Pushcart Prize. She and her husband currently reside in New York, where she teaches at the Masters School.

Monica Hsiung Wojcik is a senior at Princeton University, majoring in chemistry with a minor in French and Italian. Monica was born and raised in Brookline, Massachusetts. In addition to writing, she competes in marathons and enjoys painting and bike riding. Upon graduation she will attend medical school.

credits

Photo Credits